Family Therapy

Ensuring Treatment Efficacy

About the Authors

Jon Carlson, Psy.D., Ed.D., ABPP, is professor of psychology and counseling at Governors State University and a psychologist with the Wellness Clinic in Lake Geneva, Wisconsin. Dr. Carlson is the founding editor of *The Family Journal* and past president of the International Association of Marriage and Family Counselors. He holds a Diplomate in Family Psychology from the American Board of Professional Psychology. He has authored twenty books and more than one hundred professional journal articles.

Len Sperry, M.D. Ph.D., is professor of psychiatry and behavioral medicine and preventive medicine at the Medical College of Wisconsin. He is also director of its Division of Organizational Psychiatry and Corporate Health, and executive director of the Foley Center for Aging and Development. Dr. Sperry is board certified in psychiatry, preventive medicine and clinical psychology and is a Fellow of the Division of Family Psychology of the American Psychological Association. He has published twenty-two professional books—including *Marital Therapy: Integrating Theory and Technique*—as well as more than two hundred chapters and journal articles. He is associate editor for research of *The Family Journal* and is listed in the *Best Doctors in America: Midwest Region*. He is a member of the American Family Therapy Academy and of the Coalition of Family Diagnosis.

Judith A. Lewis, Ph.D., is a licensed psychologist and a professor in the Division of Health Administration and Human Services at Governors State University. She has authored numerous books and articles on subjects related to family, community, and health counseling. She is president of the International Association of Marriage and Family Counselors and serves as associate editor of *The Family Journal*.

Family Therapy
Ensuring Treatment Efficacy

Jon Carlson
Governors State University

Len Sperry
Medical College of Wisconsin

Judith A. Lewis
Governors State University

Brooks/Cole Publishing Company

I(T)P® An International Thomson Publishing Company

Pacific Grove • Albany • Belmont • Bonn • Boston • Cincinnati • Detroit • Johannesburg • London
Madrid • Melbourne • Mexico City • New York • Paris • Singapore • Tokyo • Toronto • Washington

 A CLAIREMONT BOOK

Sponsoring Editor: *Eileen Murphy*
Marketing Team: *Jean Thompson and Deborah Petit*
Marketing Representative: *Tom Braden*
Editorial Assistant: *Lisa Blanton*
Production Coordinator: *Fiorella Ljunggren*
Production: *Sawyer & Williams*

Manuscript Editor: *Stacey Sawyer*
Interior Design: *Michael Rogondino*
Cover Design: *Laurie Albrecht*
Indexer: *James Minkin*
Typesetting: *Stacey Sawyer and Fog Press*
Printing and Binding: *Quebecor Printing, Fairfield*

For more information, contact:

BROOKS/COLE PUBLISHING COMPANY
511 Forest Lodge Road
Pacific Grove, CA 93950
USA

International Thomson Editores
Seneca 53
Col. Polanco
11560 México D. F. México

International Thomson Publishing Europe
Berkshire House 168-173
High Holborn
London WC1V 7AA
England

International Thomson Publishing GmbH
Königswinterer Strasse 418
53227 Bonn
Germany

Thomas Nelson Australia
102 Dodds Street
South Melbourne, 3205
Victoria, Australia

International Thomson Publishing Asia
221 Henderson Road
#05-10 Henderson Building
Singapore 0315

Nelson Canada
1120 Birchmount Road
Scarborough, Ontario
Canada M1K 5G4

International Thomson Publishing Japan
Hirakawacho Kyowa Building, 3F
2-2-1 Hirakawacho
Chiyoda-ku, Tokyo 102
Japan

Printed in the United States of America

10   9   8   7   6   5   4   3   2   1

Library of Congress Cataloging-in-Publication Data

Carlson, Jon.
    Family therapy : ensuring treatment efficacy / Jon Carlson, Len Sperry, Judith A. Lewis.
        p.   cm.
    Includes bibliographical references and index.
    ISBN 0-534-16698-9
    1. Family psychotherapy.   I. Sperry, Len.   II. Lewis, Judith, A., date.   III. Title
RC488.5.C363 1997
616.89' 156--dc20

96-32435
CIP

To our families: Laura, Kirstin, Chris, Matt, Karin, Ben, Kali, Alex, Patricia, Tracey, Christen, Tim, Jon, Steve, and Keith

Contents

Preface

We believe that this book will be useful to counselors and therapists both in training and in practice. In *Family Therapy*, we present the challenges of a diverse population and describe practical strategies to assess families, develop tailored treatment plans, and maintain treatment adherence and prevent relapse.

Traditionally, counselors and therapists have lacked the process to use the vast amounts of data families can provide; thus they often end up working on only a small aspect of the family picture. This situation reminds us of the story of the blind inhabitants of Ghor who tried to learn about the elephant that had been brought to their town—a mysterious creature they had never seen and could not see (in R.E. Ornstein, *The Psychology of Consciousness*. New York: Viking, 1972, p. 143):

> The populace became anxious to learn about the elephant, and some sightless from among this blind community ran like fools to find it. Since they did not know even the form or shape of the elephant, they groped sightlessly, gathering information by touching some part of it. Each thought that he knew something, because he could feel a part. . . .
>
> Each had felt one part of many. Each had perceived it wrongly. No mind knew all; knowledge is not the companion of the blind. All imagined something, something incorrect.

Like the blind men in this story, therapists often assess couples and families on the basis of limited knowledge. However, to understand not only the individual aspects of a family but also the family as a whole in its environment, therapists need to conduct a comprehensive and thorough assessment of the situation. Such an assessment allows the therapist to tailor treatment to fit each individual family, thus ensuring treatment efficacy. Without comprehensive and accurate assessments, therapists tend to treat all families in the same fashion, according to the theory of family therapy to which they subscribe.

In addition, once treatment has taken place, many counselors feel that they have done their job. However, without implementing sound treatment adherence/relapse prevention strategies, all gains are frequently lost.

Although we are aware that family therapy methods cannot change overnight, we believe that this book can provide a beginning as well as a basis for future study. In this vein, we are reminded of Aldous Huxley's statement in the foreword to *Brave New World Revisited* (New York: Harper & Row, 1958):

However elegant and memorable, brevity can never, in the nature of things, do justice to all the facts of a complex situation. On such a theme one can be brief only by omission and simplification. Omission and simplication help us to understand—but help us, in many cases, to understand the wrong thing; for our comprehension may be only of the abbreviator's neatly formulated notions, not of the vast, ramifying reality from which these notions have been so arbitrarily abstracted.

But life is short and information endless: nobody has time for everything. In practice we are generally forced to choose between an unduly brief exposition and no exposition at all. Abbreviation is a necessary evil and the abbreviator's business is to make the best of a job which, though intrinsically bad, is still better than nothing. He must learn to simplify, but not to the point of falsification. He must learn to concentrate upon the essentials of a situation, but without ignoring too many of reality's qualifying side issues. In this way he may be able to tell, not indeed the whole truth (for the whole truth about almost any important subject in incompatible with brevity), but considerably more than the dangerous quarter-truths and half-truths which have always been the current coin of thought.

Chapter 1 helps the reader understand the new reality of professional family therapy practice by highlighting the many changes that have occurred and must be considered when developing effective treatment. Chapter 2 describes the often overlooked relationship between work and family life, a relationship that is much more involved than therapists had previously imagined. Chapters 3 and 4 stress effective understanding through accurate assessment. Chapter 3 presents the theories of family therapy—specifically, the goals, treatment process, and techniques of the various theories. This information is essential background knowledge in order to tailor treatment effectively. Chapter 4 describes how to integrate the concepts of the various models presented in Chapter 3. Chapters 5, 6, 7, and 8 describe how to tailor treatment to each family. Different models are considered, as a clear clinical protocol is developed. Issues of gender, culture, addiction, disability, abuse, and work are all highlighted. Chapter 9 concludes the text by presenting the fundamental concepts of treatment adherence and relapse prevention. When these concepts are not duly considered, initial treatment success often ends in long-term treatment failure.

We had a great deal of help in preparing this manuscript. Special thanks go to Candace Ward Howell for her valuable assistance. We are indebted to the following reviewers for their helpful comments and suggestions: James Robert Bitter, East Tennessee State University; Joseph H. Brown, University of Louisville; Kenneth M. Davis, Villanova University; Thomas L. Millard, Montclair State University; and Beth Sirles, University of Alaska–Anchorage. Additionally, we appreciate the enthusiasm and support of Claire Verduin, Eileen Murphy, and the rest of the Brooks/Cole family.

Jon Carlson
Len Sperry
Judith A. Lewis

Part 1

Challenging Treatment Issues

1

Family Therapy in the 21st Century

New Strategies for a Changing Environment

Because family therapy is such a young discipline, one may be surprised to realize that the time for a paradigm shift has arrived so soon. In fact, however, much of the conventional wisdom that guided practice in the past has lost its value in this era of rapid change. The transformation of family life can be expected to continue, making it unlikely that therapies constrained by orthodoxy will be viable in the 21st century.

In response to an evolving environmental context, the soul and spirit of what we have known as "the family" are changing at the deepest level. Just as the social context of family life has been altered, as we will discuss, so have the professional and economic contexts within which therapy takes place. These changes will lead irrevocably toward a revolution in the practice of family therapy.

The New Realities of Family Life

The practice of couple and family therapy has traditionally been built on the unexamined assumption that a model of appropriate family life exists. Unfortunately, the notion of a "normal" family not only is impractical but also may be harmful. As Bernardes points out, people whose lives fail to fit the popularized model of the family often view themselves as at fault. "The guilt and shame of these victims is the direct consequence of our own refusal, thus far, to recognize our responsibility in portraying the image of the normal nuclear family that has become such a popular yardstick against which ordinary people measure personal success and failure" (1993, p. 48). In actuality, if the conventional nuclear family of therapeutic myth ever existed, it now represents the reality of an ever-declining minority of the population (Coontz, 1992).

What are the new realities of family life?

The Question of Hierarchy

One concept of family life that remained unquestioned in the past is the assumption that a hierarchical structure is necessarily a good thing. In a recent interview (West & Bubenzer, 1993), Cloe Madanes expressed doubt about the utility of the hierarchy.

> You have to enter the family from wherever you can and to think that you want to reconstitute a hierarchy with parents in charge of the children often doesn't work. I think that this coincides with the general disillusionment about hierarchical institutions in this country. There has been a loss of respect for all the organizations that function like a pyramid. I'm thinking more of the family like a fish net with multiple interwoven threads. (p. 104)

Because a hierarchical structure provides a vehicle for the oppression of women, questioning the validity of the hierarchy becomes especially important when we consider gender roles. For example, "a therapist may 'unpack' the metaphor of 'family harmony' and expose the hierarchy by pointing out that accord within the family often is achieved through women's acquiescence and accommodation" (Hare-Mustin & Maracek, 1988, p. 461).

Of course, changes in family structure and composition have been taking place for many years, even within families that appear on the surface to adhere to tradition.

> Even the traditional family unit has seen fundamental changes. Not long ago, husbands brought home the bacon and wives cooked it. Today, only 22% of married-couple households contain a male breadwinner and a female homemaker, a dramatic decline from 61% in 1960. (Riche, 1991, p. 44)

For the most part, women have entered the workforce because their families needed additional income or because they were the sole support for their families. If social, economic, and political policies begin to be guided by reality rather than by outmoded prototypes, the families can receive the kind of environmental support that can keep them functioning effectively.

Working from the assumption that a hierarchy is the only appropriate model for families may interfere not only with a sensible view of gender roles but also with a realistic picture of children's lives. In raising her questions about hierarchical structures, Madanes pointed out that therapists often find themselves working with families in which the children are stronger and healthier than the parents (West & Bubenzer, 1993). Certainly, the lives of children today represent unknown territory to previous generations.

> Today's children are living a childhood of firsts. They are the first day care generation; the first truly multicultural generation; the first generation to grow up in the electronic bubble, the environment defined by computers and new forms of television; the first post-sexual revolution generation; the first generation for which nature is more abstraction than reality; the first generation to grow up in new kinds of dispersed deconcentrated cities, not quite urban, rural, or suburban. The combination of these forces has produced a dynamic process. Childhood today is defined by the expansion of experience and the contraction of positive adult contact. (Louv, 1990, p. 5)

Ironically, family structures now may be characterized by less intense contact between children and their parents but also by prolonged interaction. Young adults are remaining with their parents longer. In 1960, 43% of 20- to 24-year-olds were living with their parents; by 1988, 55% were living in their childhood homes (Glick, 1990).

Relationships among the generations are also being complicated by the lengthening life span of Americans. Many elderly people who have outlived younger family members are existing without a support system of care-givers. If current patterns hold, we will soon have as many as five generations living at one time, with children constituting only one of these generations. The stereotypes of aging must be recognized and abandoned as older adults become healthier (Sperry & Carlson, 1991a).

Regardless of what the future holds for parents and children, we can be sure that the traditional hierarchical structure will continue to exist only in the imaginations of an unrealistic few.

Diverse Family Forms

The subtle changes within families are joined by more radical changes in family forms. Family life today is characterized by a myriad of models, including nuclear families, singlehood, non-marital heterosexual and homosexual cohabitation, single-parent families, remarried and stepfamilies, foster and adoptive families, childless families, and multi-adult households. Diversity of family forms will become more prevalent as the result of individual needs and choices.

The expanding diversity of family forms implies that individuals will experience more family transitions over their life cycles than was true in previous generations. Divorce, remarriage, and stepfamily relationships still remain emotion-laden, creating personal and legal dilemmas for members of immediate and extended families alike (Zinn & Eitzen,

1987). Remarriage creates a different kind of family system, with children often living with one biological parent and a stepparent or dividing their family lives between maternal and paternal homes. Therapists' generalizations applied to family life in first marriages do not apply to second marriages (Visher & Visher, 1979). Yet, therapists depart with great difficulty from the traditional concept of the "normal," intact, "Dick and Jane" family with both parents and their biological offspring living together. Some therapists also have difficulty departing from the notion that divorce is an abnormality that should be avoided at all costs. Accepting the high divorce rate as a reality forces us to view family life as fluid rather than permanent and allows us to provide more effective help to families in transition.

An even more difficult adjustment for some therapists involves working with people who find their roots and their homes in non-biological, chosen families. Rather than being organized through marriage and childrearing, these families are characterized by fluid boundaries and tend not to be structured by hierarchies of gender and age. Gay and lesbian couples have pioneered in organizing the kinds of intimate kinship networks called *chosen families,* and an ever-increasing number of people can be expected to create non-biological families in the future.

Perhaps we need to define "family" by the frequency of interactions rather than on a genetic basis. For instance, a company now in Tokyo, "Japan Efficiency," specializes in renting out "families" to elderly citizens who have no offspring or whose own families are unable to visit them. One afternoon of "human warmth" with pretend kin—a son, a daughter-in-law, and a grandchild—costs the equivalent of about $350 (Blackwell, Blackwell, Guccione, & Kohut, 1992).

Therapists will also need to become accustomed to career-driven marriages. Among career-oriented people, work is a major life focus, and love and friendship needs are more likely to be met in the job environment than anywhere else (Sperry & Carlson, 1991b). Although the idea of a two-paycheck couple is not new, the idea of a dual-career couple may be. The "career" designation indicates the partners' pursuit of goal-directed work choices that often bear the seeds of intrapersonal and interpersonal conflict. Overwork and overload are common complaints in most relationships, and these phenomena are compounded in the dual-career couple. Because socially enforced gender stereotypes still abound, the greater burden continues to fall on the woman in the relationship (Goldenberg & Goldenberg, 1984). Only with the appearance of the companionate marriage model have therapists begun to imagine relationships wherein both partners can have goals of equal importance.

Variations of the career-driven couple include the commuting couple, the military couple, the executive couple, and the family-business couple (Sperry & Carlson, 1991b). Each of these models occurs within a new social context that must be assessed and understood by family therapists. At the same time, therapists need to be aware of a trend that seems to run counter to the blurring of boundaries between work and family life. More and more people are "downshifting" (Saltzman, 1991).

In the 1980s, many people embraced the notion of a fast track as the surest path to success. Today, members of a new breed of career trendsetters, "downshifters," are taking control of their careers rather than allowing their careers to control them. These people are not dropouts. They are not giving up the intellectual, emotional, and financial rewards of professional success. Instead, they are learning to limit their careers so that they can devote more time to their families, their communities, and their own needs beyond work. Many Americans will work hard at "downward mobility" in the future (Edmondson, 1991).

Multicultural Factors

Many of the assumptions we make about family life represent "culturally embedded meanings that have been disguised as universal truths" (Lewis, 1993, p. 338). However, in the 21st century, the United States will emerge as a nation with greater ethnic diversity. It is projected that 33% of the population will be "people of color," with the highest concentration of "minority" families being of Hispanic origin, followed by African Americans, Asians, and Native Americans (McCubbin, 1990). Models of marital quality and healthy family life will have to involve a new awareness that incorporates ideas from these diverse cultures. The truly effective family therapists will be only those who have learned to appreciate diverse worldviews rather than to make judgments based on the dominant culture.

Therapists will also need to examine the effects of context on ethnically diverse groups. Research will be needed on resiliency and health among families in varying ethnic groups as well as on the impact of social policy and programs on cultural values, the role of communal ties in family preservation and survival, and the processes of family adaptation to cross-cultural change.

Responses to Change

Faced with all these trends and changes, people tend to align themselves with either the pessimists or the optimists. The pessimists believe that changes in the American family are destructive and prevent the family from carrying out its functions of childrearing and the provision of stability in adult life. The optimists, in contrast, view the family as an institution that is not declining but, rather, is showing its flexibility and resilience. This group believes that traditional family structures are too male-dominated and conformity-oriented to allow for growth and that they are no longer appropriate.

Regardless of their position, however, most people still reside within a family. According to Doherty (1992),

> the world is now more oriented to individual options, particularly for women, and the family has changed accordingly. From this point of view, the main problems faced by contemporary families can be traced to the failure of society to accept that the "Leave It to Beaver" family is a dinosaur and to provide adequate support for the variety of post-Beaver families that now dominate the landscape. (pp. 32–34)

In addition to the pessimistic and optimistic views just discussed, a third orientation is emerging. This orientation agrees with the pessimistic view, says Doherty, in that the family is in trouble and a transformation of values is needed. However, it also agrees with the optimistic view in that changes in family structure are inevitable and here to stay and that both old and new family forms should receive more community support.

Doherty believes that families at the beginning of the 20th century were *institutional families* whose chief value was *responsibility*. In the mid-1920s the focus of marriage and family shifted so that the chief value became *satisfaction*. Now, we have moved to the pluralistic family that has a chief value of *flexibility* but that can also address the needs for responsibility and satisfaction. According to Doherty,

> this completes a century-long trek toward liberation of the individual, particularly women and children, from the oppressive features of the traditional family. The pluralistic family offers individuals freedom to create the family forms that fit their changing needs over life's course with little stigma about failing to conform to a single family structure and value system. (p. 35)

The New Realities of Professional Practice

Just as the realities of family life have changed, so have the conditions within which family therapists practice. Client populations have changed, and family problems have become more complex. At the same time, therapists now find themselves dealing with an ever-changing set of constraints that affects their work.

Therapists' training has always tended to prepare them for working with verbal and sophisticated clients who are able to enter into positive therapeutic relationships with little prodding. Now, however, previously underserved populations have finally found their way into treatment. Since service has become accessible, and even mandated, marriage and family therapists have begun to see very different families. People with little education, low pretreatment levels of functioning, and multiple life problems are being seen by therapists who have not been trained or compelled to treat them in the past (Garfield & Bergen, 1986).

No longer can we assume that our clients will be voluntary, socio-economically advantaged, well-educated, or functional. Mental health services at one time were sought primarily by people who wanted to change their lives. Now, treatment is often court-ordered and mandated. In comparison with their self-motivated counterparts, compulsory clients require alternative methods of treatment, assessment, and intervention (Huber, 1992).

The problems being addressed in family therapy have increased in number and complexity as the client population has become more heterogeneous. The increasing rates of drug abuse, suicide, alcoholism, divorce, teenage pregnancy, and violence are rooted in high-risk families. These multiproblem systems require solutions that go beyond palliative interventions to include public policy modifications and preventive strategies.

Just as therapists are addressing some of their most daunting challenges, they must also face the need to adapt to changes in the treatment environment. With managed care has come the pressure to be precise, efficient, and accountable. In the past, therapists and their highly motivated clients could control the course of treatment independently. Now, survival in the managed-care environment requires each treatment provider to emphasize careful assessment; to deliver treatments that have been tailored to fit the assessment; to use brief, empirically supported modalities; and to accept external review.

The need for transformation seems to many people to be both abrupt and painful. Discussing the current plight of traditionally trained therapists, Wylie (1995, p. 22) points out:

> Their teachers and mentors and role models were the secular gurus who did not so much show them what to do as pass down . . . a body of knowledge and practice, a way of life, that seemed stable as the ages. . . . Degree in hand, the fledgling therapist could count on spending the next 25, 35, 50 years doing what the field's elders had always done—seeing individual clients or families in a private office for as short or as long a period as one or both sides determined, getting paid for doing it in the general confidence that once vacated, no appointment hour would remain long unfilled. Oh, those dear, dead days.

The New Practice of Family Therapy

Today's families are most notable in terms of their variety and diversity.
No single structure or set of interactional patterns can be identified as
right or healthy for all families. If any one generalization can be made
about a healthy family, it is that the family can accomplish its own
goals, as well as those of its individual members. Family therapy,
then, must focus on helping each client system to be successful on
its own terms.

This general strategy obviously requires important changes in the
therapist's approach. Even such sacred cows as the genogram will have
to be modified to accommodate blended and non-biological families.
Clearly, the family therapist of the future will work from a new set of
guiding principles, including the following ones.

1. **Family therapists will be sensitive to the broader contexts
   within which families function.**
   Family therapists have always understood the impact of systems on
   individuals. In the future, this perspective will be widened, making
   therapists cognizant of the fact that they can help families most
   effectively if they recognize the effect of the social, cultural, and
   economic milieu. As Unger and Sussman (1990) point out, "understanding the life situations of families, identifying their problems,
   and developing new solutions require an ecological framework that
   recognizes that families are embedded in a matrix of relationships
   within community and larger social systems" (p. 1). Among the
   larger systems that will be addressed through innovative strategies
   is the workplace, which has a major effect on most families and
   which has remained largely untapped as a source of data for the
   therapeutic process.

2. **Family therapists will tailor treatment to the special needs of
   each family system.**
   The new realities of both family life and the treatment milieu must
   direct us toward tailored treatment. Given the increasing hetero-
   geneity of family forms, there is little possibility that a generalized
   package of treatment strategies could be appropriate even for one
   therapist's clientele. At the same time, the managed-care environment tends to emphasize the desirability of limiting services to what
   the specific client needs. If treatment tailoring is based on a comprehensive assessment that clarifies the family's needs and resources,
   this approach can be both right and practical.

3. **Family therapists will use ingenuity and flexibility in the design of brief interventions.**
   What is right in terms of client needs and what is practical in terms of economic feasibility can also coincide through the use of flexible treatment formats. Hoyt (1995) suggests that a "once-and-for-all cure" achieved through time-unlimited therapy is not necessarily the most appropriate goal for most clients. A more realistic approach might involve the provision of brief interventions as needed through the life cycle of the individual, couple, or family. The success of therapy can also be enhanced through attention to developing the family's own resources for maintaining positive changes over time.

4. **Family therapists will celebrate the cultural diversity that characterizes the families they serve.**
   Given the increasing diversity among families, the most effective therapists will be the ones who are best able to learn from their clients. Culturally based values guide individuals in the definitions and meanings they place on family life. When therapists are willing to explore these meanings with their clients, they are better able to assess family needs and to choose promising interventions. When therapists remain unaware of cultural differences, they run the risk of pathologizing behaviors that are understandable in the family's cultural context.

5. **Family therapists will be aware of issues related to gender role socialization.**
   Our review of current and projected alterations in family life highlighted changes in the way gender roles are perceived. In the past, therapists sometimes believed they could ignore this issue with families in the interests of objectivity. Now, more clinicians realize the stance of neutrality tends to support the status quo of inequality. Harriet Lerner pointed out (Lewis & Engle, 1994) that "a feminist perspective has been enlarging and has helped me to look more objectively at theories that I was taught were neutral and inclusive but that were, in fact, partial, distorted, and insulting to women and other marginal groups" (p. 373). As Lerner states, "it's always the case that dominant thinking is confused with what is real and true" (p. 373).

   Ultimately, the key to successful therapy may be the therapist's ability to accept the wide variety of truths on which healthy family systems can be based.

Summary

As family therapists search for the strategies that will ensure effectiveness into the 21st century, they will need to face some new realities. Family life will involve a breakdown of hierarchies, an increase in the number and variety of family forms, and a focus on multiculturalism. The professional practice of family therapy will also change, as therapists continue to work with a more heterogeneous group of clients.

What effects will all of these changes have on family therapists? New principles will guide their work as they learn to recognize the contexts within which families function, to tailor treatment that meets the unique needs of specific families, to design flexible strategies, to celebrate diversity, and to develop gender sensitivity.

References

Bernardes, J. (1993). Responsibilities in studying postmodern families. *Journal of Family Issues, 14*(1), 35–49.

Blackwell, J., Blackwell, M., Guccione, B., & Kohut, J. (1992, September). Out: Closing comments. *Spin, 8*(6), 124.

Coontz, S. (1992). *The way we never were: American families and the nostalgia trap.* New York: Harper/Collins.

Doherty, W. J. (1992, May/June). Private lives, public values. *Psychology Today,* 32–82.

Edmondson, B. (1991). Remaking a living. *Utne Reader,* No. 46, 66–77.

Garfield, S. L., & Bergen, A. E. (Eds.). (1986). *Handbook of psychotherapy and behavior change.* New York: John Wiley.

Glick, P. C. (1990). Marriage and family trends. In D. H. Olson & M. K. Hanson (Eds.), *2001: Preparing families for the future.* Minneapolis: National Council on Family Relations.

Goldenberg, I., & Goldenberg, H. (1984). Treating the dual career couple. *American Journal of Family Therapy, 12,* 29–37.

Hare-Mustin, R. T., & Maracek, J. (1988). The meaning of difference: Gender theory, postmodernism, and psychology. *American Psychologist, 43,* 455–464.

Hoyt, M. F. (1995). *Brief therapy and managed care.* San Francisco: Jossey-Bass.

Huber, C. (1992). Compulsory family counseling. *Topics in Family Psychology and Counseling, 1*(2), Entire Issue, 1–81.

Lewis, J. A. (1993). Farewell to motherhood and apple pie: Families in the postmodern era. *The Family Journal, 1,* 337–338.

Lewis, J. A., & Engle, J. (1994). Harriet Lerner: A conversation. *The Family Journal, 2,* 373–377.

Louv, R. (1990). *Childhood's future: Listening to the American family. New hope for the next generation.* Boston: Houghton Mifflin.

McCubbin, H. (1990). Ethnic and mixed race families. In D. H. Olson & M. K. Hanson (Eds.), *2001: Preparing families for the future.* Minneapolis: National Council on Family Relations.

Riche, M. F. (1991, March). The future of the family. *American Demographics,* 44–46.

Saltzman, A. (1991). *Downshifting: Reinventing success on a slower track.* New York: Harper Collins.

Sperry, L., & Carlson, J. (1991a). The family psychologist as futurist: Some facts and challenges. *The Family Psychologist, 7*(2), 30–38.

Sperry, L., & Carlson, J. (1991b). The work-centered couple. *The Family Psychologist, 7*(4), 19–21.

Unger, D. G., & Sussman, M. D. (1990). Introduction: A community perspective on families. *Marriage and Family Review, 15*(1), 1–18.

Visher, E. G., & Visher, J. S. (1979). *Stepfamilies: A guide to working with stepparents and stepchildren.* New York: Brunner/Mazel.

West, J. D., & Bubenzer, D. L. (1993). Interview with Cloe Madanes: Reflections on family therapy. *The Family Journal, 1,* 98–106.

Wylie, M. S. (1995). The new visionaries. *The Family Therapy Networker, 19*(5), 21–29, 32–35.

Zinn, M. B., & Eitzen, D. S. (1987). *Diversity in American families.* New York: Harper & Row.

2

The Workplace and Its Impact on Today's Family:

Realities and Possibilities

The portrait of the traditional American family is fading fast, yet the frame still hangs on the walls of American corporate and government offices, as well as those of psychotherapists. The portrait shows a white male with two children and a wife who doesn't work outside the home. He puts in a 9 to 5, five-day work week, and he leaves his work at the office or shop. He rarely allows family matters to impinge on his work life and vice versa.

Replacing the fading portrait is the picture of today's family. As noted in Chapter 1, the majority of today's families do not comprise a married couple with a single breadwinner and two children. Rather, many types exist, including single parents, couples without children, and dual-earner couples. The workday may really be a night shift or a rotating shift. Some or all of the work might be done at home (telecommuting or flexwork), or considerable traveling or long-distance commuting may be involved. The work week may be compressed (flextime) into four 10-hour days or three 12-hour shifts a week. More likely than not, family matters impinge on work life, and work life clearly affects family life. National surveys indicate that 72% of men and 83% of women experience significant conflict between work and family roles and demands (Cooper, 1991).

Unfortunately, most government officials, many corporate executives, and large numbers of psychotherapists have clung to the faded family portrait of the past. Although therapists admit that a sizable portion of their case loads consists of single-parent families and dual-earner couples, their therapeutic sensitivity to work-family issues and

14

practice patterns may not have appreciably changed. To date, relatively little coverage of work-family issues appears in marital and family therapy texts and journals. Therapists can effectively help today's couples and families only if they fully understand the whole range of issues faced by couples and families, and adopt a systemic approach to therapy.

Accordingly, the purpose of this chapter is to provide an overview of the connection between family and work. Three broad areas will be covered: (1) the relationship of work and family life; (2) types of work-centered families; and (3) common concerns and patterns of work-family conflicts and their consequences. This chapter will serve to revise the clinician's portrait of the family and enhance the therapeutic repertoire.

The Relationship of Work Life and Family Life

The relationship between family and work has evolved from interdependence to independence, then to dependence to counterdependence, and now, coming full circle, to interdependence again. The tension between the two primal themes of individualism and communitarianism is reflected in this evolving relationship. In many ways the history of work and family reflects the kind of boundary issues of merging, splitting, and balance that families typically experience. This section will briefly review the history of work-family relations.

In the beginning, work was centered in the home. Families—husbands, wives, and children—hunted and grew food, built shelter, and raised their young. Even with the rise of the merchant and craftsman class in the Middle Ages, work and family remained interdependent, with the craftsman/merchant working in the home or out of sheds or shops nearby. Male children apprenticed with their father, and mother and daughter often were involved in the work task.

With the dawn of the industrial revolution in the mid-1800s, a distinct split occurred between family and work. For the most part men worked away from home at a factory from dawn to dusk, while women tended the hearth and raised the children. Home thus became independent from work, a refuge from the travails of earning a living. This pattern endured for nearly 100 years, broken during World War II when women's labor was needed outside as well as inside the home. The work-family supports, such as child care centers, that emerged then were quickly eliminated when the war ended, relegating many, but not all, women once more to domestic chores.

Subsequently, the suburbs became a middle-class ghetto for women and children during the 1950s. The 1950s also witnessed the emergence of "organization men and women" as portrayed by Whyte in his sociological classic, *The Organization Man* (1956). During this period workers became dependent on their corporations, and their loyalty was rewarded with promises of long-term employment, regular salary increases and promotion, and generous benefit packages. There was an unspoken agreement that the corporation's needs always had priority over personal and family needs. Furthermore, it was assumed that family problems were the worker's concern, not the corporation's.

The rebellious 1960s and 1970s witnessed an unbridled questioning of the values and functions of all social institutions, including the workplace. Many workers concluded that their dependence on the corporation was akin to "selling their souls to the company store" in exchange for security. Not surprisingly, the reaction to this dependence was counterdependence, which led to considerable conflict between management and labor in the 1970s and early 1980s. Believing they had been taken advantage of by their corporations, many workers and executives took revenge on the organization by limiting their productivity, absenteeism, stealing, and so on.

In the middle 1980s a wave of corporate takeovers and downsizing essentially broke the earlier "psychological contract" whereby worker loyalty was rewarded by corporate security. These events reflected the demise of the "organization man" (Bennett, 1990). The corporate world turned cold and calculating as mergers, acquisitions, and downsizing escalated. Both workers and executives with decades of seniority were fired or forced into early retirement. Not surprisingly, the incidence of stress-related medical disorders, alcohol and substance abuse problems, and other indices of occupational stress increased dramatically. The seemingly secure organizational and family-like cultures of manufacturing and service corporations disappeared almost overnight. The purges seemed to be convincing proof that if corporations were worker's second families, they were hostile and dysfunctional families.

Because of the anticipated shortage of a qualified workforce, however, business has had little choice but to revise its philosophy. In light of the major changes that are affecting the workforce and restructuring the nuclear family, corporate leaders are realizing that the workplace needs to be reorganized to reflect the growing diversity of family forms.

Today, there are signs that corporate and employee needs and values may be merging, suggesting that an interdependent relationship between work and family may be re-occurring (Vanderkolk & Young, 1991). Baby boomers now constitute the largest segment of the workplace. Their values of personal development and balance among family, self, and job reflect the need for flexibility of work scheduling, family leaves, and dependent care along with adequate remuneration, benefits, and an enriched work environment. Corporations are beginning to recognize and accommodate these needs and values. Those corporations that have risen to the challenge have become healthier and more successful than their predecessors. These firms have begun to modify their corporate culture and values to reflect that family-friendly benefit policies are integral to their business strategy. This emerging partnership or interdependence between family and work is viewed as essential in recruiting and keeping the best workers and insuring the kind of corporate loyalty and productivity necessary for American corporations to maintain a competitive edge in the new global economy.

Types of Work-Centered Families

Given the trend toward interdependence between work and family life, one should not be too surprised that as work becomes the major focus of most individuals, their intimacy and social needs are more likely to be met in the job environment than anywhere else. Work has become central to our lives, partly because of longer work hours (Schor, 1991) and changes in societal norms. The designation "work-centered family" reflects these changes (Sperry & Carlson, 1991). Although work is a general defining feature of today's family, various types of definitions exist. This section focuses on the following family and couple types: the two-person career couple, the dual-earner and dual-career couple, the commuting couple, the military couple, the clergy couple, the executive or corporate couple, and the family-business couple. Finally, the single-parent worker is briefly described.

The Two-Person Career Couple

One variant of the traditional family is the two-person career couple. In this couple type, one person is employed outside the home but requires a second person to play an emotionally supportive role to ensure the success of the single career (Papanek, 1974). Typically, a well-educated wife without employment outside the home channels her talents and energies into performing a supportive role in her spouse's professional and managerial career. She does this in place of launching or advancing her own occupation or professional career. In such a traditional "egalitarian" relationship, both spouses benefit. The husband is promoted and attains increased stature and salary, while knowing that his wife's help and support were pivotal in the success. The old saying "behind every successful man there is a woman" refers to this couple type. Usually this couple, particularly the husband, is late middle-aged or older. Perhaps the most common form of this couple type is the traditional corporate or executive marriage, discussed later in this section.

The Dual-Earner and the Dual-Career Couple

Dual-earner families are the largest group of non-traditional families. In this family type, both spouses individually pursue work roles for monetary gain while simultaneously maintaining a family life. This pattern contrasts with the traditional family wherein the husband assumes the breadwinning role and the wife the homemaking role (Sekaran, 1986). Estimates indicate that dual-career couples currently make up 60–70% of the workforce and will represent 80% by the year 2000 (Johnson, 1990).

Several designations have been used to describe this type of couple: dual-paycheck family, two-job family, dual-career family, dual-provider, dual-worker, and two-career. The lack of clear differentiation among of these designations argues for more exact specification. Not to establish one hinders the comparability of findings across various studies and limits the clinical utility of the concept. Some experts advise abandoning the term "dual-career couples" and replacing it with the more precisely defined categories of *dual-professional couples*—both spouses are employed in the labor force in either professional or managerial titles; *dual-worker couples*—where both spouses have job designations that are neither professional nor managerial; and *professional/worker couples*—one spouse has a professional or managerial job designation and the other does not. This taxonomy has merit but has yet to be consistently observed. For the purpose of this text, the designation *dual-earner* couple or family will refer to marriages in which one or both spouses work in a job designated as non-professional or non-managerial. *Dual-career* couples will refer to marriages in which both spouses have jobs designated as professional or managerial. (See Table 2.1.)

Note that all dual-career couples are not the same. Looking at dual-career relationships from the perspective of a woman, one can see at least four patterns (Poloma, Pendleton, & Garland, 1981): (1) regular career, (2) interrupted career, (3) second career, and (4) modified second career. The regular career begins after college but before marriage. The woman may continue her work with minimal interruption, possibly for maternity leaves or on a part-time basis during child-rearing years. A woman's interrupted career begins like a regular career, but child rearing or some other factor effectively interrupts her career. Her career only resumes when the children are fully grown and independent. The woman with a second career often receives professional training around the time her children are grown or leaving home. Finally, the modified second career begins earlier than the second career, usually after the youngest child no longer needs full-time mothering.

Of course, when a couple has children, researchers found that it tended to limit the woman's career involvement. Sometimes promotions or relocations were turned down, or increased home responsibilities

Table 2.1 Definitions of Common Work-Family Terms

two-person career couple Couple in which one spouse is employed outside the home in a job that requires the other spouse to play an emotionally supportive role to ensure the success of the single career.

dual-earner couple General term referring to a couple in which both spouses are employed. More specifically, it refers to a couple in which both spouses work in a job designated as non-professional or non-managerial.

dual-career couple Couple in which both spouses have jobs designated as professional or managerial.

role strain Stress or strain associated with incompatible behavior, expectations or obligations.

role overload Stress associated with attempting to fulfill a greater variety of roles than energy or time permits.

role conflict Conflict and stress associated with inconsistencies or contradictions about role expectations.

role cycling dilemma Dilemma involving decisions about issues that arise at different life stages of the life cycle. Chief among these are conflicts of wanting to achieve one role—such as becoming a mother—while not wanting to compromise another—such as career advancement.

spillover Situation in which stresses experienced in either the home or workplace lead to stresses in the other domain.

crossover Situation in which job stresses experienced by one spouse lead to stresses in the other spouse at home.

required reducing hours of work. Also, as people live longer, adult children are finding they are assuming responsibility for the care of their aging parents. Again, the woman usually assumes the responsibility (Vandekolk & Young, 1991).

Generally speaking, spouses in dual-career marriages are highly committed to their careers and tend to view work as essential to their personal identity and psychological sense of self. Dual-career couples view employment as part of a career path involving progressively more power, responsibility, and financial resources. In contrast, dual-earner couples tend to view employment as providing money to pay bills, as an opportunity to keep busy, rather than as an integral element of their self-definition (Stoltz-Loike, 1992). In short, while dual-career families believe their occupations are a primary source of personal fulfillment and self-actualization, dual-earner families tend to seek satisfaction and fulfillment elsewhere, such as in hobbies, friends, or vacations (Rapoport & Rapoport, 1975). It is estimated that 20% of all dual-earner couples are dual-career couples.

What is the effect of the dual-career lifestyle on quality of life, the marriage relationship and marital satisfaction, and spousal identity? Generally speaking, quality of life is quite high for dual-career couples. Sekaran (1986) notes that quality of life is a function of the roles played by the spouses (that is, self, parent, worker, spouse) and the satisfaction experienced by the partners (that is, job satisfaction, marital satisfaction, personal satisfaction, family satisfaction). Psychological well-being is a correlate of a rewarding, satisfying job (Baker & Scott, 1992). Quality of life is generally enriched for both spouses because of the financial status derived from two incomes. From the woman's perspective, employment satisfies a number of needs, including involvement, variety, challenge, and power, that might not be fulfilled in the home-making role. From the man's perspective, being in a dual-career relationship means assuming non-traditional roles and obligations, particularly child care, which requires him to respond with nurturance and compassion. As such, this response can broaden the meaning of his life. He may also feel less pressure to succeed since he is not solely responsible for the family's financial well-being.

The dual-career lifestyle can also positively affect the quality of the marital relationship. Dual-career relationships tend to be characterized by a greater balance of power and decision making than exist in traditional relationships. Shared decision making seems to increase the couple's respect for each other as equals and brings them closer together. They experience increased self-worth and self-perception of competence (Sekaran, 1986). Since they can share career as well as non-career concerns, a sense of collegiality further reinforces the sense of equity.

Conversely, women committed to careers that are intellectually and financially satisfying may have less motivation to marry. Furthermore, financial independence increase's a woman's independence within a marriage, as well as her willingness to dissolve an unsatisfying or dysfunctional marriage (Betz & Fitzgerald, 1987). Generally speaking, both career-committed men and women tend to marry later in life, with approximately 35% of spouses in dual-career marriages having been married previously (Gilbert, 1985).

In general, marital satisfaction is higher for those in dual-career than in traditional relationships (Sekaran, 1986). Marital satisfaction is highest for women who work by choice, are better educated, work part-time, and receive their husbands' support. Husbands experience high marital satisfaction when they support their wives' choice to work and when their wives work part-time. Women with low marital satisfaction work longer hours and experience role strain and conflict (Voydanoff, 1985).

Couples experience high degrees of marital satisfaction when the husband participates in household duties and when family income is

increased. Marital satisfaction is lowest when the couple adopts traditional gender expectations of the woman's role in the home (Stoltz-
Loike, 1992). Finally, people who began their careers before marriage
tend to be more involved in each other's career after marriage, have
equal commitment to the relationship, practice equal decision making,
and have greater marital satisfaction than do people in relationships
in which the woman began her career after marriage (Ray, 1990).

Finally, identity issues can be prominent for dual-career couples.
Identity issues are more likely for couples who were not raised in dual-
career households. Gender-based roles and values internalized early in
life may conflict with the non-traditional roles couples are trying to
establish, creating role and identity confusion. For example, women
who were taught that a "good wife" stays home, raises children, and
does not compete with men may feel ambivalent about their femininity
and guilty about working (Sekaran, 1986). Nevertheless, these dual-
career couples are usually able to forge a workable identity as individuals and as a couple. It may be surprising to note that there is less sexual
dysfunction reported in dual-career couples than in traditional marriages (Avery-Clark, 1986).

In summary, Stringer (1985) lists four ingredients for success in
dual-career relationships. First, couples who have a high level of commitment to their careers report a greater degree of marital satisfaction
than traditional couples. Second, these couples tend to be flexible and
make decisions that provide mutually satisfying decisions: for example,
they are willing to relocate, commute, and make adjustments to fit each
other's career; they are interdependent; they have common interests,
sharing mutual leisure-time activities and being physically active with
each other; and they encourage the self-actualization of their spouse.
Third, they spend more time together than other couples. And, fourth,
they are realistic about their limitations and do not expect to "have it all."

Dual-career relationships can also be described in terms of life,
career, and family stages. Hall and Hall (1979) and Sekaran and Hall
(1989) offer these observations. First, couples are more likely to make
family sacrifices earlier in their career than in later stages, and family
factors tend to take priority in mid-career. Second, conflict between
career and family tends to be highest in mid-career, moderate in early
career stages, and lowest in late career. Third, considerable stress results
from asynchronism. Asynchronism is the couple's experience of being
"off schedule" with regard to expectations or norms of "timetable" of
family, organization, and society. For instance, couples who marry late
and have children late are often considered "out of sync" with the dominant culture's timetables for marriage and children. Enlightened corporate policy is a primary means of maximizing synchronism. This

includes career development policies, such as paternity as well as maternity policies that integrate and synchronize the preferred career paths of individuals and actively encourage employees to take advantage of them without stigma. Fourth, career compatibility can reduce conflict and stress. For instance, two careers are more likely to be compatible if one spouse has career as the first priority, while the other has family as the first priority. Similarly, compatibility is higher if both spouses are in similar fields; there are no children; they are at different stages of their careers, rather than at the same stage; and if both jobs allow considerable autonomy and flexibility.

It has been shown that the degree of mutual commitment to both career and family correlated strongly with marital satisfaction, and often family was required to make accommodations to career (Sekaran & Hall, 1989). Hall and Hall (1979) identified four types of couples based on their involvement in home and career. They are *accommodators*—each spouse has a different top priority, such as the family for one and career for the other; *allies*—both partners have the same top priority, family or work; *adversaries*—each partner is highly involved in work and wants the other to attend to family tasks; or *acrobats*—each partner is highly involved in both work and family. These authors believe that acrobats experience the highest level of stress in their bid to "have it all," while allies and accommodators have the lowest levels of stress.

The Commuting Couple

Sharing the same residence has long been a part of the traditional definition of marriage. However, the transformation of the modern marriage and family has affected even this tradition. For example, *commuter marriage* refers to couples who have made the difficult choice of conducting an intimate relationship while maintaining two separate residences and two independent careers (Lang, 1988a, 1988b). What are the broad consequences for the personal relationships of commuter couples at home and at work, and with friends, lovers, and family members?

Although couples have been geographically separated in the past, commuter marriage provides a new combination of four factors: equal career commitment, distance, permanence, and preference for living together. First "equal career commitment" does not mean that one spouse pursues opportunities until he or she can rejoin or send for the family. It refers to two equally career-oriented individuals who have chosen not to let their marriage force them to sacrifice individual achievement and success. Second, the spouses live at a distance great enough to require the establishment of two separate households. Third, this is seen as a permanent arrangement in the sense that they have set no specific goal achievement or length of time after which they will be back together. The fourth point is equally important: they prefer to be together. The separation is not for the purpose of working through marital problems, and, despite the permanence of the situation, they talk hopefully of the day when career options will make shared residence possible (Gerstel & Gross, 1984).

Commuter marriages impose different demands and stresses at different stages in the marriage cycle. For instance, a young married couple without children face the fact that they may not have been married long enough to build the kind of commitment that can withstand the long-term separation incurred with commuting. Not surprisingly, couples with children face many of the adjustment problems of non-commuting couples, with a great burden of care placed on the parent with the children and a sense of loss for the parent who is alone. However, the post-parental couple seem to do best as commuters.

Women often find commuter marriage freeing and exciting. Men, however, no longer have a wife at home to work for them and are likely to experience a certain deprivation. In short, commuting couples cope with problems of balance between friendship and loneliness, self-sufficiency and dependence, and togetherness and separateness (Lang, 1988).

The Military Couple

To work effectively with the military couple, the therapist needs an appreciation of the unique dynamics of the military family. Kaslow and Ridenour (1984) conceptualize four levels of military families. The first level represents the service person and his/her family of creation. At the next level is the service person and his/her nuclear family of origin. A third level comprises one's colleagues in the battalion, crew, or squadron. The fourth level incorporates the vast military establishment. Although being a member of four different families creates a sense of security and belonging, it also causes the individual to have simultaneous commitments to several different military families, which can lead to divided loyalties and produce conflict, especially within one's marriage.

In addition to the problem of divided loyalties, military families and couples frequently experience disruption caused by moves between military and civilian areas. In many areas, military families are seen as minority groups or outsiders, which creates considerable pressure on them. Growing up as a child in the military family poses special problems brought on by separation from parents, frequent moves, changes of schools, loss of friends, transcultural experiences, isolation, and sometimes child abuse and child neglect as well as parental alcoholism. However, these experiences can challenge children to become resourceful and self-reliant.

Clinicians need to be familiar with military life to effectively intervene with military couples; they need to learn the language, ranks, and hierarchy. Special problems occur when one spouse is in the military and the other is not, as well as when both are working in the service in a dual-career fashion. The pressures of military life and loyalty may force marriage to a low priority. A major hurdle to therapy is that, because of military security issues, treatment often occurs without the promise of confidentiality between therapist and client. Also, individuals who have strong needs for closeness in marriage may find military life counterproductive to this goal.

The Clergy Couple

Either partner in a couple may be ordained in the clergy. Currently, however, the majority of ministers are male. Women married to clergymen must deal not only with the role conflict and overload associated with being a wife, but also the unique role expectations associated with their husbands' ministerial careers. Traditionally, women married to clergymen have been expected to assume the roles of model spouse, mother, church and community leader, and promoter of the faith. This, of course, is an example of the two-person career couple—in this case, the wife supports the husband's ministerial career. Clergy couples and their families have been described as living in a "clerical fish bowl." Their fish-bowl existence and lack of sufficient social support are the two most significant stressors identified by clergy wives. Not surprisingly, after they are married, these women experience a loss of control over their living space, time management, and personal identities (Baker & Scott, 1992).

It is generally assumed that clergy wives are at greater risk with regard to mental health problems and lack of general well-being than women not married to clergymen. But the data do not support this belief, at least not entirely. Baker and Scott (1992) found that clergy wives were happier and more satisfied with their lives than a comparable group of non-clergy wives. More than 400 Lutheran women, married an average of 20 years, approximately half of whom were clergy wives, were studied. Each group consisted of wives who worked outside the home as well as those who did not. (Unfortunately, data on differences between two-person career couples and dual-earner career couples were not reported.)

Mickey and Ashmore (1991a; 1991b) have reported the most comprehensive and extensive data, involving 748 married clergy from a broad span of 11 Protestant denominations. They found that there was a direct correlation between a strong sense of vocational calling and the couple's, particularly the wife's, ability to cope with stress. A strong sense of vocational calling is associated with the conservative church denominations such as Baptist, Assembly of God, and so on, in which wives were more likely to accept the traditional support role in a two-person career couple. In contrast, more career conflicts between spouses and more divorce occurred in the more liberal or profession-oriented denominations such as Episcopalian, Methodist, and Lutheran.

Age seems to be another moderating factor. For instance, the typical clergyman is late middle-aged, caucasian, married to a somewhat younger spouse, and has two to three children. Generally, older clergymen and spouses were reasonably satisfied with a traditional, two-person career, whereas younger clergymen and spouses were less satisfied, preferring the dual-career option instead.

What do we know about clergy couples in which both spouses are ordained ministers? Kieran and Monro (1988) note that dual-clergy couples share a number of stressors and strains with other dual-career couples. These include identity issues, work and role overload, role cycling problems, social network dilemmas, and discrepancies between personal and social norms. However, dual-clergy couples also experience some unique stressors, including ambivalent boundaries between work and family roles, vigorous role expectations, and embeddedness of both work and family roles.

Essentially then, clergy couples from conservative denominations and older clergy couples in general seem relatively satisfied with two-person career marriages. Younger couples, couples from liberal denominations, and couples with advanced education tend to be more disposed toward dual-career relationships. These dual-career couples may experience considerably more stress than traditional clergy couples.

According to Baker and Scott (1992), factors that contributed to the well-being and satisfaction of clergy wives were few demands associated with their husbands' ministry and perceived support for individual identity. Some therapeutic implications of these findings are that clergy wives need to consider intentional strategies to cope with role strain and find support for their own personal identities. Seeking employment outside the home and ministry, acquiring additional formal education, and participation in support groups and enrichment programs—for example, time management, stress management, and self-care—which focus on dealing with changing and conflicting role expectations and demands may prove useful.

The Executive or Corporate Couple

Executive or corporate marriages tend to be either the traditional (hard-working executive husband and stay-at-home wife "supporting" both the man and the corporation) or the dual-career type. Currently, the traditional corporate couple is an example of the two-person career. Presently, traditional corporate couples slightly outnumber dual-career couples, but this will rapidly change as baby boomers advocating companionate marriages continue to displace older males in the corporate suite. Interestingly, while 90% of male executives are married, only 41% of female executives remain married (Hardesty & Jacobs, 1986). The following description focuses on traditional corporate couples.

While dual-career couples exhibit a wide range of spousal bonding, some researchers believe that traditional corporate couples are primarily bonding of a dependent wife with a controlling husband, a perfectionist-compulsive husband with a dramatic-histrionic wife (Greiff & Munter, 1980). Studies of the attributes of the traditional corporate wife are few. Kanter's (1977) findings are still representative of the traditional corporate wife over the age of 55. The wife feels the need to sacrifice personal goals for corporate goals, believes she is limited to a peripheral role in corporate life (that is, hostess) is socially active, is supportive of husband's work, and views herself differing appreciably in motivation and attitudes from career women in the corporation.

Seidenberg (1973), in contrast, notes that the corporate wife's role may not be so peripheral. Based on his consultation and therapy with corporate wives, he notes they are the third party in most decisions made by their executive husbands and companies. He believes that corporations that fail to involve the wife in corporate decisions involving her husband and subsequently herself, particularly with regard to travel and relocation, will lose or not attract the best executives. Parenthetically, Seidenberg notes that the principal "disease" of the corporate wife is loneliness.

Though feminism has had some effect on older, traditional executive couples, the challenge of working with the unique needs of such couples has not been adequately addressed in the family literature.

The Family-Business Couple

We typically associate "family business" with the "mom and pop" corner grocery or independent hardware store in the neighborhood in which we grew up. Actually, the family-owned and operated business is the predominant form or organization in the United States, accounting for 95% of all businesses, including 175 of the Fortune 500. There are two common family-business couple relationships. One is the two-person career couple, whereby the female spouse usually supports the business-owner husband. This pattern is more common among older couples. Danco (1981) adroitly describes this pattern in her book, *From the Other Side of the Bed: A Woman Looks at Life in the Family Business.* The second pattern is a variant of the dual-earner couple, in that both spouses work for the same corporation as owner/employee. Barnett and Barnett (1988) dub this relationship the "entrepreneurial couple." (The Barnetts' co-founded the National Association of Entrepreneurial Couples.) The following paragraphs describe background material on the family-business couple.

While working for a bureaucratic organization may be cold and impersonal, working in a family firm can provide a couple with a high sense of job satisfaction and personal and family well-being. Loyalty, flexible work conditions, and feeling like an "insider" are common perks. However, family firms also have their own share of problems, including complicated authority issues, trouble with boundary mainte-nence, triangulation issues, and difficulty with individuation and eman-cipation. Rosenblatt, de Mik, Anderson, and Johnson (1985) note that there is no shortage of marital or family dynamics in family firms, and they disappointingly note several reasons why counseling business fami-lies/couples may be less successful than counseling with other couple types. Freudenberger and Freedheim (1989) report that the most com-mon interpersonal problems individuals from family firms bring to psychotherapy are differing expectations, communication problems, confusion of roles, and the inability to shift roles. Rosenblatt et al. also found that marital conflict, anxiety, depression, eating disorders, sexual problems, stress-related medical problems, and role carryover are com-mon therapeutic presentations.

Succession is probably the greatest dilemma for the family business (Ward, 1987). Decisions about when and how to turn over the business represent a critical turning point in a family firm. Whether the oldest son/daughter should become president, an "outsider" should take over, or the firm should be sold are difficult, painful issues. Unlike in non-family businesses, the question of continuity and preservation of a fam-ily business's financial interest is a key consideration. Succession is further complicated if the founder of the business privately acknowl-edges the need for succession but is unable or unwilling to communi-cate these plans to an heir or other employee (Dyer, 1986); consequently, the successor may not be adequately prepared. In addition, employees may resist changing their loyalty from founder to the heir or resent being passed over for someone less experienced (Davis & Stern, 1980). Not surprisingly, the issue of succession is often the reason for engaging the services of the clinician and/or consultant.

Some experts predict that the number of family businesses may increase significantly in the coming decade (Bucholz & Crane, 1989). Because of the greatly reduced number of middle management positions (more than 35% were eliminated in the 1980s) and the extremely large cohort of middle-aged baby boomers who want to climb the corporate ladder but will not now be able to, many would-be corporate executives will opt to establish their own businesses. Many other entrepreneurial baby boomers will seek their futures in their family's business rather than strike out on their own (Benson, 1990).

Single-Parent Families and Work-Family Relations

A major trend affecting the structure of the family in recent years has been the rapidly accelerating increase in single-parent families. It is estimated that six out of ten American children will live in single-parent households at some time during their formative years. Currently about 25% of children, including about 50% of African American children, live in single-parent households according to U.S. Census Bureau figures (Burden, 1986). Such families are not a homogenous group. They are formed through death, desertion, separation, or divorce.

This family type has also been termed the one-parent, the lone-parent, and the solo-parent family. "Single-parent family" implies that a mother or father is parenting alone, which may not be the case. Goldenberg and Goldenberg (1984) describe eight possible types of single-parent families, including temporary situations such as non-separated spouses and permanent situations such as an unmarried parent. It is for this reason that more specific designations have been suggested. Feminists prefer the designation "single-parent household" (Hanson & Sporakowski, 1986), while Goldenberg and Goldenberg suggest "single-parent-led family."

While single-parent families constitute a significant family form, relatively little is known or understood about them. The majority of the limited literature focuses on dysfunction and distress in the home (Mahler, 1989), ignoring the role of work in the lives of single parents. For most single women with children, single parenthood is a transitory state in that 75% remarry within 6 years of divorce. Since at any given time only 16% of the female workforce is divorced, separated, or widowed, research studies either include single mothers within the general category of employed mother or exclude them altogether. Furthermore, about 60% of single women with children under the age of 6 are employed. Therefore, based on these indicators, Burden (1986) estimates that approximately one-third of the workforce may be single parents at some point during their work lives. Finally, besides providing economic security and the opportunity for independence and self-sufficiency, employment provides a critical social support network to the single parent.

There are, however, some data on work-family relations of single parents that may be instructive to family therapists. Burden (1986) collected data from nearly 30 employees, parents and non-parents, single and married, of large corporations. Not surprisingly, she found that single parents experienced the greatest amount of stress in handling the multiple responsibilities of work and family. Single female parents expressed the most difficulty with role strain. They spend an average of 75 hours per week trying to balance both job and family duties with little financial or emotional assistance. Despite this, they expressed higher levels of job satisfaction and equal levels of job motivation and job performance as other employees. In contrast, single male parents did not evidence the same levels of work-family stress and strain that other parent categories did. Though they worked the greatest number of hours per week on the job, they had the highest salary levels and the lowest levels of depression of all employee categories. Essentially, their responses appeared more like non-parent employees than parent employees.

Finally, although single female parent employees appear to be functioning at high levels on the job, Burden (1986) believes they may be doing so at the expense of their own physical and emotional well-being. The long-term consequences of such multiple stressors and role strain experienced by these individuals remain to be seen. Clearly, employers should provide the necessary supports and services to help employees realistically manage work and family demands. Research suggests that increasing the single parent's social supports and coping skills as well as increasing job scheduling flexibility can increase the well-being of working parents (Shinn, Wong, Simko, et al., 1989). Doing so is not only good for the single-parent worker, but good for business.

Common Work-Family Conflicts and Their Consequences

The many social changes of the 1980s have created challenges to most families trying to achieve and maintain a sense of togetherness and economic stability. In less than one generation, to stay abreast of inflation families have shifted from one-paycheck to two-paycheck households. However, real family earnings dropped significantly during this time. The two-adult family now works an average of 80 hours a week outside the home compared with 40 hours a generation ago (Googins, 1991).

The result of such changes have been an increase in the type and frequency of work-family conflicts. This section briefly reviews common work-family conflicts and their consequences for the family and other social institutions.

A variety of work-family conflicts exist. They include role strain (refer back to Table 2.1 on page 19), role overload, and role conflicts, as well as problems involving child care, elder care, and issues of balance between career, family, and personal needs. Another source of stress is the role cycling dilemma. Finally, stress can have a contagious quality, manifesting in spillover or crossover (Bolger, Delongis, Kessler, & Worthington, 1989).

Work-family conflicts exist when role pressures from work and family demands are mutually incompatible, as when participation in one role precludes participation in another. Three general classes of work-family conflict have been articulated: time-based conflicts, strain-based conflicts, and behavior-based conflicts (Greenhaus, 1987; Greenhaus & Beutell, 1985). *Time-based conflict* refers to how time devoted to one role detracts from another role, as when late night meetings conflict with a child's school conference. *Strain-based conflict* refers to the intrusion of strain symptoms such as fatigue and irritability from one role to the other. *Behavior-based conflict* refers to the incompatibility of behavior in one role with behavior expected in another, as when a worker is expected to be detached and objective on the job but warm, nurturing, and emotional in the family. Greenhaus, Paraguaman, Granrose, et al. (1989) studied strain-based and time-based conflicts and found that men and women experienced similar levels of strain-based conflict, but in different ways. Work scheduling was associated with strain-based conflict for men but not for women. Women experienced high levels of work-family conflict that greatly involved their work and did not experience as much stress when their partners exhibited high work salience; the pattern was reversed for men. Men's work-family conflicts were unrelated to their job involvement, whereas women's job involvement was clearly related to work-family conflicts.

Several types of role strains also affect inherent in dual-career relationships. These include career versus personal and family demands, competition between spouses, division of labor, child-care arrangements, time allocation, job-related geographic mobility, social networks, and identity maintenance versus identity diffusion. Shaevitz and Shaevitz (1980) list a number of questions that must be addressed. How will household tasks be assigned? Who will do what and according to what standards? Who controls the money? Separate or joint accounts? What are the rights of each in spending money? How should partners deal with job relocation? Is one spouse's commuting a realistic solution?

What if one spouse is more successful in his or her career than the other? How can partners recognize and deal with overload and burn-out? Who will be responsible for child care? Who will be available in emergencies? Are child-care facilities available in emergencies? Are child-care facilities available at all? What special things must the partners do to enhance their relationship?

Finally, whatever the source of stress or conflict, the goal of couple equity represents the ideal solution for the dual-career couple. Stoltz-Loike (1992) defines *couple equity* as the perceived balance over time between individual, couple, and family needs and goals and the sense among spouses that the relationship is fair. Equity is not equality and is not achieved through a perfect 50-50 split in responsibilities. Equity is attainable when the couple strives toward a common goal at the expense of neither spouse.

Work-family conflicts have been present throughout the history of the United States. Googins (1991) has ably chronicled the fascinating history of work-family conflicts from the 1600s to the present. However, the history reveals that the focus of work-family relations in the 1990s is unique. Furthermore, the consequences of modern changes in work-family relations and conflicts are monumental.

One such consequence is the increasing isolation of family members. Dual-earners have less time and energy to invest in others than do spouses in traditional families. Dual-earner spouses have little time for each other, their children, their elderly parents, or themselves. If they have friends, friendships tend to be with co-workers (Voydanoff, 1985). A second consequence is a change in values and priorities. Since work (paid) time has come to dominate family life, the payor's or corporation's values and expectations pervade the payee's thinking and decision making. At some level the worker thinks, "If I only could find better child care, I could pay more attention to the real priority, which is my work." Should adults have to choose between work and family or feel guilty and apologetic about rescheduling a meeting or arriving late because a child or elder is sick? A third consequence is an intergenerational "gap." Because of increased longevity and social change, three living generations of adults have grown up in totally different worlds and consequently have markedly different lifestyles and value systems. Fourth, a generation ago dual-paycheck families were primarily lower-class families; if a middle- or upper-class wife worked, her work was considered nonessential in supporting the family. Fifth, for many individuals, the workplace has come to replace the home as the haven of safety, the center of life's meaning, and the source of self worth. Previously, work provided the financial means to keep the home secure. Finally, a majority of current work-family conflicts arise because major social institutions, such as the school system and government, have organized their resources and structure around obsolete concepts of the family and society. These institutions seem complacently blind to the plight of the contemporary family.

With few exceptions, most U.S. corporations function as if the significant changes of the 1980s never occurred. Despite the increasing number of women in the workplace, many government, school, and corporate leaders seem to harbor a delusional belief that mothers are indeed not in the workplace but rather at home where they can attend to the needs of their spouses, children, and elderly relatives. As a result of this institutional blindness, families are expected to adapt, adjust, and singly manage the stresses and strains of ever increasing social, economic, political, and cultural changes. It is becoming increasingly apparent that government's hands-off-the-family policy and the corporate world's reluctance to establish realistic family policies are shortsighted and counterproductive.

As work-family conflicts increase and the balancing of work and family responsibilities becomes more complex, the need for better support systems increases. The alternative is continuing the inequitable and dysfunctioning systems currently in place. A major challenge of the 1990s will be to reshape work-family relations, increase productivity, and create new opportunities for intimacy. This challenge will require an increased awareness of and honesty about the complexity of the issues and their ownership beyond the family. No longer can government shrink from responsibility with moral claims about the sanctity of family privacy. Other social institutions that have been resistant to change must begin the process of reconfiguration and accommodation. Schools and corporations will have to change their hours and their leave policies and provide social services that they previously resisted.

Special Concerns

This last section discusses concerns about job-related travel, executive pressures, financial strain, overwork, and the effect of mother's and father's work on family functioning.

Job-Related Travel

Greiff and Munter (1980) note that professionals and executives travel for a variety of reasons beyond job demand. These personal reasons include restlessness, status, intimacy, self-esteem, release from pressure, excitement, and freedom. They also describe the psychodynamics of such travel in terms of anticipation, separation, and regeneration. Boss, McCubbin, and Lester (1979) studied the effects of the traveling (absent) husband/father from the family systems perspective. They concluded that such travel is stressful for families because departures and returns require constant change in the family system boundaries and role assignment. Their research found that corporate wives who coped best with their spouse's travel focused on self-development, interpersonal relationships, independence, and self-sufficiency and easily "fit" into the corporate scene. Lang (1988) offers a number of useful suggestions for reducing travel stress of both the executive and family.

Executive Pressures

Many dual-career couples hold executive positions. Greiff and Munter (1980) report that the most common personal pressures affecting job and family are time, money, health, value conflicts, age, and self-appraisal. They note that divorce and dual-career marriage are the most important family pressures on the executive and that performance appraisals, public speaking, the inner circle, and authoritarian bosses are the organizational pressures that most stress the executive. Cooper (1991) reports research findings that confirm most of Greiff and Munter's observations. However, while Greiff and Munter's list relates primarily to male executives, Cooper also reports on the unique pressures on female executives at home and on the job. These include threats of sexual involvement, threatened male colleagues, a patronizing male or "queen bee" female boss, being "superwoman" at home and at work, blocked promotions and the "glass ceiling" phenomenon, and overly high expectations of others and self to succeed in a male-dominated work force.

Financial Strain

Economic stress is a primary factor in marital discord. Economically stressed couples struggle with a wide variety of issues. These stressors may precipitate marital conflict or exacerbate existing marital problems. During time of financial stress a couple's communication may be considerably affected. The couples may engage in fewer rewarding exchanges, and negative communication may increase. Spouses may covertly or overtly attempt to control the other. Consequently, there is ample opportunity for disappointment and disillusion as one spouse blames the other for their financial difficulties.

Both spouses may become psychologically absorbed with the family's financial concerns. They may lack the energy needed to devote time to marital issues, as they work longer hours, attempting to deal with overdue bills. The result is a diminished amount of both time and energy to devote to family matters.

Recently, researchers have begun focusing on the family dynamics affected by economic hardship. Conger, Elder, Lorenz, Conger, et al. (1990) describe a process model of marital dysfunction involving economic hardship. They note that economic hardship leads initially to a subjective sense of "economic strain." This strain engenders cognitive, affective, and behavioral changes. Economic strain then leads to an increase in spousal hostility. As hostility continues to increase, warmth decreases, marital quality decreases, and the relationship becomes unstable. A second study (Lorenz, Conger, Simon, Whitbeck, & Elder, 1991) confirmed this model and concluded that efforts to increase warmth and decrease hostility improved relationship stability even amid financial stressors.

Although financial stress is problematic for couples of all economic levels, middle- and upper-income couples face unique challenges. Expectations and past experiences can result in middle- and upper-income couples feeling extreme disappointment following economic setbacks, particularly if the couple anticipates or experiences the threat of a reduced standard of living.

Several negative complications and consequences have been observed among middle-income families who experienced economic hardship. Three are particularly prominent: reduced self-esteem, particularly among males; projection of hostility onto the spouse; and reciprocity of negative affect among spouses (Lorenz et al., 1991). A corollary of reduced self-esteem involves self-derogation, which can invite dominating, discouraging reactions from others (Horowitz, Locke, Morse, et al., 1991). When one spouse engages in self-derogatory behavior, the other spouse may unintentionally respond with domination and negative affect, which can lead to increased marital dissatisfaction. Marital competition is another complicating factor. Although competitive feelings are often repressed or denied, they may surface during financial crises, particularly when job loss is experienced by one spouse. This competition may intensify as one spouse imagines how life might have been if only the other spouse had worked harder or was more capable. Needless to say, in relationships where competitiveness may be an issue, such as in dual-career families (Rice, 1979; Stoltz-Loike, 1992), couples will experience increasing dissatisfaction as financial stress increases.

Overwork

In 1991 the average American worked the equivalent of 1 month longer per year than his or her counterpart did in 1970 and 2 months longer than European counterparts, according to data reported by Schor (1991). Subjectively, American workers believe that they are working harder and longer and enjoying their work less. Schor, a Harvard economist, predicts that if current work patterns continue, 20 years from now the average worker will be on the job 60 hours a week, 50 weeks a year. What is the reason for the increase in working hours? Schor believes there are a number of reasons. For hourly wage earners, wages have declined so much from the mid-1970s to the mid-1990s that workers in 1991 must work roughly 200 extra hours a year to maintain their 1973 standard of living. Thus, there are more dual-earner families and more individuals working overtime or moonlighting at another job. While the professional and managerial worker has seen a real increase in wages over the past two decades, it has been at the cost of additional pressure to work longer hours because of increased competition in a difficult economic climate. Layoffs and downsizing that did not used to affect white-collar workers are now everyday concerns for managers and professionals. They are afraid they may lose their jobs so they work harder and longer.

Schor believes that this trend to increase work hours is counterproductive. Although increased effort may result in economic growth, it comes at the price of stress-related disorders, increased family problems, and stunted personal development. She suggests that Americans should trade this promised economic growth for leisure time, resulting in better health and family relations, as well as minimizing the ecological damage that continued economic growth makes inevitable.

Effect of Mother's Work on Family Life

It is not unusual for a working mother to query a clinician about the effect on her children of her working outside the home. This question may be posed in dead earnest in a therapy session or off-handedly in social conversation at a dinner party or reception. How should the clinician answer? This section briefly reviews pertinent research literature.

The first study concerns the effects of parental employment on the family and children's emotional development. Since 40% of working women have children under the age of 18, this question is of great concern to them. In her exhaustive review of the research on the effect on her family of a mother's working, Hoffman (1987) found no significant differences among these two variables. Although employed mothers spend less time with their children, there appeared to be no difference in infant/mother bonding when compared with non-employed mothers. Employed mothers of school age children were more likely to encourage independence in their children, and these children were more likely to have more egalitarian attitudes about both sexes. Furthermore, daughters of employed women were more likely to see women as competent and effective and name their mother as their adult model. The employed mother's emphasis on independence may possibly be a disadvantage for her sons. For instance, in the blue-collar class the mother's employment may diminish the father's status in their son's eyes.

Effect of Father's Work on Family Life

The question of the effect of a father's job on family life is usually raised in the context of the effects of occupation on child-rearing and conflicts between job demands and family involvement. However, compared with the amount of research being done on working mothers' effect on family life, relatively little has been published on the effect of working fathers on family life (Zedeck & Mosier, 1990).

In a literature review, Bowen and Orthner (1991) concluded that the work involvement of fathers does influence their parenting behavior and family outcomes. Specifically, men who work longer hours characteristically spend less time in parenting and shared marital activities, but this is contingent on the couple's role priorities and expectations for the marriage. For instance, the values, expectations, and demands of certain occupations are quite obvious and tend to be reflected in family rules and behavior. This is particularly common among the clergy and high-risk occupational groups such as the police and military personnel.

Furthermore, Bowen and Orthner report that although contemporary fathers are currently more likely than traditional fathers to spend time in one-on-one interactions with their children, mothers continue to carry a disproportionate level of responsibility for day-to-day child care. And even though current beliefs prescribe increased paternal involvement in child-rearing, fathers' behaviors have clearly lagged behind these expanding expectations. This delay seems to be largely due to the organizational culture of the workplace, which quietly but strongly reinforces traditional fatherhood roles and values and thereby limits the opportunities for men to take advantage of the cultural prescriptions that encourage them to take greater responsibility for and enjoyment in child-rearing.

In short, children of dual-career couples appear to be relatively more independent and resourceful and less susceptible to sex-role stereotyping than children reared in more traditional families. Ultimately, the effect of the dual-career life style on children's adjustment depends on such factors as the quality of the parent/child relationship, the quality of child care, and the personal and marital satisfaction of both parents. The employment of both spouses, if handled with care and sensitivity, can enrich the lives of the entire family.

Concluding Note

That the portrait of the American family is changing is indisputable. That clinicians and counselors working with couples and families will be sensitive and effective regarding this changing reality is another matter. A central theme of this book is that treatment efficacy can be greatly enhanced by tailoring treatment to the unique needs, circumstances, and expectations of couples and families. Tailoring treatment requires a comprehensive, integrative assessment of the unique needs, circumstances, and expectations of the client-system.

References

Avery-Clark, C. (1986). Sexual dysfunction and disorder patterns of husbands of working and non-working women. *Journal of Sex and Marital Therapy, 12*(4), 282–296.

Baker, D., & Scott, J. (1992). Predictors of well-being among pastors' wives: A comparison with non-clergy wives. *Journal of Pastoral Care, 46*(1), 33–41.

Barnett, F., & Barnett, S. (1988). *Working together: Entrepreneurial couples.* Berkeley: Ten Speed Press.

Bennett, A. (1990). *The death of the organization man.* New York: William Morrow.

Benson, B. (1990). *Your family business.* Homewood, IL: Dow Jones-Irwin.

Betz, N., & Fitzgerald, L. (1987). *The career psychology of women.* Boston: Academic Press.

Bolger, N., Delongis, A., Kessler, R., & Worthington, E. (1989). The contagion of stress across multiple roles. *Journal of Marital and Family Therapy, 51*, 175–183.

Boss, P., McCubbin, H., & Lester G. (1979). The corporate executive's wife's coping patterns in response to routine husband-father absence. *Family Process, 18*, 79–86.

Bowen, G., & Orthner, D. (1991). Effects of organizational culture on fatherhood. In F. Bozett & S. Hanson (Eds.), *Fatherhood and families in cultural contexts.* New York: Springer.

Bucholz, B., & Crane, M. (1989). *Corporate bloodlines: The future of the family firm.* New York: Lyle Stuart.

Burden, D. (1986). Single parents and the work setting: The impact of multiple job and homelife responsibilities. *Family Relations, 35,* 37–43.

Conger, R., Elder, G., Lorenz, F., Conger, K., et al. (1990). Linking economic hardships to marital quality and stability. *Journal of Marriage and the Family, 52,* 643–656.

Cooper, R. (1991). *The performance edge: New strategies to work effectiveness and competitive advantage.* Boston: Houghton-Mifflin.

Danco, K. (1981). *From the other side of the bed: A woman looks at life in the family business.* Cleveland: Center for Family Business.

Davis, P., & Stern, D. (1980). Adaptation, survival and growth of the family business. *Human Relations, 34*(4), 207–224.

Dyer, W. (1986). *Cultural change in family firms: Anticipating and managing business and family transitions.* San Francisco: Jossey-Bass.

Freudenberger, H. J., & Freedheim, D. K. (1989). Treatment of individuals in family business. *Psychotherapy, 26*(1), 47–53.

Gerstel, N., & Gross, H. (1984). *Commuter marriage: A study of work and family.* New York: Guilford Press.

Gilbert, L. (1985). *Men in dual-career families: Current realities and future prospects.* Hillsdale, NJ: Lawrence Erlbaum.

Goldenberg, I., & Goldenberg, H. (1984). Treating the dual-career couple. *American Journal of Family Therapy, 12,* 29–37.

Googins, B. (1991). *Work/family conflicts: Private lives—public responses.* New York: Arburn House.

Greenhaus, J. (1987). *Career management.* Chicago: Dryden Press.

Greenhaus, J., & Beutell, N. (1985). Sources of conflict between work and family roles. *Academy of Management Review, 10,* 76–88.

Greenhaus, J., Paraguaman, S., Granrose, C., et al. (1989). Sources of work-family conflict among two-career couples. *Journal of Vocational Behavior, 34,* 133–153.

Greiff, B., & Munter, K. (1980). *Tradeoffs: Executive, family and organizational life.* New York: New American Library.

Hall, F., & Hall, D. (1979). *The two-career couple.* Reading, MA: Addison-Wesley.

Hanson, S., & Sporakowski, M. (1986). Single parent families. *Family Relations, 35,* 3–8.

Hardesty, S., & Jacobs, N. (1986). *Success and betrayal: The crisis of women in corporate America.* New York: Simon & Schuster.

Hoffman, L. (1987). Work, family and the child. In M. Pallak & R. Perloff (Eds.), *Psychology and work: Productivity change and employment.* Washington, DC: American Psychological Association.

Horowitz, L., Locke, K., Morse, M., et al. (1991). Self-derogations and interpersonal theory. *Journal of Personality and Social Psychology, 61,* 68–79.

Johnson, A. (1990). Relocating two-earner couples: What companies are doing. *The Conference Brand.* Research Bulletin #247.

Kanter, R. (1977). *Men and women of the corporation.* New York: Basic Books.

Kaslow, F., & Ridenour, R. (1984). *The military family.* New York: Guilford Press.

Kieran, D., & Monro, B. (1988). Handling greedy clergy roles: A dual clergy example. *Pastoral Psychology, 36*(4) 239–248.

Lang, D. (1988). *The phantom spouse: Helping you and your family survive business travel and relocation.* NewYork: Dodd, Mead, 1988.

Lorenz, F., Conger, R., Simon, R., Whitbeck, L., & Elder, G. (1991). Economics pressure and marital quality. *Journal of Marriage and the Family, 53,* 375–388.

Mahler, S. (1989). How working single parents manage their two major roles. *Journal of Employment Counseling, 26*(4), 178–185.

Mickey, P., & Ashmore, G. (1991a). Denominational variation on the role of the clergy family. *Pastoral Psychology, 39*(5), 287–294.

Mickey, P., & Ashmore, G. (1991b). *Clergy families: Is normal life possible?* Grand Rapids, MI: Zondervan.

Mirkin, M. P. (1990). *The social and political contexts of family therapy.* Boston: Allyn & Bacon.

Papanek, H. (1974). Men, women, and work: Reflections on the two-person career. *American Journal of Sociology, 78,* 852–872.

Poloma, M., Pendleton, B., & Garland, T. (1981). Reconsidering the dual-career marriage: A longitudinal approach. *Journal of Vocational Behavior, 2,* 205–224.

Rapoport, R., & Rapoport, R. (1975). Men, women and equity. *The Family Coordinator, 24,* 421–432.

Ray, J. (1990). International patterns and marital satisfaction among dual-career couples. *Journal of Independent Social Work, 4*(3), 61–73.

Rice, D. (1979). *Dual-career marriage: Conflict and treatment.* New York: Free Press.

Rosenblatt, P., de Mik, L., Anderson, R., & Johnson, P. (1985). *The family in business.* San Francisco: Jossey-Bass.

Schor, J. B. (1991). *The overworked American: The unexpected decline of leisure.* New York: Basic Books.

Seidenberg, R. (1973). *Corporate wives-corporate casualties.* New York: Amacom.

Sekaran, U. (1986). *Dual-career families.* San Francisco: Jossey-Bass.

Sekaran, U., & Hall, D. (1989). Asynchronism in dual-career and family linkages. In M. Arthur, D. Hall, & B. Lawrence (Eds.), *Handbook of Career Theory* (pp. 159–180). Cambridge: Cambridge University Press.

Shaevitz, M., & Shaevitz, H. (1980). *Making it together as a two-career couple.* Boston: Houghton-Mifflin.

Shinn, M., Wong, N., Simko, P., et al. (1989). Promoting the well-being of working parents. *Journal of Community Psychology, 17*(1), 31–55.

Sperry, L., & Carlson, J. (1991). The work-centered couple. *The Family Psychologist, 7*(4), 19–21.

Stoltz-Loike, M. (1992). *Dual-career couples: New perspectives in counseling.* Alexandria, VA: American Association for Counseling and Development.

Stringer, D. (1985). Counseling the dual-career couple. In D. Myers (Ed.), *Employee problem prevention and counseling* (pp. 191–206). Westport, CT: Quorum.

Vanderkolk, B., & Young, A. (1991). *The work and family revolution: How companies can keep employees happy and business profitable.* New York: Facts on File.

Voydanoff, P. (1985). *Work and family life.* Beverley Hills, CA: Sage.

Walker, L., Rozee-Koker, P., & Wallston, B. (1987). Social policy and the dual-career family: Bringing the social context into counseling, *Counseling Psychologist, 15*(1), 97–121.

Ward, J. L. (1987). *Keeping the family business healthy.* San Francisco: Jossey-Bass.

Whyte, W. (1956). *The organization man.* New York: Simon and Shuster.

Zedeck, S., & Mosier, K. (1990). Work in the family and employing organization. *American Psychologist, 45*(2), 240–251.

3

Theories of Family Therapy
Goals, Treatment Process, and Techniques

Therapists must be able to explain family functioning in a manner that makes sense to the family seeking treatment. For example, we are often presented with families in which the problem/dysfunction is easy to describe, and yet the family cannot or does not seem to find any meaning in the explanation or treatment that we first give. It is therefore necessary to use alternative explanations. The many alternative theories of family therapy have well-developed rationales and strategies and their own proponents. Each perceives the family and explains its functioning in a somewhat different fashion. Some theories clearly explain certain phenomena but are vague about others. However, in spite of their differences, family therapy theories are similar in that they are all *interpersonal models*. These models are distinct from the traditional intrapsychic, or individual, models. Both types of models (interpersonal and intrapsychic) are based on very different philosophical assumptions and therefore have distinct methods of conceptualization and technique. They are both valuable and effective, given the appropriate context.

Most professional therapists were trained in the intrapsychic model and may have difficulty switching to an interpersonal, systemic paradigm (Huber, 1994). Family therapy approaches are based on a family systems model of therapy and have the following common tenets.

1. The whole is greater than the sum of its parts.

2. Individual parts of a system can be understood only within the context of the whole system. Since human behavior arises within a social system, it can be understood only within this context.

3. Traditional models of linear cause and effect are replaced by notions of circular, simultaneous, and reciprocal cause and effect.

4. Change in one part of a social system (for example, an individual family member) will affect all other parts of that system (for instance, the entire family).

5. Systems have a tendency to seek homeostasis, or equilibrium. This balance-seeking function serves to maintain stability and sometimes prevents change.

6. When a family is out of balance, or equilibrium, feedback mechanisms attempt to bring the family back into balance.

7. The methods used to restore equilibrium (for example, the identified attempts of patient to solve problems) can become problems themselves.

8. Interventions from an interpersonal/family systems perspective focus on relationships within the entire family system rather than on one individual in the family (that is, on the identified patient) (Walsh & McGraw, 1996).

The purpose of this chapter is to provide a brief description of some of the major family therapy theories—their goals in treatment, treatment process, and techniques. Additionally, intrapersonal theories (that is, behavioral and object relations) that also address family work are included, because many of their goals, treatment processes, and techniques may be used by the family therapist. We hope the reader will develop in-depth knowledge of each of these theories by reading from the corresponding additional resources sections. Therapists must have a broad knowledge base to know when and how to use techniques. Treatment cannot be tailored unless the therapist understands the full range of strategies.

Adler

According to Alfred Adler, all behavior is purposive and interactive. Both individuals and social systems are holistic, and individuals seek significance by the manner of their behavior in social systems. The basic social system is the family. It is from the family that individuals learn how to belong and interact.

Problems, or dysfunctions, in families result from discouragement or lack of acceptance within the family. The treatment process stresses education to promote growth and change. The therapist addresses the interactions within the family system and changes the interpersonal system.

Family dynamics (Walsh & McGraw, 1996) include a wide variety of concepts related to the interplay of structural and functional components in a family system. They include the following:

- *Power:* The lines of movement through which the family and each of its members strive toward goals. Mechanisms in the family through which power is channeled include decision making, manipulation, and negotiation.

- *Boundaries and intimacy:* The degree of physical and emotional closeness and inclusion or exclusion among family members.

- *Coalitions:* Two or more people joined together for mutual support or to oppose one or more other individuals. These arrangements may take the form of open alliances or hidden collusions.

- *Roles:* Reciprocal characteristic patterns of social behavior that members of a social system expect from one another.

- *Rules:* Implicit or explicit guidelines that determine what behavior is acceptable or not acceptable in a family. Rules are related to a family value system and may vary with different roles in the family. Natural or logical consequences provide corrective feedback.

- *Complementarity and differences:* Dissimilar roles in a family that may be integrated by a process of cooperative reciprocity. Individual differences among members of a system can lead to an interaction of thesis and antithesis and ultimately result in a new synthesis.

- *Similarities:* Qualities of a family, including shared vocabulary and a common perception of experience, that enhance family cohesiveness and identity.

- *Myths:* A family's subjective representational model of reality. Rules and roles in a family arise from the family's myths.

- *Patterns of communication:* Verbal and non-verbal communications that form the basis of interactions in a family. Faulty communication due to double messages, withholding information, or over-generalizing can lead to misunderstanding and problems in the system. (pp. 104–105)

Goals

The general goal of Adlerian family therapy is to promote change in both individuals, as well as the family as a whole. The specific goals differ with each family; however, basic ones are as follows:

- To promote new understanding and insight about purposes, goals, and behavior

- To enhance skills and knowledge in areas such as communication, problem solving, and conflict resolution

- To increase social interest and positive connections with others

- To encourage commitment to ongoing growth and change

According to Sherman and Dinkmeyer (1987), the goals of family therapy may be attained by change at several levels:

1. In perceptions, beliefs, values, and goals

2. In play, structure, and organization

3. In social interest, feelings, and participation

4. In skills and behavior

5. In the use of power

Treatment Process

The treatment process of Adlerian family therapy is organized into four phases. In the first phase, the therapist gains access to the family system and uses joining and structuring to set the stage for the remainder of the therapeutic process. The second phase is devoted to assessment. In this phase information is gathered, and tentative hypotheses about the family dynamics are formulated. During the third phase, the family gains increased understanding of their problems and develops awareness and commits to reorientation. In the fourth phase, the changes achieved in therapy are solidified, and the therapist begins to disengage from the family system and to develop a process of relapse prevention.

Techniques

According to Grunwald and McAbee (1985), the key techniques of Adlerian therapy are as follows.

- *Family constellation:* Information is obtained about the birth order of all family members and about siblings, relationships to and between parents, the family climate, additional parental models, and physical, academic, sexual/gender, and social development in childhood, as well as life meanings in childhood. The role of the adult is often formed by his or her birth order and the influence of the personalities of siblings and parents.

- *Early recollections:* Each family member is asked to share eight memories from early childhood. The description of these memories are analyzed according to theme and developmental maturity. Often family members construct memories, but they are still helpful in identifying the unconscious psychological goals of the person and the ideal self.

- *Typical day:* Parents or other family members are asked to detail events in a complete typical day.

- *Encouragement:* Techniques are used that convey respect and equality and that support understanding, having faith in family members, asking for help, using logical consequences, honesty, the right to make decisions, setting goals, the right to give encouragement, consistency, and the use of encouraging words.

- *Paradoxical intention:* A therapist assigns the symptom as a homework assignment.

- *Use of family council:* Family meetings are held on a regular basis in which all family members participate in the discussion of issues so that each person's views are taken into consideration in the making of decisions.

- *Use of logical or natural consequences:* Parents are taught how to use natural consequences with their children without arguing or criticizing them. For example, a child who is late for dinner may not eat until the next meal.

- *Confrontation:* The therapist points out mistaken personal logic.

Additional techniques are intended to promote improved communication. All family members are requested to adhere to communication guidelines:

- Speak for yourself and do not suggest what others may think or feel

- Speak directly to others, not through a third party or in vague generalities

- Do not scapegoat or blame

- Listen and be empathic

- Continue to build improved communication in the family (Dinkmeyer & Dinkmeyer, 1991)

Further Resources

Carlson, J., & Slavik, S. (Eds.) (1997). *Techniques of Adlerian psychology.* Washington, DC: Taylor & Francis.

Dinkmeyer, D., & Carlson, J. (1984). *Time for a better marriage.* Circle Pines, MN: American Guidance Service.

Dinkmeyer, D., & McKay, G. D. (1989). *STEP: Parents' guide*. Circle Pines, MN: American Guidance Service.

Sherman, R., & Dinkmeyer, D. (1987). *Systems of family therapy: An Adlerian integration*. New York: Brunner/Mazel.

Bowen/Intergenerational

Bowen and his followers see the family as an emotionally interdependent unit. A change in one part of the family system will evoke changes in other parts and in the family as a whole. Behavioral patterns are created over time and are frequently repeated for several generations. Each family exerts pressure (that is, homeostasis) to force the conformity of each member's behavior. The family creates the emotional climate and behaviors that members will duplicate outside the family setting.

Goals

In the Bowenian model, therapists have goals of treatment for themselves that are crucial to the family's attainment of their goals. According to Kerr and Bowen (1988), the primary goals are (1) to reduce the anxiety of the family, allowing family members to improve their ability to function independently and to reduce their symptomatic behaviors and (2) to increase each family member's basic level of differentiation, enabling each to respond more effectively to emotionally intense situations. Symptom reduction and decreased anxiety can occur relatively quickly in treatment. Improvement in the basic level of differentiation is a long-term process that can take many years. The main goal, however, is to assist one or more members of the family to move to a greater level of self-differentiation.

Treatment Process

If the therapist is able not to be triangulated, and the family is able to interact in an atmosphere of low anxiety and reactivity, Bowen believed that progress would occur. Bowen's theory contains two main variables: degree of anxiety and degree of self-integration. Most organisms can adapt to acute anxiety of short duration; however, chronic anxiety over long periods of time can lead to differentiation of self and to physical illness, emotional symptoms, or social delinquency. This anxiety is infectious and can spread to other members of the family. People can seem normal at one level of anxiety; however, they will become ill or abnormal at more intense levels of anxiety.

The therapist may work with a marital couple, the entire family, or just one individual from the family. The configuration of individuals seen by the therapist may change as treatment progresses. According to Bowen (1978), progress in therapy depends on the therapist's ability to relate meaningfully to the family without becoming emotionally entangled in the family system (p. 312). Bowen listed the five main functions of the therapist in the treatment process with the family as follows:

1. Define and clarify the relationship between spouses (that is, develop and use the genogram)

2. Keep self detriangled from the family's emotional system

3. Teach the functioning of emotional systems using the tenets of the model

4. Demonstrate differentiation by managing self during the course of therapy

5. Resolve cut-offs (Papero, 1991, p. 61)

Techniques

- *Talk to therapist, not to each other:* This is done to keep emotional reactivity and anxiety in the sessions low.

- *Person to person relationship:* The therapist establishes a relationship with each person that allows him or her to share personal thoughts and feelings directly with the therapist while his or her partner and/or other family members observe. In this way, the spouses begin to develop a person-to-person relationship in their marriage, rather than creating an emotional divorce. Each person learns to focus on self, rather than talking or gossiping about a third person.

- *Asking frequent factual questions:* This technique serves to focus on thinking and intellectual processes. The thinking of family members is externalized so that members of the family system can hear one another's perspectives.

- *Emotional neutrality:* The therapist remains emotionally neutral and avoids taking sides, thus remaining detriangled from the family emotional system. The therapist also maintains neutrality in the sessions through the use of modeling, non-verbal behavior, and the appropriate use of humor (Bowen, 1978).

- *Genograms:* A genogram is a map representing the process and structure of at least three generations of a family. Genograms are used to organize information about a family and provide a means to track a family's progress in therapy.

- *Detriangling:* This refers to the process of remaining objective in response to the family. The therapist is able to share his or her own thoughts and feelings without becoming offensive or putting down the views of others. The therapist remains calm in response to reactions by other family members.

Further Resources

Bowen, M. (1978). *Family therapy and clinical practice*. New York: Jason Aronson.

Kerr, M. E., & Bowen, M. (1988). *Family evaluation: An approach based on Bowen theory*. New York: W. W. Norton.

Papero, D. V. (1990). *Bowen family systems theory*. Boston: Allyn & Bacon.

Communication/Satir

The hallmark of Virginia Satir's work is to increase the self-esteem of individuals in a family in order to change the interpersonal system. She found a direct correlation between self-esteem and communication, with low self-esteem being associated with poor communication. The family is viewed as a holistic system. Roles have a major effect on the effectiveness of family functioning by influencing rules, communication processes, and responses to stress. When family members become aware of what they are experiencing in the present, they can grow, both as individuals and as a family.

Goals

Satir's therapeutical goal was increased maturity. Her main aim was to integrate the growth of each family member with the integrity and the health of the family system. Specifically, she wanted (1) to assist the family to gain hope, awakening dreams of what the future can be like; (2) to strengthen the coping process and the coping skills of family members; (3) to make it clear to all that individuals can make choices and take responsibility for the outcomes of those choices; and (4) to promote good health in the individual family members and the family system (Satir & Baldwin, 1983). Specifically, Satir focuses on releasing and redirecting blocked energy by facilitating the development of increased self-esteem, improved communication skills, and more tolerant rules.

The outcome of family therapy in general terms is stated quite clearly by Satir (1983) as follows:

Treatment is completed:

- When family members can complete transactions, check and ask for feedback
- When they can correctly interpret hostility
- When they can see how others see them
- When one member can tell another how he/she manifests him/herself
- When one member can tell another what he/she hopes, fears, and expects from him/her
- When family members can disagree
- When they can make choices
- When they can learn through practice
- When they can free themselves from harmful effects of past models
- When they can give a clear message—that is, be congruent in their behavior with a minimum of difference between feelings and communication and with a minimum of hidden messages (p. 176)

Treatment Process

The treatment process is consistent with the goals of treatment in that family work is a process of facilitating effective communication and building self-esteem in a rational context. Satir and Bitter (1991) indicate that as therapy becomes more successful, the anxiety levels decrease significantly, and the family learns how to see change as an expected part of family life. The five stages of treatment are as follows:

1. Establish trust with the family. Develop an assessment and treatment plan early to gain the confidence of the family. Satir referred to this as *making contact.*

2. Develop awareness through experience. The therapist helps the family develop new awareness about their functioning by asking specific questions or using specific techniques. This Satir called *chaos.*

3. Create new understandings in family members through new or increased awareness of their family dynamics.

4. Have family members express and apply these new understandings through different behaviors during the session.

5. Have family members use the new behaviors outside the therapeutic environment—what Satir referred to as *integration*.

Techniques

*   *Family-life fact chronology:* A holistic family history is made extending from the birth of the oldest grandparents to the present.

*   *Family maps:* Visual representations similar to genograms are created of family structure over three generations. In Satir's use of this technique, three family maps are drawn: mother's family of origin, father's family of origin, and the current family.

*   *Ropes*: Ropes representing relationships with other family members are tied to the waist of each member until each has as many ropes as there are family members. The other ends of the ropes are tied to each of the other family members. All the family members become aware of how they are connected and how tension is created in the ropes. Often entanglements occur. This provides concrete representation of the dynamics in the family system.

*   *Metaphor:* A word used to represent an idea and the idea itself are discussed by analogy. For example, Satir would use the word "pod" as a metaphor for a person's self-esteem and then ask how full a person's pod was at a given time.

*   *Touch:* Satir used touch with family members, shaking hands with each person at the beginning of therapy. However, she was careful not to violate the boundaries of individuals, because some people consider touch to be a violation.

*   *Sculpture:* A family member is asked to describe his or her relationship to one or more family members using bodily positions and gestures to represent degrees of closeness and communication patterns. When movement is added, the family sculpture becomes a stress ballet. All entities that affect the family dynamics, including pets, extended family, and friends, are symbolically brought into the sculpture through the use of role-playing and fantasy.

*   *Drama:* Family members are asked to act out a scene in the life of the family or an individual. These enactments of significant events in the family history again provide an opportunity for a new perspective and for more insight.

- *Family reconstruction:* Similar to drama, family reconstruction involves enactment of events from the family history based on information derived from the family-life fact chronology or the family maps.

- *Reframing:* The therapist creates a shift in the perceptions of family members. The therapist decreases the threat of blame by accentuating the ideas of puzzlement and good intentions.

- *Humor:* Humor can be used to promote contact between therapist and family, as well as among family members. It can mitigate intensity, clarify exaggerated dynamics, and encourage movement in a way that decreases defensive action. Satir would use a light touch of humor to keep a relaxed atmosphere for learning.

- *Verbalizing presuppositions:* The therapist overtly states presuppositions that are evident in a family's behavior. For example, Satir would verbalize the hope and expectation for change a family manifests by virtue of their involvement in therapy.

- *Denominalization:* This involves obtaining specific behavioral descriptions for words such as "love" and "respect" and discovering exactly what must be done for the person to perceive that he or she is receiving love and respect. The clarified answer is often related to the individual's primary sensory-base representational system (that is, visual, auditory, or kinesthetic).

- *Anchoring:* Anchoring refers to a learned association between a stimulus and a response or between one response and another. This technique serves to bring feelings to the level of interpersonal physical experience.

- *Multiple family therapy:* Numerous unrelated families are brought together for joint family sessions.

- *Communication stances:* Satir would ask family members to participate in an exercise in which each person plays the physical position of a certain stance: placater, blamer, computer, distractor, and congruent person. Family members share feelings associated with using various stances and with responding as recipients to stances. In this way, family members increase their awareness of effective communication and learn how to become congruent.

- *"I" statements:* Satir would encourage family members to own their feelings. Often people use passive forms such as "it is confusing." Satir would model the active form, "I am confused," in family therapy and develop exercises in which family members would practice using such "I" statements.

Further Resources

Satir, V. (1972). *Peoplemaking*. Palo Alto, CA: Science & Behavior Books.

Satir, V. M. (1983). *Conjoint family therapy* (3rd ed.). Palo Alto, CA: Science & Behavior Books.

Satir, V. M. (1988). *The new peoplemaking*. Palo Alto, CA: Science & Behavior Books.

Satir, V. M., & Baldwin, M. (1983). *Satir: Step by step*. Palo Alto, CA: Science & Behavior Books.

Satir, V., Baxmen, J., Gerber, J., & Gomori, M. (1991). *The Satir model: Family therapy and beyond*. Palo Alto, CA: Science & Behavior Books.

Experiential

Carl Whitaker used an atheoretical and practical approach to families. He emphasized experiencing and expressing emotions in the here and now, promoting the natural growth tendency in families, and recognizing the struggle between autonomy and interpersonal belonging within the family group. Using a metaphor, Whitaker and Bumberry (1988) compare symbolic-experiential family therapy to the telephone lines, water pipes, and gas mains of a city—the infrastructure. The impulses and symbols that flow through the infrastructure affect the surface life of the city in a pervasive way. By participating in symbolic-experiential family therapy sessions, family members become comfortable with their impulses and can integrate them into everyday life. The therapist focuses on experiencing and discussing these impulses and symbols in the therapy session. The family will need to make decisions about how they will live. Life involves decision and struggle. The therapist cannot do it for them: they will need to do it themselves.

Goals

The goals of treatment in family therapy are to simultaneously increase the perception of belonging on the part of the family members and the freedom for each family member to be a separate individual (Whitaker & Keith, 1981). To accomplish this overall goal of increased belonging and individuation, therapists attempt to do the following:

1. Expand the symptoms, escalating interpersonal stress

2. Develop a sense of family nationalism

3. Improve relationships with past generations of the extended family

4. Increase contact with the community and its members, in particular the culture group

5. Understand expectations of the family and family boundaries

6. Increase the separation between generations

7. Encourage the family and its members to learn to play

8. Provide a model of a continuous joining, separating, and rejoining

9. Confront the myth of individuality

10. Encourage family members to be themselves

Treatment Process

Since creativity is emphasized, therapy sessions are unpredictable. Often the relationship between parents is one of the primary targets of the work. Whitaker and Bumberry (1988) maintain that men are raised to relate to objects, such as cars, computers, and activities, not to intimacy and close relationships as women are. The therapists show that relationships are bilateral. Each person can change the relationship by what is done and said. By withdrawing and assuming that a relationship is only unilateral, the spouse sentences the relationship to deterioration. By involvement and hard work, relationships can improve.

Techniques

- *Joining:* The therapist makes contact with each family member, beginning with the most distant, typically the father. If the therapist forms a relationship with the father, the family usually stays in therapy.

- *Homework:* The only assignment is to refrain from discussing therapy and relationships between sessions and to stop being therapists to one another.

- *Use of self:* One of the main characteristic techniques of symbolic-experiential therapy is the use of the self by therapists. Therapists are in touch with themselves and share their personal processes with the family. They never betray themselves by losing themselves in the family.

- *Additional techniques:* According to Thomas (1992), the following techniques are often used:
  (1) Redefining symptoms as attempts to grow
  (2) Encouraging family members to talk about fantasy alternatives (such as how one spouse might kill the other)

(3) Converting an intrapersonal problem to an interpersonal stress by the use of fantasy (for example, ask what the other family members might do if one family member committed suicide; the therapist initiates the fantasy and asks the suicide-prone individual to complete it)

(4) Increasing and exaggerating the pain of a family member

(5) Playing with children in the interview

(6) Using feelings to confront people (such as telling parents to "bug off" when they interrupt the play between the therapist and one of the children)

(7) Sharing spontaneous primary process suggestions as they arise

(8) Playing with family roles (encouraging family members to reverse roles)

(9) Seeing love and hate not as opposite but as yoked feelings (pp. 226–227)

Further Resources

Napier, A., & Whitaker, C. A. (1978). *The family crucible.* New York: Harper & Row.

Simon, R. (1985). Take it or leave it: An interview with Carl Whitaker. *The Family Therapy Networker, 9*(5), 27–37, 70–75.

Whitaker, C. A., & Bumberry, W. M. (1988). *Dancing with the family: A symbolic-experiential approach.* New York: Brunner/Mazel.

Milan

The Milan group became fascinated by Bateson's (1972) concept of cybernetic circularity (the idea that the family system was constantly evolving) and developed an interview method of circular questioning to scan for difference and to tap the pattern of circularity used by the living system of each family. The therapist would remain neutral in an effort to assess the map or belief system of the families. Families appeared stuck because of epistemological errors—that is, outdated belief systems. Goals of the therapist were to develop a hypothesis from the data obtained in the questioning sequence and to introduce new information into the system that would allow families to change their belief systems.

The systemic school of family therapy takes its name from the cybernetic systems theory on which Bateson based his work. The information theory and theory of games of which Bateson often wrote are important in this approach. Accordingly, human beings in reciprocal interactions through time are becoming each other; on viewing the river, one *is* the river. People are neither good nor evil. The family is always changing its members, who remain connected with one another, influencing one another continuously over time.

The Milan group would be considered the purest application of the systems work of Bateson in that every technique or practice represents a particular application of his systemic theory. Presenting problems are recognized as serving a function in the family system. Patterns of interaction are passed on through generations; therefore, the history of the family is important in cognitive processes. Ideas, beliefs, perceptions, and fantasies are addressed, along with behaviors.

Goals

Change is seen as a random discontinuous process and there is no way to predict the creative, alternative ways families will find to evolve. By changing the thinking patterns and cognitive maps, it's possible to stimulate the family to find its own way of solving their problems. An overriding goal for the therapy team is to have the family discover, interrupt, and eventually change the rules of their game. The family may create a solution to their problem that is different from the therapist's goal. The parental couple is encouraged to regain the skills that will enhance their leadership function.

Treatment Process

In the treatment process, the therapist remains neutral. Frequently the therapeutic process involves more than one therapist. The Milan system treatment process uses extended breaks between sessions, often one month or more, to allow prescriptions to fully effect the family system.

Techniques

- *Telephone chart:* The telephone chart is an assessment tool developed by the Milan group. Information is obtained from the family over the telephone before they make an appointment. During this interview, the Milan group talks with the family member requesting treatment for at least 15 to 30 minutes. This is done to obtain information necessary to generate a hypothesis before the therapy team meets with the family and to decide whom the family should invite to the first session.

- *Circular questioning:* The role that the symptom is playing and has played in the family system is assessed using circular questions asking each family member to comment on or speculate about other family members' beliefs, feelings, and behavior. The therapist uses circular questions to find out the reactions of family members and determine their perceptions of the problem.

- *Hypothesizing:* An hypothesis is an educated assessment of a family's thinking patterns and myths that are holding them back. Hypothesizing is a process whereby the therapy team speculates, in advance of the family session, about what might be responsible for causing the family's problems. The therapists, therefore, come to each session prepared with hypotheses to be tested. This prevents the family from imposing their faulty problem definition on the therapy session and thereby preventing solutions.

- *Positive connotations:* The attribution of positive motives for an individual's or family's symptomatic behavior patterns is critical to success in the Milan model. (Different terms used to describe a similar process in other models include *reframing, noble ascription,* and *positive attribution.*)

- *Prescriptions:* Prescriptions are paradoxical interventions whereby the family or certain family members are directed to perform the symptomatic behavior, thereby demonstrating that the symptom is under voluntary control. If the directive is resisted, the family gives up the troubling symptom.

- *Split team intervention:* This is a type of prescription whereby the family is told that the therapy team has different opinions or ideas regarding a particular family dynamic. This process allows the family game to be uncovered, gives the therapist in the session leverage, and allows the family to find their own resolution.

- *Ritual and ceremony:* These are methods of prescription whereby family members put into action a series of behaviors designed to alter the family game. The therapists spell out the specifics of the prescription in minute detail. This is the type of prescription that directs the family members to change their behavior under certain circumstances. Thus the therapist hopes to change the cognitive map, or meaning of the behavior.

- *Counterparadox:* This technique is used to instill a therapeutic double bind in a family system to undo a preexisting family double bind message. For example, a common counterparadox is to inform the family that even though the therapists are change agents, they do not want to alter what seems to be a workable homeostatic balance in the family and consequently prescribe no change for the time being (Selvini-Palazzoli et al, 1978).

Further Resources

Bateson, G. (1972). *Steps to an ecology of mind.* New York: E. P. Dutton.

Boscolo, L., Cecchin, G., Hoffman, L., & Penn, P. (1987). *Milan systemic family therapy: Conversations in theory and practice.* New York: Basic Books.

Selvini-Palazzoli, M., Boscolo, L., Cecchin, G. F., & Prada, G. (1978). *Paradox and counterparadox: A new model and therapy of the family in schizo-phrenic transaction.* New York: Aronson.

Selvini-Palazzoli, M., Cirillo, S., Selvini, M., & Sorrention, A. M. (1989). *Family games: General models of psychotic processes in the family.* New York: W. W. Norton.

Simon, R. (1987). Good-bye paradox, hello invariant prescription: An interview with Mara Selvini-Palazzoli. *The Family Therapy Networker,* September/October, 17–33.

Constructivist/Narrative

This model of family therapy, based on constructivism, examines how individuals can re-author their life stories in a way that externalizes the concern that brought them to therapy. Therapists assist families to create new stories by asking them to explain unique outcomes (that is, situations in which the family has attained their goals on found solutions). The process of developing new stories creates a sense of personal urgency for family members that enables them to better manage future struggles. This therapeutic process also promotes an appreciation of the subjective nature of human histories. Constructivist family therapy contradicts the typically held position that the family system causes the problem; instead, it believes that the problem promotes the formation of the family's belief system (that is, the family system evolves around it).

Goals

This approach is still in the process of being developed; however, many theorists—for example, Goolishian and Anderson, and White and Epston—use portions of this approach. The overall focus is to develop new meanings or stories about our lives and our roles in life. Problems are seen as the stories that people have agreed to tell themselves. Constructivist/narrative therapists believe that stories of misery and personal failure are not so much approximations of the truth as they are life constructions made up of stories, metaphors, and the like (Gergen, 1991). Narrative therapists are less interested in objective claims and more so in the social utility that the stories have in explaining one's life. Constructivist therapy then has a goal of reconstructing new stories or developing alternative stories in order to promote changes in behavior.

Treatment Process

The process of therapy can take the form of Goolishian and Anderson's seeing themselves as learners and conducting therapy from a position of not knowing. This is not to say that the therapist lacks knowledge or is without therapeutic skills, but rather he or she does not begin with any preconceived ideas about what should change. The family and the therapist work together to co-create stories different from those previously held. The therapy takes its shape from the emergent qualities of the conversations that it inspires.

White and Epston, in contrast, have specific stories that they want families to adopt. Such stories highlight the family's past, present, and future, putting people and the family, not the problems, in charge. White and Epston use externalization to help the family see themselves as separate from the problems that brought them into treatment.

Techniques

- *Externalizing:* In this process, families achieve a non-pathological view of the problem, one in which no one is to blame. The family is offered an empowering opportunity to develop a new narrative that provides an alternative account of their lives.

- *Deconstruction:* This process unravels the history of the problem that has shaped the lives of the family members.

- *Reconstruction/re-authoring:* This is the process by which a new story is developed.

- *Letters:* Following therapy, letters are written to the family that summarize the sessions, invite reluctant members to attend future sessions, and address the future. This serves the purpose of extending conversations while encouraging family members to record or map out their own futures.

- *Unique outcomes:* In this process, the family is asked to identify exceptional events, actions, or thoughts that contradict their dominant problem-saturated story and to develop alternative stories in which the problem does not defeat them or even exist.

- *Reflecting team:* One or more times during the therapy session, a group of other professionals who have been observing the session (that is, the reflecting team) talk in front of the family and therapist so that they, in turn, may become observers of the process that they have been a part of. The team members talk about the family conversation they have just observed. This allows family members to shift between an inner and outer dialogue process and develop new perspectives on the same event, which often leads to a therapeutic breakthrough.

- *Questions:* Many of the questions used by Michael White are designed to elicit specific responses. They help people to realize (1) they are separate from the problem, (2) they have power over the problem, and (3) they are not who they thought they were. The use of questions allows the family to reach empowering conclusions.

Further Resources

Anderson, H., & Goolishian, H. (1988). Human systems as linguistic systems: Preliminary and evolving ideas about the implications for clinical theory. *Family Process, 27*, 371–393.

Bubenzer, D. L, & West, J. D. (1993). Kenneth J. Gergen: Social construction, families, and therapy. *The Family Journal, 1*(2), 177–187.

Bubenzer, D. L., West, J. D., & Boughner, S. R. (1994). Michael White and the narrative perspective in therapy. *The Family Journal, 2*(1), 71–83.

O'Hanlon, B. (1994). The third wave. *The Family Therapy Networker,* November/December, 19–29.

West, J. D., Bubenzer, D. L., McQuistion, R. R., & Cox, J. A. (1995). Harlene Anderson: A conversation on language systems in therapy and training. *The Family Journal, 3*(2), 164–175.

White, M., & Epston, D. (1990). *Narrative means to therapeutic ends.* New York: W. W. Norton.

Wylie, M. S. (1994). Panning for gold. *The Family Therapy Networker,* November/December, 40–48.

Solution-Focused

The philosophy behind the solution-focused model is based on the idea that change is constant and inevitable. The emphasis in therapy is on what is possible and changeable, rather than what is impossible. This model focuses on taking small steps to initiate change, and as the process progresses, changes will occur. According to this model, deShazer, for example, states that the solutions people are using are the problem, not the presenting problems themselves. Therefore, the focus is on solutions and competencies, rather than on problems. In this model, meanings are negotiable. The goal of therapy, therefore, is to choose meanings that will lead to change.

Goals

The goals of this type of brief therapy are to alter the world view of the family in subtle ways and to change family members' behavior so that a solution to the problem evolves and the problem is resolved. The primary goal is addressing the family's presenting concern. Formation of goals with the family is a crucial component of the solution-focused model and begins in the first session. It is preferable that the goals be specific, measurable, attainable, and challenging.

Treatment Process

The general treatment process allows for variation and still follows a fairly structured course. In the initial session, introductions are made, structure is imposed, and a statement of the complaint is elicited—specific information is collected from each family member. Then a discussion ensues about what goes on when the family is not experiencing the problems described in their complaint. Once the therapist gains sufficient background information, he or she may use "the miracle question," which asks the family how things would be different if a miracle occurred and the problem were solved. This encourages the family to think about change. Next the therapist develops compliments and tasks. The compliments prepare the family to be responsive to homework tasks.

Techniques

- *Deconstructing:* This refers to creating a doubt in the family's frame of reference regarding the complaint, which creates a need and expectation for change, making the consideration of new behaviors possible.

- *Clue:* Intervention that mirrors the behavioral responses of the family is called a *clue*. If the family operates using double binds or paradoxes, then intervention would be a *counterparadox*. If the family behaves in a straightforward manner and takes direction well, the prescription of a task to be completed would constitute the clue.

- *Confusion:* Each family member is asked in detail about family differences, especially as they relate to goals in therapy, and the therapist admits confusion without reaching any resolution of the differences.

- *Past successes:* The therapist compliments the client on particular past successes but does not directly link these to the resolution of the present problem.

- *Skeleton keys:* These formal interventions or stock prescriptions can be used with many different types of problems.
  (1) *Write/read/burn:* on odd-numbered days of the month, the client is to spend 1 hour writing about all the bad and good times that the client experienced with the ex-spouse, for example, on even days of the month, the client spends 1 hour reading what has been written and then burns it.
  (2) *Structured fight:* to decide the order of a fight, toss a coin. The winner complains for 10 straight minutes. Then the other person gets a turn for 10 minutes. Ten minutes of silence are maintained before the coin is tossed for a second round.
  (3) *Do something different:* the therapist directs the client to do something different related to the specific problem situation between the current session and the next session.
  (4) *Overcoming the urge:* clients who are tempted to eat too much or to return to drinking alcohol or taking drugs are directed by the therapist to observe whatever they are doing when they overcome the desire to indulge.
  (5) *Intervention before the initial session:* clients are asked to pay attention to whatever is occurring in their lives—in marriage, family, or relationships—that they would like to have continue so that they can describe it in detail at the initial session. (deShazer, 1985)

- *Miracle question:* Ask the family how things would be different if a miracle occurred and the problem were solved. This question encourages the family to think about change and exactly what *would* happen if changes occurred.

- *Scaling:* The therapist has the family provide numerical ratings regarding the state of affairs in the family. On a scale from 1 to 10, with 1 being as bad as it could be and 10 being as good as it could be, where do they rate the situation now? Ongoing scaling used in sessions presupposes change and provides feedback on differences among family members.

Further Resources

Berg, I. K., & Miller, S. (1992). *Working with the problem drinker: A solution-focused approach.* New York: W. W. Norton.

Bubenzer, D. L., & West, J. D. (1993). William Hudson O'Hanlon: On seeking possibilities and solutions in therapy. *The Family Journal, 1*(4), 365–379.

deShazer, S. (1982). *Patterns of brief family therapy: An ecosystemic approach.* New York: Guilford Press.

deShazer, S. (1985). *Keys to solutions in brief therapy.* New York: W. W. Norton.

deShazer, S. (1988). *Clues: Investigating solutions in brief therapy.* New York: W. W. Norton.

deShazer, S. (1991). *Putting differences to work.* New York: W. W. Norton.

deShazer, S. (1994). *Words were originally magic.* New York: W. W. Norton.

Miller, S., & Berg, I. K. (1995). *The miracle method.* New York: W. W. Norton.

Strategic

The strategic family therapy model is based on the idea that families are rule-governed systems and can be best understood in this context. Furthermore, the presenting problem serves a function in the family that must be recognized. Symptoms are system-maintained and system-maintaining, and destructive ongoing cycles of interaction prevent the family or couple from achieving its basic purposes. Developmental stages in the family life cycle warrant consideration because halted development can lead to problems later. In strategic family therapy, the focus is on the present; insight into the cause of the problem is less important than effecting a change in behavior or functioning.

Goals

The goal of treatment is to solve the presenting problem of the family. The problem is defined as a sequence of behaviors among family members within a social context. It is the therapist's responsibility to plan interventions that resolve the problem within the social context of the client. A secondary goal of treatment is to help the family members move to the next phase of the family life cycle, as well as their own individual life cycles. For example, the stage of a young adult's leaving home is a particularly difficult one for the person and for the family.

Treatment Process

Therapeutic process is practical, brief, and conducted by the therapist. The objective of the treatment process is to interrupt behavioral sequences to promote goal attainment. According to Haley (1987), there are five stages of therapy.

1. *Social stage:* The therapist talks to each person, asking his or her name and obtaining a response, similar to a hostess or a host encouraging guests to feel comfortable. The therapist looks at the seating arrangement that the family has chosen, mentally drawing tentative hypotheses, and also matches the mood of the family to vocal tone and gestures.

2. *Problem stage:* The therapist asks formal questions about the problem.

3. *Interaction stage:* The therapist asks family members to talk with one another about the problem and observes who talks to whom, who remains silent, and who interrupts whom, but does not share any tentative hypotheses with the family.

4. *Goal-setting stage:* The therapist finds out what changes are expected by family members as a result of therapy, specifying these in clear behavioral terms.

5. *Task-setting stage:* The therapist gives the family a directive. This may be practiced in the session, but is more often a homework assignment to be completed between sessions. An appointment for the next session is set during this stage, and the therapist specifies which family members are to return.

Problem-solving therapy follows these stages until the presenting problem and any other problems are resolved.

Techniques

*   *Directives:* In strategic therapy, the predominant technique is the use of *directives*, also occasionally called *prescriptions*. Directives are orders the therapist gives, either directly or indirectly, hoping for either compliance or its opposite, rebellion. The goal is to help people change their behavior, thereby changing their subjective reality. Directives serve three basic functions in therapy: (1) to promote behavior change and new subjective experiences for family members; (2) to intensify the therapist/client relationship through the use of tasks; and (3) to gather useful information about the family by noting the family's responses to the directives.

*   *Paradoxical directives:* The therapist assigns tasks in which success is based on the family defying instructions or following them to an extreme point and ultimately recoiling, thus producing change. Typically these tasks are assigned when the therapist has reason to believe the family will resist straightforward directives.

- *Reframing:* This is also referred to as *relabeling, positive interpretation, positive connotation,* and *reattribution.* In this intervention, the therapist offers a different view of the presenting problem that enables the family members to think and behave differently within the next context.

- *Prescribing the symptom:* In this paradoxical intervention, the client is directed to perform the symptomatic behavior.

- *Pretend techniques:* These are paradoxical interventions in which clients are directed to pretend to have the problem behavior—for example, a father that fears having a heart attack is told to pretend he is having one during the therapy session. Since the behavior was the result of pretending, it may be reclassified as voluntary and unreal.

- *Restraining changes:* In these paradoxical interventions, the therapist attempts to discourage the family from moving too fast. He or she may even deny the possibility of change.

- *Ordeals:* The therapist issues a directive that tells the client to do something that is more severe than having the symptoms of the problematic behavior. Typically the directive refers to something that is good for the person. For example, a woman who feels anxious is required to exercise for several minutes.

- *Metaphor for tasks:* These are directives that involve activities or conversations that symbolically relate to the presenting problem and thereby indirectly facilitate change.

- *Devil's pact:* This is a task to which the family must commit before the therapist discloses it. The family is advised that the task is extremely demanding, and therefore they must decide whether or not they really want to resolve their problems.

Further Resources

Haley, J. (1963). *Strategies of psychotherapy.* New York: Grune & Stratton.

Haley, J. (1973). *Uncommon therapy: The psychiatric techniques of Milton H. Erickson, M.D.* New York: W. W. Norton.

Haley, J. (1984). *Ordeal therapy: Unusual ways to change behavior.* San Francisco: Jossey-Bass.

Haley, J. (1987). *Problem solving therapy* (2nd ed.). San Francisco: Jossey-Bass.

Madanes, C. (1981). *Strategic family therapy.* San Francisco: Jossey-Bass.

Madanes, C. (1984). *Behind the one-way mirror: Advances in the practice of strategic therapy.* San Francisco: Jossey-Bass.

Simon, R. (1986). Behind the one-way kaleidoscope. *The Family Therapy Networker*, September/October, 19–29, 64–67.

West, J. D., & Bubenzer, D. L. (1993). Cloe Madanes: Reflections on family therapy. *The Family Journal, 1*(1), 98–106.

Structural

Structural family therapy focuses attention on the present and the future. According to this theory, the history of the family is manifest in the present, and therefore it is accessible through interventions in the here and now. Humans are viewed as social creatures and must be viewed holistically within the context of their social systems. Environmental factors are given priority over hereditary factors. The reciprocal nature of systemic causality (that is, the situation whereby an individual's behavior influences and is influenced by his or her social system) is acknowledged.

There is also an emphasis on process over content. Family structure is seen as comprising sets of family transactions. Transactions determine how family members relate; they can be verbal or non-verbal, known or unknown. Transactions regulate behavior in two ways: (1) a power hierarchy exists that dictates authority and decision making in a family; and (2) and mutual expectations formed by negotiations over time are determined and fulfilled by individuals in a family.

Components of the family structure that exist to carry out various family tasks are called *subsystems*. Subsystems can be formed on the basis of generation, interest, or specific family function. It is possible for family members to belong to several subsystems at the same time. The most important subsystems are the adult, parental, and sibling subsystems. Subsystem boundaries are constructed by a set of rules that define who participates in the subsystem and how individuals participate. The nature of the boundaries has a significant effect on the functioning of the subsystem as well as the entire family unit. There are three types of boundaries that lie on a continuum: (1) rigid boundaries; (2) clear boundaries; and (3) diffuse boundaries.

The rules of the family provide the structure by which operations can occur that meet the needs of the family as a whole. Substructures within the family system interact according to the rules that serve as boundaries between the subsystems. Internal and external stressors necessitate adaptation of the family structure to maintain homeostasis. In addiition, the developmental process creates a predictable stressor for most family systems.

Goals

The overriding goal of structural family therapy is to solve problems in the family and to change the underlying systemic structure. By bringing about changes in the structure of the family, one can solve the presenting problems. Structural family therapy emphasizes action over insight. In particular, action occurs in the session. By restructuring family transactions directly in the session, one effects change in the family structure. Through homework assignments, families continue to change through action.

Treatment Process

Minuchin (1974) sees treatment as structural change that modifies the family's functioning so it can better perform necessary tasks. Once the therapist has initiated change, new processes will be maintained by the family's self-regulating mechanisms. Since the family is a dynamic system in continual movement, the steps in the therapeutic process may overlap and recycle. Typical steps in the treatment process of structural family therapy are as follows:

1. *Joining and accommodating:* The therapist adjusts to the communication style and perceptions of family members to join with the system. The goal in this stage is to establish an effective therapeutic relationship with the family.

2. *Structural diagnosis:* This refers to the continuous process of observation and hypothesis-testing and reformulation relevant to the family's structure and transactions. The goal in this stage is to provide a framework of information relevant to the problem in the family system that is amenable to structural intervention.

3. *Restructuring:* The therapist uses therapeutic interventions that bring about change through modification in the family structure. The goal in this stage is the development of a family structure capable of appropriately dealing with future stressful situations.

Techniques

- *Joining:* The primary goal of joining or accommodating techniques is to establish an effective therapeutic relationship. This involves acting out the predominant mood of the family. To accomplish this end, three restructuring functions occur:
  (1) *Maintenance:* supporting specific behaviors and verbalizations to increase the strength and independence of individual subsystems and alliances.

(2) *Tracking:* using clarification, amplification, and approval of family communication to reinforce individuals and subsystems.

(3) *Mimesis:* adopting the family's communication style and conforming to its affective range (for example, if the family frequently uses expletives, the therapist adopts this mode of speaking).

- *Restructuring:* This is a process of changing the structure of the family. It can be accomplished through enactments, delineating the boundaries, unbalancing (by forming a coalition with some family members against another family member), and complementarity. Walsh and McGraw (1996) lists the following as restructuring techniques used by Minuchin:

  (1) *Enactment:* having family members recreate an interaction. The interaction may be relatively innocuous or may directly relate to the presenting problem. Enactments are used to diagnose family structure, increase intensity, and restructure family systems.

  (2) *Actualizing family transactional patterns:* stimulating naturalistic family interactions so the therapist can observe the typical transaction. This may be achieved by directing the family to have a conversation or by the therapist refusing to answer a question.

  (3) *Marking boundaries:* strengthening diffuse boundaries and increasing the permeability of rigid boundaries to enhance healthy subsystem interaction. This can be accomplished by helping the family members to set new rules, renegotiate old rules, and establish specific functions for each subsystem.

  (4) *Escalating stress:* heightening tension in a family to force them to accept restructuring. This can be achieved by encouraging conflict when it occurs, joining alliances against other family members, and blocking dysfunctional transactional patterns that serve to decrease stress in a system.

  (5) *Assigning tasks:* assigning specific tasks for individuals or subsystems to be accomplished in the session and at home.

  (6) *Utilizing symptoms:* altering the function a symptom serves in the family system by encouraging, deemphasizing, or relabeling the symptom. This might also remove the secondary gain that may be inherent in the symptomatology.

  (7) *Paradoxical injunction:* imposing a directive that places the client in a therapeutic double bind that promotes change, regardless of client compliance with the directive. This technique is typically used when resistance to the directive is anticipated.

  (8) *Manipulate mood in the family:* modeling an exaggerated reflection of a frequently manifested mood in the family. For example,

if yelling is frequently used in the family, to create a volatile
mood the therapist may yell even louder.

(9) *Support, education, and guidance:* providing direct instruction to
the family to behave differently.

- *Reframing:* In reframing, a positive connotation is given to a negative behavior. For example, a mother may yell at her son to do his
homework. The yelling on the part of the mother is reframed as concern about her son. Reframing is an important interpersonal skill; it
shows that there are advantages and disadvantages of every behavior. By accepting the behavior, the person will often decrease the
behavior.

- *Relabeling:* If the blaming projective stance is typical of families in
treatment, an adjective that is positive in connotation is substituted
for an adjective that is negative in connotation. For example, if the
wife screams at the husband that he is controlling, the therapist
relabels by saying the husband is overburdened.

- *The family lunch*: Minuchin, Roseman, and Baker (1978) developed
a technique for working with anorexic families in which the therapist actually eats with the family and enacts the parents attempting
to force the anorectic person to eat.

Further Resources

Minuchin, S. (1974). *Families and family therapy*. Cambridge, MA: Harvard
University Press.

Minuchin, S., & Fishman, C. H. (1981). *Family therapy techniques*. Cambridge,
MA: Harvard University Press.

Minuchin, S., & Nichols, M. P. (1993). *Family healing*. New York: Free Press.

Minuchin, S., Roseman, B., & Baker, L. (1978). *Psychosomatic families: Anorexia
nervosa in context*. Cambridge, MA: Harvard University Press.

Simon, R. (1984). Stranger in a strange land: An interview with Salvador
Minuchin. *The Family Therapy Networker, 8*(6), 21–31, 66–68.

West, J. D., & Bubenzer, D. L. (1993). Salvador Minuchin: Practitioner and theo-
retician. *The Family Journal, 1*(3), 277–282.

Behavioral and Cognitive-Behavioral

Behavioral and cognitive-behavioral family therapists believe that families and couples are influenced solely by their environments. Behavioral
patterns are learned; therefore, dysfunctional behaviors can be replaced

by more adaptive ones. In marriage and family therapy, therapists and the family can specify behavioral goals, assess present patterns, and develop new patterns. Cognitive-behavioral therapists have gone beyond a focus just on observable actions to include the words people say to themselves and others. They have developed specific techniques for confronting irrational ideas espoused by family members.

Behavioral and cognitive-behavioral approaches are linear. They address the thoughts and behaviors of individuals who pursue goals in logical ways. The family is not viewed as a separate system with properties of its own (Thomas, 1992, p. 312).

Goals

The goals of cognitive-behavioral therapy are as follows:

1. Assess present patterns and teach families how to assess behavioral interactions and/or thoughts.

2. Teach new adaptive patterns such as communication skills, problem resolution, competencies, behavioral exchange, contracting, negotiation of rules and roles, and managing conflict.

3. Weaken or decrease maladaptive behavior.

4. Create and maintain reinforcement patterns that create a collaborative reciprocity.

Treatment Process

The therapeutic process involves a clear analysis and assessment of the family's functioning. The cognitive-behavioral therapist uses assessment before initiating therapy, during the initial session, throughout the therapy process, at termination, and often in follow-up many months after therapy is terminated. The therapist functions as an educator and role model to teach the family how to assess their own relationships and implement the strategies of behavioral/cognitive change and to use their own resources to strengthen their relationships. This is essentially a teacher and learner model.

Techniques

- *Completing inventories and presenting ground rules:* This technique is used at the beginning as well as throughout the treatment process. An assessment is made of the expectations for treatment, as well as what is going on in the present relationship. Developmental history is of a secondary nature and only of interest as it affects the present.

- *Caring days:* Couples do counseling exercises, in which each spouse is asked to describe exact behaviors his or her partner should show for the spouse to know his or her partner cares. For example, each spouse is required to clearly state "I feel loved when you. . . ." Rules stipulate that the requested behaviors be small and exhibited at least daily and that they have not been the cause of recent conflicts, are not chores, are positive, and are specific (Stuart, 1980).

- *Communication skills training:* Behavioral and cognitive-behavioral therapists teach couples to listen, to make constructive requests using "I" statements, to give positive feedback complimenting a spouse on a particular positive behavior immediately after it occurs, and to use clarification and questions to check out non-verbal and verbal behaviors.

- *Contracting:* Using a win-win approach, families are encouraged to negotiate a holistic contract. Each family member is required to make requests of the others for specific positive behaviors. Other family members rephrase the request and ask for clarification of meaning. After reaching a consensus, they record their request in contract form and sign it.

- *Decision-making skills:* Each person identifies those areas where they exercise power and those areas where they ideally would like to exercise power. The family then negotiates who will control what area, under what conditions, and in what situations. Families may use a "powergram" to discuss those areas that each member controls alone, those that each controls after consulting others, and those that are controlled equally.

- *Conflict management skills:* Discussions are confined to the present, rather than expanding to related incidents or issues from the past. The stages of conflict include trigger, reflex, fatigue, commitment, reconsolidation, and rapprochement.

- *Maintenance of therapeutic outcome:* This process includes the following components:
    (1) explaining the rationale for each intervention and the principles of relationship change
    (2) modeling techniques during the therapy that the clients themselves can apply in the future in their relationship
    (3) teaching family members how to assess interaction and change the relationships so that they can continue these processes after termination
    (4) helping families to anticipate predictable relapses
    (5) identifying supports in the environment by encouraging the family to spend 1 hour a month assessing the family relation-

ship, rewarding one another for the gains that have been made, and making new requests for additional desirable behaviors

(6) equipping the family with reminders of ways the family has successfully handled problems in the past, such as a written summary of the interventions used and the changes made by each person on the completion of an experiential "what-if" exercise.

- *Cognitive restructuring:* Family members are encouraged to become observers of their own interpretations of family events and to develop skills to test the validity of these interpretations through collecting and processing data (Epstein, Schlesinger, & Dryden, 1988).

Further Resources

Beck, A. T. (1988). *Love is never enough.* New York: Harper & Row.

Epstein, N., Schlesinger, S. E., & Dryden, W. (Eds.) (1988). *Cognitive-behavioral therapy with families.* New York: Brunner/Mazel.

Freeman, A. (Ed.) (1983). *Cognitive therapy with couples and groups.* New York: Plenum.

Stuart, R. (1980). *Helping couples change: A social learning approach to marital therapy.* New York: Guilford Press.

Object Relations

The essence of object-relations theory is quite simple: We relate to people in the present partly on the basis of expectations formed by early experience. This theory is based on Freudian theory and the later work of theorists such as Kohut, Mahler, Fairbairn, and Winnicott. The theory conceptualizes current relationship difficulties as originating in early parent/child interactions. This model attempts to bridge intrapsychic and interpersonal approaches by using object-relations concepts such as individual development, projection, and ego identity within a relations context. The general goal of this model is to provide a therapeutic environment in which the family can understand and resolve unconscious issues that are problematic to current family functioning.

Goals

The goal of object-relations family therapy is to make conscious the unconscious patterns established in the family of origin. This is done through interpreting patterns of transference and counter-transference, which leads to increased awareness and elimination of blocks.

Treatment Process

Stages of object-relations therapy involve:

1. Establishment of a therapeutic contract.

2. Development of therapeutic alliance.

3. Working through defenses and resistances—family members' object relations from the family of origin are played out and talked about, leading to increased understanding of any interlocking pathologies.

4. Termination issues dealing with loss and separation.

Techniques

Object-relations therapists are a diverse group that share the idea that internal images derived from significant relationships in the past produce faulty, unsatisfying, or distorted dealings with people in the present. This approach is characterized by four basic techniques:

- *Listening:* The therapist resists the pressure to do something and maintains analytic neutrality, which promotes an atmosphere of listening and understanding. No demands are placed on the family to change.

- *Empathy*: The analyst works very hard at understanding the world from the family's point of view.

- *Interpretation:* Interpretations are used to clarify hidden and confusing aspects of experience.

- *Maintaining analytical neutrality*: The therapist suspends involvement with the outcome and maintains an atmosphere of analytic exploration.

Further Resources

Framo, J. (1992). *Family of origin therapy: An intergenerational approach.* New York: Brunner/Mazel.

Scharff, D. E., & Scharff, J. S. (1987). *Object relations family therapy.* Northvale, NJ: Jason Aronson.

Slipp, S. (1988). *The technique and practice of object relations family therapy.* Northvale, NJ: Jason Aronson.

Slipp, S. (1984). *Object relations: A dynamic bridge between individual and family treatment.* New York: Jason Aronson.

Summary

This chapter has presented the major approaches to family therapy. Each was presented in terms of a brief description of approach, goals, therapeutic process, and techniques. Readers can refer to this overview to develop a general intervention plan before developing a more tailored plan. The remaining chapters of the book describe the process of tailoring therapy plans to meet individual family needs.

References

Bateson, G. (1972). *The steps to an ecology of mind.* New York: E. P. Dutton.

Bowen, M. (1978). *Family therapy and clinical practice.* New York: Jason Aronson.

deShazer, S. (1985). *Keys to the solution in brief therapy.* New York: W. W. Norton.

Dinkmeyer, D., & Dinkmeyer, J. (1991). Adlerian family therapy. In A. M. Horne & J. L. Passmore (Eds.), *Family counseling and therapy.* Itasca, IL: F. E. Peacock.

Epstein, N., Schlesinger, S. E., & Dryden, W. (1988). Concepts and methods of cognitive-behavioral family treatment. In N. Epstein, S. E. Schlesinger, & W. Dryden (Eds.), *Cognitive-behavioral therapy with families* (pp. 5–48). New York: Brunner/Mazel.

Gergen, K. J. (1991). *The saturated self: Dilemmas of identity in contemporary life.* New York: Basic Books.

Grunwald, B. B., & McAbee, H. V. (1985). *Guiding the family: Practical counseling techniques.* Muncie, IN: Accelerated Development.

Haley, J. (1987). *Problem solving therapy.* (2nd ed.) San Francisco: Jossey-Bass.

Huber, C. H. (Ed.) (1994). *Transitioning from individual to family counseling.* Alexandria, VA: American Counseling Association.

Kerr, M. E., & Bowen, M. (1988). *Family evaluation: An approach based on Bowen's theory.* New York: W. W. Norton.

Minuchin, S. (1974). *Families and family therapy.* Cambridge, MA: Harvard University Press.

Minuchin, S., Roseman, B., & Baker, L. (1978). *Psychosomatic families: Anorexia nervosa in context.* Cambridge, MA: Harvard University Press.

Papero, D. V. (1991). The Bowen theory. In A. M. Horne & J. L. Passmor (Eds.), *Family counseling and therapy.* Itasca, IL: F. E. Peacock.

Satir, V. (1983). *Conjoint family therapy* (3rd ed.). Palo Alto, CA: Science & Behavior Books.

Satir, V., & Baldwin, M. (1983). *Satir step by step: A guide to creating change in families.* Palo Alto, CA: Science & Behavior Books.

Satir, V., & Bitter, J. R. (1991). Human validation process model. In A. M. Horne & J. L. Passmore (Eds.), *Family counseling and therapy* (2nd ed.). Itasca, IL: F. E. Peacock.

Selvini-Palazzoli, M., Boscolo, L., Cecchin, G. F., & Prada, G. (1978). *Paradox and counterparadox: A new model and therapy of the family in schizophrenic transaction.* New York: Aronson.

Sherman, R., & Dinkmeyer, D. (1987). *Systems of family therapy: An Adlerian integration.* New York: Brunner/Mazel.

Stuart, R. (1980). *Helping couples change: A social learning approach to marital therapy.* New York: Guilford Press.

Thomas, M. D. (1992). *An introduction to marital and family therapy.* New York: Charles Merrill.

Walsh, W. M., & McGraw, J. A. (1996). *Essentials of family therapy: A therapist's guide to eight approaches.* Denver: Love Publishing Company.

Whitaker, C. A., & Bumberry, W. M. (1988). *Dancing with the family: A symbolic-experiential approach.* New York: Brunner/Mazel.

Whitaker, C. A., & Keith, D. V. (1981). Symbolic-experiential family therapy. In A. S. Gurman & D. P. Kniskern (Eds.), *Handbook of family therapy* (pp.187–225). New York: Brunner/Mazel.

4

Integrative Treatment with Couples and Families

The Basis for Treatment Efficacy

In each treatment session, the therapist is confronted with a barrage of information: verbal and non-verbal behavior, intrapsychic and interpersonal processes, transactional patterns, attitudes, and more. The multitude of processes that occur in the individual, the subsystem, the family, and the therapeutic system are so complex and multidimensional that no one could possibly attend to all or even most of them. Neither is it possible for any therapist to reflect on all these perceptions, to perfectly formulate them, to decide on the best possible intervention plan and strategies. Therefore, the therapist limits his or her observations, reflections, and interventions to a reasonable and manageable number of variables and selectively decides on which processes, patterns of behavior, and structure to focus. These decisions are often determined by the therapist's own life history, personality structure, philosophy of life, and professional training.

An important aspect of professional training is the theory or theories of family therapy that the therapist espouses. These theories serve to organize clinical information, concepts, and experiences in a way that limits reality to a limited number of concepts and processes that allows plausible effect and goal-means-results thinking and conclusions to be made (Textor, 1988). In short, the adopted theories greatly influence what the therapist perceives, formulates, and reports or describes and how he or she intervenes. Thus, because of this selectivity factor, each theory of family therapy is necessarily limited and one-sided. Since no theory can explain and predict all the behavioral patterns and intrapsychic and interpersonal processes a therapist may observe, similarly no theory or approach is suited for the treatment of all behavioral, intrapsychic, and interpersonal problems.

Most introductory family therapy texts detail various theories, schools, and approaches to family therapy. Some of these approaches have engendered considerable support. However, the loyalty of supporters tends to be based more on evangelical fervor than scientific rigor. Historically, the early development of each individual therapy approach seems to have gone through an evangelical phase in which the new approach is viewed as transcending the mistakes of previous therapy systems and seeming to possess unlimited therapeutic potential. Proselytizing of converts to the new approach actually begins with workshops, publications, independent training institutes, and then university training programs. Psychoanalysis went through such an era between 1900 and 1930, while the mid-1950s to the early 1970s were the evangelical years of behavior therapy.

The shortcomings of the various family therapy approaches have prompted the search for more comprehensive and integrative theories of family therapy—the topic of this chapter. The first section focuses on the history, terminology, and profile of therapists who function from an integrative perspective. The second section surveys two meta-analyses of the family therapy literature regarding integrative concepts. The third section overviews a number of integrative family therapy approaches, including three clinical research models.

Integration: History, Terminology, and Proponents

Since 1970 we have witnessed evangelical fervor in the field of marital and family therapy. Too often the proponents of the psychoanalytic, systems, and behavioral family therapy models have espoused purism and denounced attempts toward eclecticism and integration. Haley (1987) is one of the strongest opponents of integration. He believes that those who espouse integration are essentially unable and unwilling to understand the unique nature of family therapy. Thankfully, this evangelical era in family therapy is passing, and the expectation that family therapists must adhere to a particular model of family therapy is lessening (Lebow, 1987). More and more therapists are concluding that no single theory or set of interventions can be applied to all cases. The shifting therapeutic scene and the increasing number of non-traditional families presenting for therapy have hastened this conclusion. The question now is this: how can the insights of different theories and approaches be

combined and systematically be integrated to yield a r
sive and useful theory to guide therapeutic work with

The early 1990s have been replete with published .
ingenious and successful efforts at integrating the concepts an.
niques of the traditional models of family therapy. However, these
efforts at integration are often hampered by conceptual and termino-
logical confusion. The following section attempts to clarify concepts
and terminology.

The term *integration* is similar to but still different from the related
concepts of *eclecticism, tailoring,* and *matching. Eclecticism* refers to
a philosophy of treatment in which the clinician selects concepts and
treatment methods from a variety of theoretical sources. There is an
element of pragmatism in this approach. In other words, eclectic clinicians practice the way they do because they have found that such an
approach works. *Integration* refers to a treatment philosophy in which
the clinician incorporates and combines discrete parts of theories and
treatment processes. The purpose of theory integration is the construction of a more useful model that maximizes the therapist's understanding and ability to intervene effectively in changing a specific family
system (Aradi & Kaslow, 1987).

Integrators are eclectics, but not all eclectics are integrators. Both
eclectic and integrative positions are basically clinician-centered, which
is to say that the clinician develops a particular way of personalizing
therapeutic concepts and techniques to meet his or her own needs
for therapeutic effectiveness, intellectual synthesis, or whatever. In
contrast, tailoring refers to the philosophy of basing treatment decisions
on what is best for the client or system. Gordon Paul's (1987) classic
formulation describes the focus of tailoring: "What treatment, by
whom, is the most effective for this individual or couple with that
specific problem and under which set of circumstances" (p. 111).
Essentially, tailoring is basically a client or couple-centered orientation
to treatment planning and intervention. Furthermore, tailoring can be
distinguished from matching. Technically, *matching* means assigning
a client-couple or family to a specific clinician or treatment modality
most likely to increase therapeutic efficacy, whereas *tailoring* means
specifically adapting treatment methods to client-couple or family needs
once matching has occurred. Nevertheless, the two terms are often used
interchangeably.

Another way of thinking about integration is in terms of the
"process" of integration—how integration takes places—and the "content" of integration—what is being integrated (Case & Robinson, 1990).
The family therapy literature describes the content of integration in at

.ast four distinct ways: (1) combining individual and family therapy (Feldman, 1985; Feldman, 1992; Pinsof, 1983); (2) developing a specific method of treatment that combines elements from different family therapy schools (Boszormenyi-Nagy & Krasner, 1986; Duhl & Duhl, 1981); (3) creating meta-theoretical models (Levant, 1984; Sluzki, 1983; Stanton, 1984); and (4) matching family therapy models with family style or level of functioning (Doherty, Colangelo, & Hovander, 1991; Weltner, 1988).

The process of integration can involve a number of strategies. Colapinto (1984) describes three such strategies: (1) the recipe book approach, based on the belief that a particular problem dictates a particular method; (2) the spontaneous approach, based on the clinician's intuitive judgment about what might work best at a given time; and (3) the model building approach, whereby the clinician chooses a unifying conceptual core as a central organizing principle supplemented by specific techniques or ideas from other approaches.

Norcross (1986) estimates that approximately 40% of psychotherapists classify themselves as favoring an integrative perspective. He cites survey data of the integrative orientation among professional disciplines: 40% of counseling psychologists; 35% of clinical psychologists in independent practice; 42% of behavioral therapists; and 54% of clinical social workers. No data seem to be available to indicate the percentage of family therapists who primarily identify themselves as operating from an integrative perspective.

Norcross found no differences, except for clinical experience, between those espousing an eclectic perspective and those adopting a non-eclectic perspective. Clinicians espousing integration tended to be older and more experienced than their non-integrative counterparts. Robertson (1979) identified six factors that appear to facilitate the adoption of an integrative viewpoint. The first is a lack of pressure in training and professional environments to bend to a doctrinal position. This includes the absence of charismatic figures to emulate. The second factor is length of clinical experience. As therapists gain experience with a heterogeneous client population and a wide variety of problems, they tend to reject a single theory or model approach. The third factor involves the extent to which their practice of psychotherapy is perceived as a career versus a vocation and personal philosophy of life. Robertson believes that integrators are more likely to represent the former position. The last three factors are personality variables. Integrators have an obsessive/compulsive desire to synthesize all the interventions in the therapeutic universe. They have maverick temperaments allowing them to move beyond their therapeutic model of origin. Finally, integrators possess a skeptical attitude toward the status quo.

Integrating Concepts from Various Family Therapy Models

All couples and family relationships can be characterized in terms of three meta-constructs that essentially combine and integrate concepts and principles of most marital and family therapy schools and approaches. These three constructs are boundaries or inclusion, power or control, and intimacy (Doherty, Colangelo, Green, & Hoffman 1985; Fish & Fish, 1986).

Boundary issues in families center on membership and structure: membership in the sense of who is involved in the marital or family system and to what degree; structure in terms of the extent to which family members are part of but at the same time apart from the couple subsystem or family unit. Boundary issues also refer to interpersonal boundaries, specifically the degree of intrusiveness that will be accepted in the relationship. For a married couple, commitment to their relationship is a core boundary issue, as is the partners' relative commitments to jobs, extended family, friends, and other outside interests. For children, boundaries usually center on the sense of belonging to the family, while at the same time having a sense of being recognized as an individual.

Power issues include responsibility, control, discipline, decision making, and role negotiation. Family interactions continually involve overt as well as covert attempts to influence decisions and behavior. Control or power issues are typically tied to issues of money, reward, and privileges. They also manifest themselves in more subtle ways such as escalation of conflict or one-upmanship in efforts to regulate another family member's behavior. Couple interaction also involves struggle for control of the relationship in various ways. Essentially, the basic dynamic in marital conflict involves who tells whom what to do under certain circumstances. Both couple and family interactions range from positive to negative emotionally, and from laissez-faire to democratic to autocratic (politically). Thus, power becomes a meta-rule for all decisions about boundaries as well as intimacy. It determines which member or partner will pursue and which will distance, and how this is accomplished.

Intimacy issues in families are evident in areas like self-disclosure, friendship, caring, and appreciation of individual uniqueness. Intimacy involves negotiating emotional as well as physical distance between partners or among family members. In either instance, the goal is to balance a sense of autonomy with feelings of belonging. When issues of affection in a family become a source of difficulty, they can be manifest in various ways ranging from complaints such as: "You don't understand my feelings," "I'm being taken for granted," or "The romance has gone out of the relationship."

Using similar categories to Fish and Fish, Doherty et al. (1985) analyzed 13 models of family therapy according to the dimensions of inclusion, control, and intimacy. (These 13 models were previously described by Gurman and Kniskern [1978].) The terms of inclusion, control, and intimacy are the basis of Schutz's FIRO model (Fundamental Interpersonal Relationship Orientation Theory; Schutz, 1958). The terms *boundary* and *inclusion* are essentially synonomous, as are the terms *control* and *power*, whereas *intimacy* involves the same dimension in both Doherty's and Fish and Fish's taxonomies. Analyzing 13 major models of marital and family therapy according to these three dimensions has yielded the following classification of therapy models (Doherty et al., 1985):

Inclusion-Boundary	Control-Power	Intimacy
Contextual	Strategic	Couples contract (Sager)
Bowen	Behavioral	Family of Origin (Framo)
Structural	Problem-centered (McMaster Model)	Symbolic-experiential (Whitaker)
Functional	Interactional	Integrative (Duhl and Duhl)
		Communications (Satir)

Basically, the conceptual analysis of the 13 models indicates that four of these models primarily emphasize inclusion or boundary as the primary focus, four emphasize the control or power dimension, and five primarily emphasize the issue of intimacy. Doherty et al. also rated the secondary and tertiary emphases of each of the 13 models. They believe that this conceptual analysis provides a guide for therapists wishing to become more eclectic or integrative in their clinical practice, by suggesting a way to match therapy techniques from different family therapy models to the presenting couple or family issue that each model emphasizes most strongly.

Clinical Research Models of Family Therapy

The traditional approaches to family therapy were developed from clinical work with couples. Usually, the clinicians who pioneered a new approach were dissatisfied with the methods they had been employing, and so they gradually developed their own unique approach. Often the development of their approach followed a pragmatic and experiential rather than experimental line of inquiry. For the most part, research was not a consideration or priority in the early stages of theory development. That came later, after the theory and approach were sufficiently developed. It was then that researching the effectiveness of the approach, usually in comparison with other approaches, became a consideration.

However, the three approaches presented on the following pages have a different history. These theoretical approaches were developed in a clinical research format. This means that theory, methods of assessment, and treatment strategies and techniques stemmed from a more inductive and experimental rather than experiential approach. These models are excellent examples of clinical research approaches to marital theory and therapy. They are the McMaster model, Olson's circumplex model, and the Beavers system model.

The McMaster Model of Family Function and Therapy

The McMaster model of family functioning was developed in the early 1960s by Epstein, Bishop, and Levin (1978) at McMaster University. The corresponding therapy model is called *problem-centered family systems therapy*. Both will be described in this section, beginning with the family functioning model, which is a useful tool for evaluating marriages and families and is based on the systems approach. As such, it describes the structure, organization, and transactional patterns of the family and marital unit. It allows an examination of a marriage or family relations along the total spectrum ranging from healthy to the severely pathological. Unlike other models that conceptualize family behavior in terms of a single dimension such as communication, power, boundaries, or intimacy, the McMaster model considers six aspects of family functioning:

1. Problem solving

2. Communication

3. Roles

4. Affective responsiveness

5. Affective involvement

6. Behavior control

1. Problem Solving   This dimension is defined as a couple's ability to resolve problems at a level that maintains effective family functioning. A family problem is seen as an issue that threatens the integrity and functional capacity of the family. Problems are divided into instrumental and effective types. Instrumental problems involve everyday issues like finance and housing, whereas affective problems are those related to feelings. There are seven stages that are operationally defined as components of the problem solving process. They are identification of the problem; communication of the problem to the appropriate person or resource; developmental alternative action; decision on one alternative action; action; monitoring the action; and evaluation of success of the action. The most effective couple and family will be able to carry out all seven stages, while the least effective couple or family usually cannot even identify the problem.

2. Communication   *Communication* is defined as the manner in which the couple and family exchange information. The focus is solely on verbal exchange. Verbal communication can then be subdivided into instrumental and affective types. Epstein reports that couples and families can have marked difficulties with affective communication and still function adequately with instrumental communication, but that the reverse is rarely seen. Communication is assessed on two other vectors: clear versus masked and direct versus indirect. These dimensions yield four patterns of communication: clear and direct; clear and indirect; masked and direct; and masked and indirect. The McMaster group proposes that the most effective communication is that which is clear and direct. The more masked and indirect the communication pattern is, the more ineffective the couple's and family's functioning will be.

3. Roles   *Roles* are defined as the repetitive pattern of behavior by which individuals fulfill marital and family functions. Functioning is divided into the instrumental and affective areas, with all the implications previously mentioned. The functions are then subdivided into necessary family functions and other family functions. Necessary functions are those that the couple and family will have to address repeatedly if they are to function well. They include instrumental, affective, and mixed types. Necessary functions include (1) provision of resources; (2) life skills development; (3) nurturance and support; (4) sexual gratification of marital partners; and (5) systems management and maintenance. Couples and families may also develop functions that are unique. Such functions are those that and arise in the course of daily living but that are not necessary for effective couple functioning. Effective couple and family functioning occurs when all necessary functions have both clear allocation to appropriate individuals and built-in accountability. In contrast, in the least effective couples and families, functions are not addressed or allocated and no accountability is maintained.

4. Affective Responsiveness   Affective responsiveness is defined as the ability to respond to a range of stimuli with appropriate quality and quantity of feelings. Two classes of responses are welfare feelings and emergency feelings. Love, tenderness, happiness, and joy are examples of welfare emotions, whereas fear, anger, sadness, disappointment, and depression are examples of emergency emotions. The most effective family will have the broadest repertoire of affective responsiveness; the least effective family will have the narrowest repertoire of affective responsiveness.

5. Affective Involvement   The degree to which the couple and family show interest in and value the activities and interests of individual members is called *affective involvement.* The focus here is on how much and in what way individuals express and invest themselves with one another. The six styles identified for this range of involvement are (1) lack of involvement; (2) involvement of a void of feelings; (3) narcissistic involvement; (4) empathic involvement; (5) over-involvement; and (6) symbiotic involvement. Empathic involvement is viewed as the most effective form, with involvement designations moving to both ends of the spectrum, implying increasingly ineffective forms of functioning.

6. Behavior Control   This dimension is defined as the pattern the couple adopts for handling behavior in three specific situations: those involving physical danger; those involving psychobiological needs, such as eating, sleeping, sex, and aggression; and those involving socializing behaviors both within and outside the family. The standard for acceptable behavior determines the style of behavior control of the particular couple or family. The four styles of control can be classified as rigid, flexible, laissez-faire, and chaotic. Obviously, flexible behavior control is considered the most effective form and chaotic the least effective. To maintain their style of behavior control, couples tend to develop a number of functions to enforce what they consider acceptable behavior, and this style of behavior control becomes part of the system maintenance and management role of function mentioned earlier.

In addition to the conceptual model of couple and family functioning, Epstein and his colleagues have proposed the corresponding treatment model which they call *problem-centered family systems therapy (PCFST).* This model provides the therapist with a detailed and systematic approach to family therapy that stresses directness and collaboration between the couple and a therapist in accessing and resolving specific problems of the family system. Therapy is conceptualized as having two phases: macro stages and micro moves. Macro stages refer to the large sequential blocks of the treatment process, such as assessment or closure. Micro moves involve the numerous interventions made by the therapist while carrying out the macro stages and would include techniques for labeling, focusing, and clarification. PCFST focuses primarily on the macro stages of treatment—on specific problems of the family system and requires a direct involvement of individual members in identifying, clarifying, and resolving these difficulties. It stresses the need for the family's collaboration with the therapist at each stage, insuring that members understand, accept, and are prepared for each step of treatment. This process tends to foster a positive response to the treatment. Usually the treatment is short term, consisting of approximately 6 to 12 sessions. The model provides the couple with an implicit approach to problem-solving that they can generalize and use in resolving difficulties in the future.

There are four macro stages to therapy: assessment, contracting, treatment, and closure. Each stage contains a sequence of substages, the first of which is always orientation. After a general orientation, each substage is approached systematically with the therapist guiding the process. On completion, the therapist and couple review and reach agreement before moving onto the next stage. Epstein and his colleagues indicate that this model has proven useful in a variety of clinical settings, training programs, and research projects.

The McMaster group has developed the Family Assessment Device (FAD) (Epstein, Baldwin, & Bishop, 1983), a questionnaire designed to evaluate families according to the McMaster model of family functioning. It is made up of seven scales including the six areas of functioning plus a scale designated as "general functioning."

Olson's Circumplex Model

Olson and colleagues (1979; 1983) have described a "circumplex" model for understanding and assessing couples and families. This model builds on the "interpersonal circumplex," which is a circular classificatory system for personality characteristics generated from factor analytic study and analysis. Olson's research began at the National Institute of Mental Health (NIMH), where he began studying normal families. At the present time the Olson group has not articulated a treatment approach. Therefore, this section will describe the circumplex model and assessment system.

After an intensive review of literature, Olson and his colleagues identified two aspects of family and marital behavior, cohesion and adaptability, which they believe are basic to understanding marital and family processes (Sprenkle & Olson, 1978). *Cohesion* is a measure of the emotional bonding that family members have toward one another. Cohesion is represented on a continuum from high to low functioning. At the high end, the family is over-identified intellectually, emotionally, and/or physically. In other words, they are an enmeshed system. And at the other end of the continuum there is low cohesion, and the members are disengaged. Olson and his colleagues assume that a moderate degree of couple or family cohesion is most conducive to effective functioning. This concept is similar to the "enmeshment-disengagement" continuum described by Minuchin (1974).

Adaptability is the ability of the marital and family system to change its power structure or role relationship and relationship rules in response to situational or developmental stresses. It is a measure of the degree to which a family tolerates change and the extent to which it requires stability. Adequate functioning requires both an element of stability and the capacity to change.

Assessment Methods

A couple or family can be assessed with either a structured interview or an inventory, such as FACES, PREPARE, or ENRICH, all developed by Olson and his colleagues. These instruments will be described in some detail in the chapter on assessment. After assessment the couple or family can be rated on two axes as noted in Figure 4.1. This figure illustrates how couples or families can be grouped into 16 possible types. The central area of the figure is the one in which the most well functioning families or couples are expected to be situated. These four types—flexibly separated, flexibly connected, structurally separated, and structurally connected—represent various combinations of adaptability and cohesion. Within the limits of this inner circle, couples or families are free to move in any direction as the situation or life cycle demands. The four extreme types, in the corners of the figure, are those most likely to be associated with marital problems or problems in an individual spouse or family member. These are the chaotically disengaged, chaotically enmeshed, rigidly disengaged, and the rigidly enmeshed. Olson and his colleagues believe that the relationship between the two central dimensions of cohesion and adaptability are curvilinear, that is, too little or too much cohesion or adaptability is not optimal.

This is a controversial issue (Beavers & Voeller, 1983; Green, Kolevzon, & Vosler, 1985); early evaluations of the curvilinear hypothesis have yielded conflicting results. However, a large-scale study with an adequate sample size failed to support the curvilinear hypothesis (Green, Harris, Forte, & Robinson, 1991a). As a result, Olson and his associates (1991) have revised his theory and introduced the three-dimensional circumplex model and revised scoring system for FACES-III. The three dimensions are cohesion, adaptability, and functional level. There are three functional levels: balanced family types (high scores on cohesion and adaptability), extreme family types (low scores

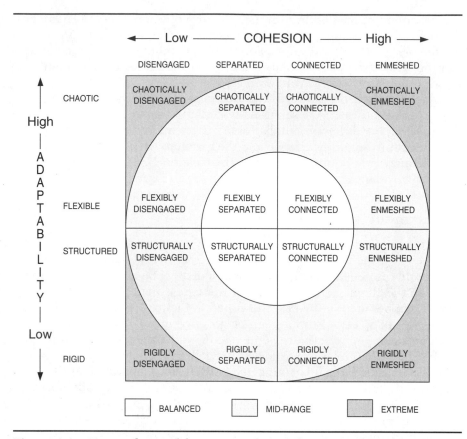

Figure 4-1 Circumplex Model: 16 Types of Marital and Family Systems (From "Circumplex Model of Marital and Family Systems: VI. Theoretical Update," by D. Olson, C. Russell, and D. Sprenkle, 1983. In *Family Process*, *22*, pp. 69–83. Copyright © 1983 by Family Process, Inc.)

on both dimensions), and mid-range family types (moderate scores on both dimensions). This elaboration of a third dimension appears to improve the model conceptually, methodologically, and clinically, and makes it more similar to the Beavers system model and the McMaster family model. It also helps clarify why FACES-III is correlated to Beavers' Self-Report Family Inventory and the McMaster Family Assessment Device. Although Green's research group had been highly critical of the circumplex model and FACES-III in the past, they have announced their intention to join with Olson in the development of a more methodologically sophisticated but clinically useful self-report instrument, to be called FACES-IV (Green, Harris, Forte, & Robinson, 1991b).

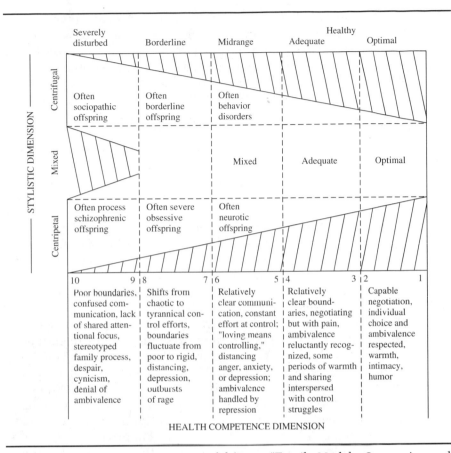

Figure 4-2 The Beavers System Model (From "Family Models: Comparing and Contrasting the Olson Circumplex Model with the Beavers System Model," by W. Beavers and M. Voeller, 1983. In *Family Process, 22,* pp. 69–83. Copyright © 1983 by Family Process, Inc.)

Beavers System Model

This model, initially described by Beavers in 1981, grew out of research on normal family functioning conducted by the Timberlawn group. This model was developed to provide a classification system for therapists based on an integration of systems research and healthy and disturbed couple and family style and competence. The model thus has two axes (see Figure 4.2). One involves "stylistic quality family interaction," classified as centripetal, mixed, or centrifugal. This represents a curvilinear continuum along which optimal couple and family functioning involves a mix of centripetal and centrifugal interaction, rather than extremes of centrifugal or centripetal interaction. The other axis is called the "health competence dimension," a continuum ranging from the extremes of severely dysfunctional to healthy. Five types of competence are derived: severely disturbed, borderline, mid-range, adequate, and optimal.

In *Successful Families: Assessment and Intervention,* Beavers and Hampson (1990) offer updated descriptions of family types based on their extensive research. Nine groupings of families are described in terms of the dimensions of centrifugal—enmeshing—or centripetal—lacking cohesion—and five levels of functioning. Furthermore, they note that individuals tend to marry partners who have similar family rules regarding distancing and intimacy. These five levels of family functioning are briefly described.

1. Severely Dysfunctional Families   Beavers states that this group represents about 20% of the families that he treats in his private practice but that many more are seen in public agencies. Among these families, coherence and hope are the primary deficiencies. Enmeshment, lack of gratification, nonexistent choice, and unresolved ambivalence characterize these couples. The severely disturbed centrifugal family is described as denying the need for warmth and closeness, whereas severely disturbed centripetal family members tend to deny their anger and desire for separateness. For the centripetal family being loving means both spouses believe they must think and feel the same.

Psychosis is occasionally an issue in the severely disturbed families. In the case of both bipolar disorder (manic depressive illness) and schizophrenia, Beavers treats patients in couple and/or family context. In addition to medication, Beavers finds that his general approach focusing on relationships, communication, boundaries, and choice is effective and relatively safe with these couples and families. Finally, he notes that triangles, particularly involving the parents and child, are ordinarily tenacious and persistent in the severely disturbed family.

2. Borderline Families   These families constitute about 40% of his practice and he notes that they are the most difficult of the groups to treat. Many of them have had several treatment experiences before. They are identified by their extreme concern with control, often of a bizarre nature. Beavers finds that relatively few centrifugal borderline families remain in treatment, particularly after a crisis is settled. He notes that this group tends to be seen more often in public clinics and usually in an individual, rather than a marital, treatment mode. The central issue for the centripetal borderline family in therapy is the power struggle. Because of this, Beavers is likely to use indirect methods such as paradox and storytelling.

3. Mid-range Families Beavers notes that this group makes up about 40% of his patient load. He notes that they are the easiest and most gratifying of families to treat. As with other types of families, the mid-range centrifugal family seldom stays in treatment. The mid-range centripetal family is less demoralized and has had more successful experiences with intimacy than any of the other groups of couples and families previously described. With these families, Beavers ties the control issue to the intimacy issue and helps the individuals see that intimidation is a method that ultimately reduces and eliminates any possibility of intimacy.

4. Adequate Families Having more characteristics of the optimal family, adequate families show a relatively low incidence of individual psychiatric morbidity. However, they have family diminished negotiation skills, are more control oriented, and tend to resolve conflict by intimidation or direct force. Interventions produce less intimacy, trust, spontaneity, and respect. Males are typically viewed as powerful, unemotional, and conventional, while females are seen as more emotional, less powerful, and the providers and seekers of nurturance. Parents in the adequate family care about parenting and work hard on it.

5. Optimal Families These well-functioning families have a strong sense of individuation with clear boundaries. Their hierarchical but flexible structure is well defined and acknowledged by family members. In these adaptive families, intimacy is sought and usually found along with respect, capable negotiations, and clear communications. Not surprisingly, such families are seldom seen by clinicians.

Assessment Methods

Two assessment methods have been developed with the Beavers approach. The Beavers/Timberlawn Family Evaluation Scale is a therapist-rated scale. The Self-Report Family Inventory is a 36-item self-rated instrument. Factor analytic studies show the Self-Report Family Inventory to be a reasonable screening device to assess a family member's view of overall family competence with a high degree of consistency in discriminating clinical from non-clinical families (R = .62) (Beavers & Hampson, 1990). In comparisons of therapist ratings with family members' self-report ratings involving a handicapped child, for example, the father's assessment was most congruent with the therapist's assessment; however, in other non-clinical, intact families, mothers tended to view the family quite similarly to the trained observer. Not surprisingly, self-rating clinical families tend to show much less similarity with the therapist (Beavers, 1989).

Evaluation of the Clinical Research Models

Both the Olson circumplex model and the Beavers systems model are cross-sectional, process oriented, and capable of providing the structure for both family theory research and family therapy. Both have been evaluated by a number of other research teams. Beavers and Voeller (1983); Green, Kolevzon, and Vosler (1985); and Green, Harris, Forte, and Robinson (1991a) level a number of criticisms at the circumplex model. These authors indicate that the Beavers model appears to conform better to clinical reality than does the circumplex model. They also believe the Beavers model can easily interface systems theory, whereas the two dimensional circumplex model cannot. Finally, they note that the adaptability scale is curvilinear rather than unilinear. In short, they believe that Beavers model is designed to take into account increased couple functioning potential, whereas Olson's curvilinear model allows only for "adjustment."

The three models—the McMaster, circumplex, and Beavers— represent major advances in the field of family dynamics, therapy, and research. There have been numerous published commentaries on these models that have led to further refinements in each. For example, Lee (1988) describes an integrated model synthesizing features of both Beavers' and Olson's models. Lee focuses on the concept of "adaptability" as measured by the Beavers and Olson models and concludes that several levels of adaptability are implicit in the circumplex model.

The search for a conceptually mature and research-based model of family functioning continues. The goal is to develop an assessment method that best fits the reality of family functioning and dysfunction. Beavers and Olson both acknowledge that the evolution of a workable family model will follow a progression similar to the American Psychiatric Association's evolution of a diagnostic scheme for classifying individual diagnoses from DSM-I, published in 1952, to DSM-IV, published in 1994 (American Psychiatric Association, 1994). Evolutions in the McMaster model—for example, Will and Wrate (1985)—further attest to this progression.

It has been only a few years (Beavers, 1981; Epstein, Bishop, & Levin, 1978; Sprenkle & Olson, 1978) since the first versions of the McMaster, Olson, and Beavers models were first widely disseminated. The years from 1986 to 1996 have easily been the most exciting years in the history of family theory and therapy. The next 10 years should witness the evolution of even more mature and clinically useful theory and treatment approaches for clinicians working with families.

Integrative Clinical Models of Family Therapy

The four approaches described in this section are examples of attempts to integrate several of the traditional approaches to family therapy. By far the most common integrative efforts involve attempts to combine two systems, such as the psychoanalytic and the behavioral models (Feldman, 1985; Pinsof, 1983; Sager, 1976; Segraves, 1982) or the psychoanalytic and systems models (Framo, 1982; Kirschner & Kirschner, 1986). (The reader is referred to these other sources for a description of these two system integration attempts.) Historically, such efforts have been necessary but not sufficient to develop a truly integrative approach.

Feldman's Integrative Multi-Level Family Therapy

Feldman (1985; 1989; 1992) has proposed integrative multi-level therapy. Theoretically, Feldman offers a comprehensive integration of the interpersonal and intrapsychic by combining the psychodynamic, cognitive, behavioral, and family systems perspectives. Clinically, Feldman presents a model for determining the optimal use of individual therapy and family therapy interventions for particular distressed individuals, couples, and families.

Feldman believes that problems experienced by individuals and families are the result of both intrapsychic and interpersonal processes that synergistically interact, and that ignoring or minimizing either process results in an incomplete understanding of individual and family dysfunction. He believes intrapsychic processes are best understood from a psychoanalytic and cognitive perspective, whereas interpersonal processes are best understood from a behavioral and family perspective.

From a psychoanalytic perspective, clinical problems are defensive reactions to unconscious anxiety—signal anxiety, separation anxiety, or intimacy anxiety—that become associated with internal representatives of significant others and self. These anxiety-generated fantasies are projected onto others, that is, transferred to current relationships, including marital and family relationships.

From a cognitive perspective, clinical problems result from dysfunctional cognitions. These distorted perceptions and dysfunctional thoughts are derived largely from unrealistic expectations, which are based on implicit assumptions about self and the world.

From a behavioral perspective, individual and interpersonal problems are primarily the result of interpersonal stimulation and problem reinforcement processes. Interpersonal problem stimulations are behaviors by one or more individuals that lead to the arousal of dysfunctional cognitions, affects, and behaviors in another and are derived from low levels of positive responses to constructive behaviors. The lack of positive responsiveness is frustrating and demoralizing and, in time, leads to dysfunctional behavior.

From a family system perspective, clinical problems are viewed in terms of dysfunctional family interaction patterns. These include dimensions of boundaries, power, and intimacy, as well as family rules, roles, and structure.

Essentially, dysfunctional behaviors are stimulated intrapsychically by conscious and preconscious dysphoric emotions aroused by unconscious perceptual and cognitive distortions. They are stimulated interpersonally by the behaviors of other family members. They may take the form of excessively rigid or permeable boundaries or roles, insufficient reinforcement of constructive behavior, unclear or inconsistent communication, overprotective or overintrusive behavior, or verbal, physical, and/or sexual abuse. These intrapsychic and interpersonal problem-stimulation processes interact in a reciprocal, circular pattern. Family members' dysfunctional behaviors are directly stimulated by conscious and unconscious cognitions and emotions that are stimulated, in part, by members who respond to their own conscious and unconscious cognitions and emotions that are, in part, reciprocally stimulated by the interpersonal behaviors of the family member(s). For example, distressed and conflicted couples are often unable to implement agreed-on behavioral changes because of each spouse's cognitive distortions (that is, denial of their own dysfunctional behavior) and anxieties and emotions (that is, narcissistic vulnerability and intimacy anxiety). Accordingly, therapeutic reduction of these dysfunctional cognitions and emotions can greatly facilitate behavioral and interpersonal change.

Based on this multi-level, integrated theoretical understanding, the therapist undertakes a detailed assessment of both intrapersonal and intrapsychic processes. The initial assessment includes individual, family, and family sub-group interventions. Based on these interviews the therapist develops a formulation of the problem, of the stimulation and reinforcement processes, and of individual and relational strengths. The therapist then meets with the couple or family to discuss the formulation and treatment.

In integrative multi-level family therapy, change is conceptualized as a multilevel process. At the intrapsychic level, the main change processes are identification, cognitive restructuring, confrontation, insight, and working through. At the interpersonal level, major change processes are joining, enactment, problem-solving training, paradox, reframing, suggestions, and reinforcement. Feldman contends that both levels of change processes are essential, and if either is ignored or minimized, therapeutic power is significantly reduced (Feldman, 1985).

To promote both the intrapsychic and the interpersonal change processes, conjoint and individual sessions are combined, which can optimally facilitate the therapist's effectiveness. Therapy is formulated as either a symmetrical or an asymmetrical combination of session formats. In symmetrical integration, each format occurs with equal frequency, whereas in asymmetrical integration, one format occurs more often than the other(s). (Cf. Feldman [1992] for a protocol for making such decisions.)

The structure of therapy is arrived at by a process of collaboration between the therapist and the couple or family. After a mutually satisfactory therapeutic structure has been agreed on, it is implemented on a time-limited basis—usually 1 month—and is evaluated and changed, if necessary, based on mutual decision. Session frequency is generally weekly with the duration of treatment from 1 to 6 months—sometimes up to 1 year or more, depending on the therapeutic needs of the particular couple or family.

Unlike the other integrated approaches previously described, Feldman's approach offers a comprehensive theory of dysfunctionality that provides a sophisticated incorporation of compatible concepts from four different psychotherapeutic perspectives. It is, furthermore, unique in proposing a multi-level method of assessment and intervention based on well-articulated premises. Furthermore, Feldman (1989) provides a review of empirical studies that support the theory and practice of integrative multi-level family therapy.

Walsh's Integrative Family Therapy Approach

Walsh (1991) offers what he calls "an integrative approach" to family therapy. It is a structural format for working with a family from the initial phone contact to the first follow-up contact. He outlines a format for evaluating the dynamics of a family and for making a working assessment with specific treatment recommendations. Walsh proposes a comprehensive "theory of personality" described as the characteristics all families have in common. Walsh describes integrative family therapy as a second-generation theoretical model, a "blending of several interpersonal models with an intrapsychic component" (1991, p. vii). Walsh believes that "once the primary aspects of a well-functioning family are identified, deviations from that norm can be isolated and treated" (1991, p. 3).

Theory is based on an integrative evaluation. This evaluation is guided by five factors: family structure, roles, communication and perceptions, themes related to the problem(s), and the personality dynamics of significant individuals. The therapist is encouraged to summarize this five point evaluation in one page.

The family structure factor is based on Minuchin's work and includes an examination of the functioning of the three subsystems (marital, parental, and sibling), as well as the nature of the boundaries of the family subsystem and system.

The communication and perception factor is modified from Satir's work on communication and Barnhill's (1979) work on information processing—an elaboration of Satir's work that includes a perceptual component. Communication is seen as the transmission of a message; perception is the act of receiving it. Faulty perception occurred in 90% of the treatment families assessed, whereas poor communication was present in approximately 50% (Walsh & Wood, 1983).

The role responsibility factor is a particularly important component of integrative family therapy. A *role* is defined as the identity and set of expectations a family member assumes in order to complete a task. Since completion of tasks is essential for a family to fulfill its various functions, role responsibility is central to effective functioning. The lack of clearly defined and articulated expectations for family members is a leading cause of disruption, particularly in adolescence (p. 15). Clear expectations and consequences for failure to meet expectations are an important focus of this approach to family therapy. Walsh calls this *role unresponsibility.*

Family themes need to be identified by the family therapist. Themes are issues that occur frequently in a family that focus their interest, attention, and energy. They may be positive or negative. Walsh notes that themes are related to the psychoanalytic concept of repetition compulsion. Positive themes involve the family in constructive activities and lead to growth. They are characterized by early resolution of conflicts and healthy channeling of tension toward goal accomplishment. Negative themes are characterized by non-resolution of conflict and increased tension. All families have several identifiable, major themes, both positive and negative. Walsh notes that three to five negative themes are the norm in severely dysfunctional families. It is important for the dysfunctional family to be made aware of positive themes. An example of themes for a recently married blended family are irresponsibility of the spouses toward parental roles, lack of family time together, and independence versus dependence issues.

Individual personality dynamics refer to strategies that individual family members use to organize, understand, and complete the tasks of daily living. In part based on Ackerman's work, individual personality dynamics are considered critical in integrative family therapy. Walsh believes therapists using his approach should choose an individual psychotherapy model—whether it be psychoanalytic, Adlerian, rational-emotive, or phenomenological—to account for intrapsychic influences of each family member's behavior in order to gain a complete diagnostic picture. Walsh (1991) notes that individual dynamics "have been central to change in approximately 50% of the families seen in therapy" (p. 19).

The five factors just discussed constitute the theoretical framework of integrative family therapy from which all change strategies emanate. Therapeutic goals and intervention methods are directly based on this five-part evaluation. Walsh states that much of this evaluation is shared with the family, and their involvement is actively solicited so that a mutually motivated change process can begin, usually by the second or third session. With integrative family therapy, the average number of sessions is 10. The therapist organizes the therapeutic encounter according to stages and tasks. The stages are developmental in that for each stage the therapist prepares the family to move forward toward the tasks in the next stage. The five stages are (1) structuring; (2) observation and assessment; (3) intervention; (4) change maintenance; and (5) review and termination. Major interventions include discussion and enactment of specific problem situations, confrontation technique to aid effective communication, communication check to ensure accurate perception, clarification of roles and expectations, help for the family to set rules to govern daily interactions, and encouragement of regular family meetings to supplement therapeutic contacts. The five stages are organized to facilitate the accomplishment of the two major treatment goals of remediating specific immediate difficulties and concerns and constructing an effective problem-solving process for individuals and the family unit.

In summary, integrative family therapy is a goal-directed approach that is straightforward and relatively structured. It may be viewed as too confining for some, yet it appears to be a useful approach for instructing therapists-in-training to think and function from an integrated perspective.

Nichols' Integrative Approach to Marital Therapy

William Nichols (1988) has proposed a form of marital therapy that not only integrates the systems approach with the behavioral and the psychoanalytic orientation but also integrates the understanding of the individual spouse with the subsystem of the marriage and the family system. This is by far the most ambitious of the integrative approaches to marital therapy. Nichols believes that the theoretical foundation for a truly integrative marital therapy approach has to deal with the contexts in which personality and marriage evolve and function, with intimate attachment processes and with the processes of motivation, change, and learning.

Nichols states that his efforts to develop a workable theoretical perspective of marital interactions evolved from his clinical work with couples and was supported by theoretical and empirical research on marriage and marriage interactions. Nichols indicates it was quite difficult to synthesize concepts from three different orientations to explain marital interaction. He uses the metaphor "lumps in the oatmeal" to reflect the idea that various concepts do not necessary blend into a homogeneous whole without some lumps and bumps. A smooth blend can be obtained only at the expense of eliminating certain data and distorting some of the realities that show up in practice, research, and theoretical work.

Nichols synthesizes concepts from systems theory, object-relations theory, and social-learning theory. Systems theory provides Nichols with the chief contextual explanation for the conduct of marital therapy. He describes eight concepts from systems theory: wholeness, boundaries, hierarchy, communications, equifinality, circular casualty, nonsummativity, and change. (The reader will find a description of these and other systems concepts in the chapter on systems orientation.) In deriving therapeutic interventions from the systems orientation, Nichols indicates that any of the structural and strategic techniques and methods for clarification, strengthening, or reworking boundaries and power alliances can be used with most couples. He focuses on the total system or its parts, its structure, its processes, or all of these, depending on what the marital system requires. Specific techniques ranging from sculpting, genograms, family rituals, and reframing to paradoxical maneuvers are all possible interventions.

Object relations refers to early interpersonal relationships that are internalized by the child and become a model for later intimate interpersonal relationships. The object-relations factors that have greatest implication for marital therapy are the understanding of how mate-selection choices were made originally, how partners are held together at the present time, and how their needs are/were not being met in the relationship. For Nichols, the object-relations approach is a useful bridge between individual systems and the marital system. Nichols notes that five concepts are particularly useful for the marital therapist. They are splitting, projective identification, collusion, ambivalence, and model of relationship. The last term is adapted from Skynner (1976) and refers to the internalized models that each spouse brings to the marriage relationship. These are models of how a parent should act, models of what effective interaction between spouses should be, and models of how parents should act as a system. Such models are learned through the direct experience of observing the behaviors of others and identifying with them.

Nichols uses three therapeutic interventions derived from the object-relations/psychoanalytic approach. They are interpretation of unconscious fears (that is, fears that bring about defensive reaction in the spouse); confrontation of the spouse's mispreconceptions; and the use of family of origin sessions in which both spouses are seen with their parents and other family members for the purpose of altering internalized perceptions from the past.

The third stream contributing to Nichols' integrative approach comes from social-learning theory. This approach emphasizes the environment and the importance of learning in therapy. The goal is to define the problem clearly in behavioral terms and to develop problem-solving solutions. Nichols uses four concepts from social-learning theory: behavior exchange and reciprocity; contingencies; modeling; and positive reinforcement. Behavior exchange is basically a quasi-economy theory applied to marital relationships. Spousal behavior can be seen as being primarily a function of consequences with specific cost and benefits. The reward/cost ratio determines the amount of marital satisfaction experienced by each spouse. The concept of reciprocity requires involvement by both spouses to secure change and develop cooperation with each other. Nichols indicates that there are therapeutic interventions that the integrative marital therapist can derive from the social-learning approach. They are contingency, contracting, and communication and problem-solving training. He also indicates that the therapist's ability to tailor interventions of the particular needs is greatly enhanced by the tenets of social-learning theory.

Integrated Family Therapy: Problem-Centered Psychodynamic Family Therapy

The problem-centered psychodynamic family therapy approach (PCPFT) blends the object-relations model and two systems models. Will and Wrate (1985) combined the structural model of Minuchin (1974) with the problem-centered systems model of the McMaster group. The purpose was to establish an approach in which the therapist can work collaboratively with the couple or family to openly explore, understand, and work with the homeostasis of the marital or family system. They describe this focus on collaboration as open, directive family therapy in contradistinction to strategic therapy, in which there is often no attempt to establish a negotiated, collaborative relationship with the family or couple.

Blending object-relations concepts and techniques allows the therapist to make a bridge between the family as a system and family members as individual persons. The blending of three models provides a depth of understanding that cannot be derived from the system approaches alone. The range of therapeutic techniques available in PCPFT make it possible to "tailor" therapy to suit the needs of different couples and families. Choosing the emphasis of specific therapeutic techniques used depends both on the general characteristics of the family and on the nature, meaning, and causes of the family's difficulty. Therefore, treating multi-problem families in which disorganization affects basic problem-solving skills often entails extensive use of clear setting of tasks between sessions. In contrast, relatively stable families with basically affective issues such as unresolved grief might better be treated with the use of interpretation.

However, during the course of therapy, both types of techniques—systems and object relations—prove necessary for most families. Some families may respond more readily to action-oriented techniques such as task setting, while others may respond more readily to interpretation. In PCPFT, the therapist can move along a technical continuum that extends from the most basic action-oriented techniques to the use of interpretation that links the present with the remote past.

Will and Wrate, like the McMaster group, have provided a useful treatment manual for family therapists. Although primarily taught and practiced in Canada, the PCPFT approach deserves widespread dissemination. Of particular benefit is Will and Wrate's 1985 discussion of the common difficulties that two teacher/clinicians have encountered in attempting to teach and practice an integrative psychoanalytic/systems approach to family therapy. They note four common problems facing trainees who have some experience in psychoanalytic theory. The most common initial difficulty is to conduct individual interviews with one family member while not including other family members. The second is not being appropriately active throughout the course of therapy. This, of course, is rarely a problem for the systems-trained therapist. However, psychodynamic therapies are based on a passive interviewing style designed to encourage the individual patient's free-flowing associations. The third problem is the tendency to devalue the power of reality-oriented techniques. Dynamically trained therapists are trained to intervene at the "deep" levels of psychological functioning. Therefore, they experience a certain degree of dissatisfaction when intervening at the level of "surface behavior" rather than at the deeper level of motivation and meaning. However, the authors note that this attitude is usually modified after the therapist experiences the results of systems interventions. The last occupational hazard of the psychoanalytically trained therapist is the tendency to focus on the couples pathology rather than on its strength. Analytically oriented therapists tend to view couples through the prism of psychopathology, seeing only traumas, fixations, and infantile defenses, thus blinding them to the assets, strengths, and achievements of the family. The authors note that these difficulties in integration of analytic and systems thinking can be overcome. In fact, they know that previous experience in psychoanalytic treatment is often very helpful for training in PCPFT.

Concluding Notes

How can the insights of different theories and approaches be combined and systematically integrated to yield a comprehensive and useful guide for therapeutic work with families? In answer to this question, several models and approaches to integration have been reviewed in this chapter. This review suggests that individual theories or models of family therapy are necessarily limited and parochial. It also implies that integrative family approaches discourage parochial thinking and shortsightedness with regard to assessment, formulation, and intervention (Mikesell, Lusterman, & McDaniels, 1995). Specifically, the assessment process will, of necessity, be multidimensional and comprehensive. Furthermore, matching and tailoring of intervention require a comprehensive, integrative assessment. This theme will be continued in the following chapter on tailoring treatment.

References

American Psychiatric Association (1994). *Diagnostic and Statistical Manual of Mental Disorders* (4th ed.). Washington, DC.

Aradi, N., & Kaslow, F. (1987). Theory integration in family therapy: Definition, rationale, content and process. *Psychotherapy, 24*(3), 595–608.

Barnhill, L. (1979). Healthy family systems. *Family Coordinator, 28,* 94–100.

Beavers, W. (1981). A systems model of family for family therapists. *Journal of Marital and Family Therapy, 7,* 299–307.

Beavers, W. (1989). Beavers system model. In C. Ramsey (Ed.), *Family Systems in Medicine.* New York: Guilford.

Beavers, W., & Hampson, R. (1990). *Successful families: Assessment and intervention.* New York: W. W. Norton.

Beavers, W., & Voeller, M. (1983). Family models: Comparing and contrasting the Olson circumplex model with the Beavers system model, *Family Process, 22,* 85–98.

Boszormenyi-Nagy, I., & Krasner, B. (1986). *Between give and take: A clinical guide to contextual therapy.* New York: Brunner/Mazel.

Case, E., & Robinson, N. (1990). Toward integration: The changing world of family therapy. *American Journal of Family Therapy, 18*(2), 153–160.

Colapinto, J. (1984). On model integration and model integrity. *Journal of Strategic and Systemic Therapies, 4,* 38–42.

Doherty, W., Colangelo, N., Green, A., & Hoffman, G. (1985). Emphasis of the major family therapy models: A family FIRO analysis. *Journal of Marital and Family Therapy, 11,* 299–303.

Doherty, W., Colangelo, N., & Hovander, D. (1991). Priority setting in family change and clinical practice: The family FIRO model. *Family Process, 30*(2), 227–240.

Duhl, B., & Duhl, F. (1981). Integrative family therapy. In A. Gurman & D. Kniskern (Eds.), *Handbook of Family Therapy* (pp. 483–513). New York: Brunner/Mazel.

Epstein, N., Baldwin, L., & Bishop, D. (1983). The McMaster family assessment device. *Journal of Marital and Family Therapy, 9,* 171–180.

Epstein, N., Bishop, D., & Levin, S. (1978). The McMaster model of family functioning. *Journal of Marriage and Family Counseling, 4,* 19–31.

Feldman, L. (1985). Integrative multi-level therapy: A comprehensive interpersonal and intrapsychic approach. *Journal of Marital and Family Therapy, 11,* 357–372.

Feldman, L. (1989). Integrating individual and family therapy. *Journal of Integrative and Eclectic Psychotherapy, 8,* 41–52.

Feldman, L. (1992). *Integrating individual and family therapy.* New York: Brunner/Mazel.

Fish, R., & Fish, L. (1986). Quid pro quo revisited: The basis of marital therapy. *American Journal of Orthopsychiatry, 56,* 371–384.

Framo, J. (1982). *Explorations in marital and family therapy.* New York: Springer Publishing.

Green, R., Harris, R., Forte, J., & Robinson, M. (1991a). Evaluating FACE-III and the circumplex model: 2,440 families. *Family Process, 30,* 55–73.

Green, R., Harris, R., Forte, J., & Robinson, M. (1991b). The wives date and FACES-IV: Making things appear simple. *Family Process, 30,* 79–83.

Green, R., Kolevzon, M., & Vosler, N. (1985). The Beavers-Timberlawn model of family competence and the circumplex model of family adaptability and cohesion: Separate but equal? *Family Process, 24,* 385–398.

Gurman, A., & Kniskern, D. (1978). Research on marital and family therapy: Progress, perspective and prospects. In S. Garfield and A. Bergin (Eds), *Handbook of psychotherapy and behavior change.* New York: J. Wiley.

Haley, J. (1987). The Disappearance of the individual. *The Family Therapy Networker, 11,* 39–40.

Kirschner, D., & Kirschner, S. (1986). *Comprehensive family therapy: An integration of systematic and psychodynamic treatment models.* New York: Brunner/Mazel.

Lebow, J. (1987). Developing a personal integration in family therapy: Principles for model construction and practice. *Journal of Marital and Family Therapy, 13*(1), 1–14.

Lee, C. (1988). Theories of family adaptability: Toward a synthesis of Olson's circumplex and the Beavers system model. *Family Process, 27,* 73–85.

Levant, R. (1984). *Family therapy: A comprehensive overview.* Englewood Cliffs, NJ: Prentice-Hall.

Mikesell, R., Lusterman, D., & McDaniels (Eds.) (1995). *Integrating family therapy: Handbook of Family Psychology and Systems Theory.* Washington, DC: American Psychological Association.

Minuchin, S. (1974). *Families and family therapy.* Cambridge: Harvard University Press.

Nichols, W. (1988). *Marital therapy: An integrated approach.* New York: Guilford.

Norcross, J. (1986). Eclectic psychotherapy: An introduction and overview. In J. Norcross (Ed.), *Handbook of Eclectic Psychotherapy.* New York: Brunner/Mazel.

Olson, D. (1991). Commentary: Three-dimensional (3-D) circumplex model and revised scoring of FACES-III. *Family Process, 30,* 74–79.

Olson, D., Russell, C., & Sprenkle D. (1983). Circumplex model of marital and family systems: VI. Theoretical update. *Family Process, 22,* 69–83.

Olson, D., Sprenkle, D., & Russell, C. (1979). Circumplex model of marital and family systems: I. Cohesion and adaptability dimensions, family types and clinical applications. *Family Process, 18,* 3–28.

Paul, G. (1987). Strategy of outcome research on psychotherapy. *Journal of Consulting Psychology, 31,* 109–118.

Pinsof, W. (1983). Integrative problem-centered therapy: Toward the synthesis of family and individual psychotherapies. *Journal of Family Therapy, 9,* 19–35.

Robertson, M. (1979). Some observations from an eclectic psychotherapist. *Psychotherapy: Theory, Research and Practice, 16,* 18–21.

Sager, C. (1976). *Marriage contracts and couples therapy: Hidden forces in intimate relationships.* New York: Brunner/Mazel.

Schutz, W. (1958). *FIRO: A three-dimensional theory of interpersonal behavior.* New York: Holt, Rhinehart, and Winston.

Segraves, R. (1982). *Marital therapy: A combined psychodynamic-behavioral approach.* New York: Plenum.

Skynner, A. (1976). *Systems of family and marital psychotherapy.* New York: Brunner/Mazel.

Sluzki, C. (1983). Process, structure, and world views: Toward an integrated view of systemic models in family therapy. *Family Process, 22,* 469–476.

Sprenkle, D., & Olson, D. (1978). Circumplex model and marital systems: An empirical study of clinic and non-clinic couples. *Journal of Marriage and Family Counseling, 4,* 59–74.

Stanton, M. (1984). Fusion, compression, diversion and the workings of paradox: A theory of therapeutic/systemic change. *Family Process, 23,* 135–167.

Textor, M. (1988). Integrative family therapy. *International Journal of Family Psychiatry, 9*(1), 93–106.

Walsh, W. (1991). *Case studies in family therapy: An integrated approach.* Boston: Allyn and Bacon.

Walsh, W., & Wood, J. (1983). Family assessment: Bridging the gap between theory, research, and practice. *American Mental Health Counselors Journal, 5,* 111–120.

Weltner, J. (1988). Different strokes. *Family Therapy Networker, 12,* 53–57.

Will, D., & Wrate, R. (1985). *Integrated family therapy: A problem-centered psychodynamic approach.* London: Tavistock.

Part **2**

Tailoring Treatment with Couples and Families

5

Tailoring Treatment
for Couples and Families
Models and Protocols for Tailoring and Matching

Tailoring treatment to the specific needs of the client-system has long been an ideal. As early as 30 years ago it was hoped that psychotherapy research would focus on "what treatment, by whom, is most effective for this individual with that specific problem and under which set of circumstances" (Paul, 1967, p. 111). To date there has been some notable progress in meeting Paul's challenge, but "we are just beginning to see the tip of the tailoring iceberg, and there's more to be seen" (Clarkin, 1992, p. 15).

What is tailored treatment and what does it have to do with families and couples? Clinicians are asking this question in their quest to provide more effective and cost-efficient treatment. Although tailoring, matching treatment, and differential therapeutics are prominent in the practice of individual psychotherapy, the same cannot yet be said about couples or family therapy. This chapter will briefly sketch the emerging trend of tailoring treatment in both individual and marital/family therapy. The first section distinguishes tailoring from similar phenomena and delineates some of the resistance to the tailoring trend. The second and main section describes several perspectives on tailoring treatment. The third section describes an assessment and treatment planning protocol as the basis for tailoring treatment.

Tailoring: Terminology and Resistance

As we mentioned in the last chapter, tailoring is similar to but still different from the related concept of matching. Worthington (1992) uses a sartorial analogy to make the distinction. Matching is choosing an appropriate suit from the rack, wheras tailoring involves custom fitting the suit to the individual. In other words, in matching a couple or family is "assigned" to a specific treatment approach based on important client variables. Tailoring involves modifying that treatment approach to "fit" the couple or family so they are more likely to benefit from the treatment. Matching typically precedes tailoring and is accomplished early in the course of treatment, usually during or after the initial evaluation. Tailoring, in contrast, occurs throughout the course of treatment. In some clinics and group practices, matching is often done in case staffing, when cases are assigned to therapists; in private practice it may involve referral to another therapist. Tailoring usually involves the flexible use of therapeutic strategies and tactics after a particular therapeutic approach has been chosen.

Tailoring has three goals. The first goal is to enhance the therapeutic relationship. The second is to create an environment in which a couple or family can benefit from therapeutic suggestions and directives. The third is to deal with specific therapeutic impasses such as noncompliance or resistance (Worthington, 1992).

Tailoring is also distinct from integration and integrative approaches. Integrative approaches are basically clinician-centered. Clinicians develop a particular way of personalizing therapeutic concepts and techniques to meet their own needs for therapeutic effectiveness, intellectual synthesis, or whatever. Tailoring, however, refers to the philosophy of basing treatment decisions on what is best for the client, couple, or family system. Paul's (1967) dictum clearly specifies what the focus of tailoring should be: the particular needs and styles of the individual, couple, or family. Essentially, tailoring is basically a client or couple-centered orientation to treatment planning and intervention.

Individual psychotherapies have been found to be more effective when matched to the client's dispositional needs, presenting problems, and treatment expectations than when a single theory or treatment modality is used without regard to these client features (Beutler & Clarkin, 1990). The literature on tailoring individual treatment is continually expanding. Significant contributions have been made by Beutler (1983); Frances, Clarkin, and Perry (1984); Perry, Frances, and Clarkin (1990); and Beutler and Clarkin (1990) to name a few.

Tailoring the therapy also increases the therapy's effectiveness for couples and families. The basic motivation for tailoring treatment should be the clinician's concern that the couple or family receive the most effective and appropriate treatment. Unfortunately, family therapy clinicians and researchers have been more resistant to the prospective of tailoring than individual psychotherapy clinicians and researchers. There are a number of reasons for such resistance. First, marital and family theory and therapy are relatively recent additions to the therapeutic landscape. Most clinicians are just learning, or have recently learned, the theory and skills of this "new" area. Consequently, few have become dissatisfied with the shortcoming of standardized, non-tailored treatment. Second, there has been relatively little theorizing about tailoring as witnessed by the near absence of citations about tailoring in family therapy literature. Third, the couple and family therapy movement is still strongly parochial in its belief in the universal applicability of its dominant theories (Worthington, 1989). Consequently, a clinician's allegiance to a dominant theory or approach almost guarantees that treatment will be clinician-centered, rather than client-centered, which is incompatible with the basic principles of tailoring. Finally, education and training in marital and family therapy typically occur within theory-consistent programs that further reinforce a non-tailoring view of treatment.

Perspectives of Tailoring

Only recently has the process of tailoring been described in marital and family literature (Sperry, 1986). There are several bases for tailoring. This section overviews tailoring approaches based on (1) level of family functioning; (2) level of relational conflict; (3) individual functioning; (4) level of readiness; (5) level of distress; and (6) differential therapeutics.

Tailoring by Level of Family Functioning

Weltner (1985) believes in tailoring treatment to a couple's or family's level of systems functioning. He describes four levels of functioning in terms of treatment issues and then proposes a corresponding intervention strategy and set of techniques for each level. The first two levels describe two kinds of under-organized couples or families, while the third describes the overorganized couple and the fourth the adequately functioning couple.

Weltner contends that intervention must first address the level of a couple's most basic problem before moving on to higher level intervention. He believes that the effective therapist must be sufficiently conversant with the major therapeutic approaches to marital therapy in order to mix and match techniques appropriately to a specific level, rather than unilaterally applying one approach to all couples or families.

For level one, the main issue involves parental capacity to provide basic nurturance and protection. Therefore, the basic treatment strategy is to mobilize available outside support to assist the single parent or the strongest member of the family facing severe stress or illness, including alcoholism. The therapist's role is that of advocate, convener, teacher, and role model. Structural interventions and support are key interventions.

In level two, issues of authority and limits are prominent for the couple and family. Expectations may be unclear or unmet. The basic strategy is to clarify expectations and power issues by means of such techniques as written contracts, formation of coalitions, and behavioral reinforcers.

Level-three families and couples are more complicated. They have a structure and a style that appear to be functional, yet issues regarding boundaries are prominent. Resistance to change is another hallmark of this type of family or couple. The basic strategy is to create sufficient inner space for a spouse or specific family member and to protect that spouse, family member, or subsystem from over-involvement. Therapeutic techniques at this level include rebuilding alliances, paradox, and developing generational boundaries.

Issues for level-four couples and families are usually focused on intimacy and inner conflict. Whereas families and couples at levels one to three are immersed in day-to-day survival issues, level-four couples are able to consider self-actualizing concerns. Insight is a basic therapeutic strategy, and techniques include marital and family enrichment, gestalt and experiential marital therapies, or even individual psychodynamically oriented psychotherapy.

Schultz (1984) has proposed a similar model of family and couple functioning based more specifically on DSM-III psychopathology. Schultz likewise describes four levels. He labels the first level of family functioning as "psychotic" and matches this with the family transactional approach as developed by Wynne and Singer. The second level is labeled as "immature" and is matched with the structural-system approach, such as Minuchin's. The third level is called "neurotic" and is matched with various strategic methods. Finally, the fourth level is labeled "mature" and is matched with growth-focused approaches, such as Satir's communication approach, the symbolic-experiential approach of Whitaker, or the psychodynamic approaches.

Tailoring by Level of Relational Conflict

Guerin, Fay, Burden, and Kautto (1987) believe that marital conflict differs significantly from one couple to another, not only with respect to specific issues but more importantly with respect to the duration and intensity of the conflict. Accordingly, they tailor treatment to the level of severity (that is, intensity and duration) of marital discord. They describe couples in terms of four levels of marital discord.

The first level involves couples who demonstrate preclinical or minimal degree of marital conflict. Often this conflict has lasted for less than 6 months, and most often the couples are newlyweds. These couples readily respond to information focusing on how marriages work and do not work and are able to apply this information to positively change their relationship for the better. Thus, therapy for this level is primarily group psychoeducational intervention. Occasionally, a few couples sessions are necessary as an adjunct to the group sessions. This psychoeducational treatment involves six weekly sessions of 1½ hours each. Developed in the Bowenian tradition, the sessions focus on such concepts as multigenerational transmission, triangles, behavior styles, and differentiation, as well as specific common problems that couples are likely to present in the beginning stages of a marriage.

Level two consists of couples who are experiencing significant marital conflicts lasting longer than 6 months. Although their communication patterns remain open and adequate, criticism and projection have increased. When the therapist dissects the conflict-ridden marital process, however, both spouses can generally move to a self-focus within six to eight sessions, after which the intensity of the conflict can be substantially reduced. Therapy in level two provides a structure for the couple that lowers emotional arousal and anxiety and helps the spouses reestablish self-focus.

Level-three couples present with severe marital conflict. Often the conflict is of more than 6 months duration, and projection is intense. Anxiety and emotional arousal are high, as well as the intensity and polarization of surrounding triangles. Communication is closed with marked conflict. The degree of criticism is high, and blaming is common. Therapy at this level is primarily focused on controlling the couple's reactivity—their tendency to react to each other emotionally without thinking. Even when a positive result is obtained through therapy, a recycling of conflicts inevitably occurs within the ensuing 6 to 8 months. Guerin notes that such recycling is a common phenomena at all levels of marital conflict, but particularly at this stage. When this recycling continues to occur, both spouses have probably lost most of their resilience and tend to be unresponsive to further treatment.

Finally, couples at level four are characterized by extremes in all the criteria that Guerin uses for a marital evaluation of conflict. Communication is closed, information exchange is poor, criticism and blaming are very high, and self-disclosure is basically absent in the relationship. Relationship time and activity together are either minimal or non-existent. The definitive marker for this level is the engagement of an attorney by one or both spouses. Such a situation is likely to be more adversarial than conciliatory. In the vast majority of cases, attempts to keep the marriage from dissolving are doomed. Therefore, treatment is aimed at diminishing emotional damage to the spouses, their children, and their extended family. The goal becomes the successful disengagement from the relationship. In short, mediation is the treatment of choice.

Guerin and his associates detail treatment protocols in which specific dynamic, behavioral, and systems interventions are used with couples at different levels of functioning. Assessment of each of the four levels of couple functioning is aided by specific behavioral indices. These indices are criteria likely to ensure that an accurate assessment of the levels of marital discord is made and that appropriately tailored treatment will follow.

Tailoring Based on Individual Functioning

Lazarus (1981; 1985) advocated the matching or tailoring of therapeutic techniques to seven specific areas of individual functioning. These areas of functioning are represented by the acronym BASIC-ID: behavior, affect, sensory, imagery, cognitive, interpersonal, and biological (identified as D and referring to drugs in particular and physical health in general). The therapist's role is to assess these areas of functioning, to develop a problem list, to prioritize their importance to the spouses' functioning, and to direct a focus intervention for each. Lazarus' orientation is an eclectic form of cognitive-behavioral therapy. Research studies attest to the effectiveness of focused multimodal intervention as compared to unimodal intervention (Lazarus, 1981). Lazarus notes that couples constitute the overwhelming majority of referrals to his practice. The BASIC-ID profile provides both couples and therapists with a blueprint map for assessing the individual's as well as the couple's or family's current level of functioning and for setting clear objectives for change. This unique methodology aids the therapist in establishing a one-to-one correspondence between diagnosis and treatment. Each item on the problem list is matched or tailored with a specific treatment intervention.

The couple or family is seen together in the initial interview to discuss the main presenting problems. They are then helped to prepare a list of undesirable behaviors that they note in themselves and in their spouse. Then each individual independently fills out a Life History

Questionnaire, which is discussed with the therapist as a subsequent individual session. During this session a Modality Profile is constructed. A conjoint session follows to compare the two profiles and to tailor the treatment process.

Tailoring Based on Level of Readiness

Adaptive counseling and therapy (ACT) is a developmental and systems model developed by Howard, Nance, and Myers (1987) and adapted by Myers (1992). Basically, ACT requires clinicians to adapt the degree of "direction" and extent of "support" they provide client couples or families. Clinician direction and support will vary with the couple's or family's readiness to accomplish the particular therapeutic tasks involved in the therapeutic process. Myers specifies three criteria for the family's "readiness": willingness, ability, and confidence. First, the family's willingness to participate in therapy is assessed. A family that is self-referred would have a higher degree of willingness to participate in treatment than a family who refused voluntary treatment but came because the court ordered them to obtain compulsory counseling. Second, the family's ability to participate is measured by the adequacy of their verbal skills for participating in talking therapy. Third, the family's confidence in a positive therapeutic outcome is reflected by the strength of their belief that they can make needed changes in their family relationships.

Four levels of family readiness are noted. The highest level involves high levels of willingness, ability, and confidence, while the lowest level involves the absence of these three criteria. Myers views a family's readiness as a trait contingent on specific tasks, rather than on a fixed global characteristic.

For Myers, the therapist tailors treatment, particularly therapeutic style, based on the family's level of readiness. Four therapeutic styles are specified based on the extent of direction and support supplied by the therapist. The styles are telling, teaching, supporting, and delegating. Thus, a therapist would respond in a delegating style to a family with a very high level of readiness. This contrasts with the therapist responding in a telling style to a family with the lowest level of readiness.

Tailoring Based on Level of Distress

Worthington (1989; 1992) describes a method for matching treatment based on the family's distress. Since couples and families often seek therapy during times of upheaval owing to normative or non-normative events, Worthington bases treatment matching on an assessment of the family's response to the event. Three variables characterize the way a family responds to transitions: (1) the degree of disruption in the family members' schedules; (2) the number of decisions about which the family members disagree; and (3) the degree of ongoing conflict. Worthington uses these three variables, dichotomized as high or low, to predict eight categories of a family's response to treatment that can then be matched to six specific treatment strategies. For example, enrichment strategies are matched to families in which degree of disturbance is small. Crisis-oriented strategies are matched to families experiencing schedule disruption. Experiential strategies can be matched to all situations except for those of high conflict. Psychoeducational strategies are good matches for families experiencing severe disturbances regarding power issues. Structural and process strategies are matched with families with unstable power structures and high conflict. Finally, psychodynamic strategies are matched with families with disturbances in intimacy.

Worthington (1992) recognizes that family members may not respond uniformly to life transitions. In such instances, the therapist must be mindful of subsystems and carefully tailor the strategy.

Finally, Worthington (1989) has carefully indexed the likelihood of success for each of the six therapeutic strategies based on the eight levels or types of family distress.

Tailoring Based on Differential Therapeutics

A somewhat different perspective on tailoring is provided by Perry, Frances, and Clarkin(1990), who believe that all forms of treatment have five inherent axes that should be considered in treatment selection: setting; format; duration and frequency; treatment method; and the need for somatic treatment. *Setting* refers to where treatment occurs: inpatient, outpatient, partial hospitalization program, and so on. *Format* is determined according to who directly participates in the treatment: individual, marital, family, or group. *Duration* and *frequency* refer to both the length of the session and frequency in terms of number of sessions per week or month. *Treatment method* refers to the type of psychosocial strategies and tactics employed: exploratory, supportive, cognitive-behavioral, or psychoeducational. *Somatic treatment* refers to prescribed medications, diet and exercise, electroshock therapy, and so forth. A meta-decision overrides the previous five factors: the matter of whether the couple or family should be offered treatment or the "no treatment" option. These authors offer specific guidelines for making informed, tailored decisions.

A Clinical Protocol for Matching and Tailoring Treatment

The previous review suggests that although there have been creative clinical innovations and even clinical research efforts to match and tailor treatment, there is currently no scientifically validated protocol for tailoring psychotherapeutic treatment. Until such a validated protocol is available, therapists will continue to use their clinical acumen and best judgment for matching/tailoring treatment.

The following protocol has been employed by the authors in their clinical practice, supervision, and teaching. It will be described here and illustrated with clinical case material in subsequent chapters. This matching/tailoring protocol involves four steps:

1. Comprehensive assessment

2. Matching of therapeutic strategy(ies) based on the comprehensive assessment

3. Tailoring the chosen therapeutic strategy to couple/family needs, circumstances, treatment capacity, and response to therapist and treatment

4. Implementation, review, and revision of matching/tailoring efforts

Comprehensive Assessment

As mentioned previously, an important value of the integrative approaches to marital and family therapy is that they discourage parochial thinking and shortsightedness. Practically speaking, integrative approaches require more multidimensional than undimensional assessment. Matching and tailoring require multidimensional and comprehensive assessments. A therapist who questions the value of a comprehensive assessment would do well to seriously consider the statistics on treatment failure in family therapy. In *Failures in Family Therapy*, Coleman (1985) notes that 83% of treatment failures could be primarily attributed to inadequate initial assessments.

The following assessment schema is derived from a biopsychosocial assessment model (Sperry, 1989). There are five basic dimensions of this comprehensive assessment schema. The schema is visually represented as follows:

> comprehensive assessment = situation/severity + system + skill + style/status + suitability for treatment

These five assessment dimensions and associated factors are listed in Table 5.1 and described on the following pages.

Table 5.1 Comprehensive Assessment in the Evaluation of Couples and Families

---

A. Situation/severity

 1. Presenting complaints and problems
 2. Couple or family demographics: age, number of members, and sociocultural and financial status
 3. Level of family functioning

B. System

 4. Family history, developmental stage, and genogram
 5. Boundaries, power, and intimacy

C. Skills

 6. Self-management skills
 7. Relational skills

D. Style/status

 8. Personality style
 9. Individual psychological and health status

E. Suitability for treatment

 10. Formulations of problem and distress
 11. Expectations for treatment
 12. Readiness and motivation for treatment

Situation/Severity *Situation/Severity* refers to assessing the symptoms and severity of stressors the family is experiencing along with demographic factors and the family's level of functioning.

1. *Presenting complaints and problems:* Families who seek family therapy or are referred for a family evaluation and/or treatment present with relatively similar concerns: communication; child and adolescent conflicts; sex; finances; physical, sexual, or verbal abuse; or various crises related to the death of a relative or family member, job, health problem, and so on. The presenting complaints are not always identical to the problem(s) that distress the family. More often the vagueness of their difficulty, as well as their inability to alleviate their discomfort by themselves, may be part of the presenting complaint (Nichols, 1988).

2. *Couple or family demographics: age, size, sociocultural, and financial status:* Family demographics may exacerbate or buffer the family from internal and external stressors. Generally speaking, an inverse relationship exists between spousal age at time of marriage and the probability of divorce. Those who marry at a very young age have the highest divorce rates, probably because they have not developed sufficient maturity and/or relational skills (Stuart, 1980). Similarly, families with very young children, irrespective of the age of the par-

ents, tend to be more stressed than families with adult children. Family size tends to correlate with family problems and divorce proneness. A U-shaped distribution is noted in which childless couples and those with large families were more likely to divorce than those with families of moderate size (Thornton, 1977).

Economic hardship in large families might explain their proneness to divorce, since financial issues can be a source of considerable family stress. Financially stressed families struggle with a wide variety of issues including marital instability (Lorenz, Conger, Simon, & Whitbeck, 1991). The recent and current trend of corporate mergers, downsizing, and layoffs has added additional burdens to an increasing number of families including those from the managerial and professional class who have been virtually immune to job loss, or the fear of job loss, since the end of World War II. When job loss is noted, its psychosocial effect must be fully assessed (Kates, Greiff, & Hagen, 1990).

Family income is more strongly and negatively associated with family conflict and divorce then any other census variable (Levinger, 1976). Too little income or a decrease in income because of job loss or wage cutback, relative to the family's expectation and standard of living, are common precipitants of discords.

Cultural values and socioeconomic status combine to shape the character of a family, particularly role expectations of its members, and the nuances of daily experience. Cultural values stem from early socialization experiences and are reinforced daily by others in the subculture in which the family resides (Laner, 1978). Social class differences also greatly affect attitudes and behavior. Lower-class families tend to have superficial contacts with more outsiders than do middle-class families, who have deeper contacts with fewer individuals outside their family (Stuart, 1980).

3. *Level of family functioning:* Level of family functioning should be initially assessed and then monitored throughout the course of treatment. Level of functioning is a key variable in matching a particular therapeutic strategy to a particular family. Earlier in this chapter three methods of assessing level of functioning were described: Weltner (1985) and Schultz (1984) for the entire family and Guerin et al. (1987) for the couple.

System   *System* refers to the family's history and developmental stage, as well as the system factors of boundaries, power, and intimacy.

1. *Family history, developmental stage, and genogram:* It is useful for the therapist to have some understanding of how the family has come to be where it is today. Much of this information can be gathered in

the course of constructing a genogram. The therapist may begin the history taking with questions about parents' births and childhoods, especially what their family lives were like as children, how they did at school, and life after leaving school. Information about their parents and siblings is also noted, as well as how the couple met and courted. The course of the marriage, including information about births of children and the children's development to date, is also noted.

The family's stage in its life cycle, as well as transition points, usually can be noted at this point in the assessment. McGoldrick and Carter's (1982) family life cycle stages provide a useful model: (1) unattached young adult; (2) joining of families through marriage; (3) family with young children; (4) family with adolescents; (5) launching children and moving on; and (6) family in later life.

Of course, intergenerational influences affect families. Exploration of each spouse's family of origin and their parents' families of origin in the presence of the family is frequently helpful in clarifying current issues and bringing them into the therapeutic arena. This can be accomplished in several ways. A common method is the use of the genogram. In this case, the genogram (McGoldrick & Gerson, 1985) is a visual depiction of the family tree covering at least three generations for both spouses. Important information is reported on the genogram such as names, ages, marital status, divorces, separations, and year of deaths. Typically, the therapist constructs a genogram of one spouse and has the second spouse fill in information and make comments following the initial disclosure of the first spouse. Then the process is reversed, and the second spouse's family of origin is explored with input from the first spouse.

2. *The factors of boundaries, power, and intimacy:* Berman and Leif (1975) and Fish and Fish (1986) suggest a series of questions therapists can ask themselves during the evaluation to determine three critical systems factors in families. These questions involve boundaries, power, and intimacy.

   Questions regarding boundaries include: Who else is considered to be part of the family system? What's being excluded from family relationships and assigned to grandparents, relatives, or others? Who and what events or things are intruding into the family?

   Questions of power involve: Who is in charge? How do the parents deal with power in their relationship and in relationships with the children?

   And finally, questions regarding intimacy include: How near, how far, and how do family members tolerate or respond to the needs and desires of one another for intimate contact and close-ness? What is their pattern of vacillation in emotional and geographical distance as family members struggle with their need for closeness?

Answers to these questions provide significant data for the therapist in assessing the family system. Inventories such as the Family Adaptability and Cohesion Evaluation Scale (FACES-III) (Olson, Portner, & Labee, 1985; Olson, Sprenkle, & Russell, 1979) and the Self-Report Family Instrument (SFI) (Beavers, Hampson, & Hulgus, 1985) are also useful in clarifying family system factors.

Skills   *Skills* refers to the level of self-management and relational skills that family members possess and use within the family. Family members may effectively use a skill such as assertiveness outside the family but not within the family or with a particular family member. Others cannot use a particular skill within or outside the family because they never acquired the skill. The therapist assesses skills and their use directly through observation of enactments and indirectly through the family members' self-report. Two classes of skills are noted: self-management and relational.

1. *Self-management skills:* A number of skills are necessary for family members to function effectively as individuals. Deficits in these skills can greatly affect family group functioning. These skills are assertiveness, problem solving, managing money, time management, making conversation, developing friendship, finding and maintaining a job or remaining in and succeeding in school, and other aspects of self-responsibility.

2. *Relational skills:* At least five skills appear necessary to sustain effective, healthy family functioning. They are encouragement, congruent communications, empathic listening, conflict resolution, and negotiation and consensus building. Nichols (1988) lists additional skills he believes are necessary for effective couple functioning: caring, commitment, and volunteering. Dinkmeyer and Carlson (1986) list many of these skills as necessary for a growing marriage relationship.

Style/Status   *Style/Status* refers to the individual system dimension. In addition to assessing family system functioning, the therapist should also assess the style and functioning of individual family members. This would include personality style and physical and psychological health status.

1. *Personality style: Personality style* refers to the enduring stylistic pattern of perceiving, responding, and thinking about the world, other people, and oneself. Personality style can be thought of as a continuum with one end characterized by healthy, flexible, and adoptive functioning and the other end by unhealthy, rigid, and maladaptive dysfunctioning. (Extreme dysfunction is referred to as an *Axis II personality disorder* in DSM-IV.) Each family member manifests a dominant personality style, or disorder, often with traits or features of other styles. Personality styles and disorders can be assessed through clinical observation and developmental history, as well as through standard interview schedules and personality inventories such as the Millon Clinical Multiaxial Inventory II (MCMI-II)

2. *Individual psychological and health status:* One or both spouses may present for treatment with a psychiatric disorder along with relational dysfunction. Even while marital and family therapists may prefer to formulate problems systemically, the fact is individual psychopathology exists that affects relational functioning. A handbook on such disorders, entitled *The Disordered Couple,* has recently been published (Carlson & Sperry, 1996).

   Accordingly, psychological functioning on Axis I and II should also be assessed. With regard to couples, Stuart (1980) notes that assessing the level of potential depression in both spouses is the most critical factor affecting the process of marital therapy. Treatment will be hindered if a diagnosable psychiatric disorder in a family member is not properly evaluated and considered in the treatment plan (Beavers, 1985).

   The importance of assessing physical health factors cannot be overstressed. Current acute and chronic medical conditions, medication use (both prescription and non-prescription), drug and alcohol use, exercise and diet, sleep patterns, and job stress can greatly affect family functioning. These factors must be assessed (Doherty & Baird, 1987).

Suitability for Treatment   *Suitability for treatment* refers to the adequacy of the family's explanation or formulation of its problems and dysfunction, as well as their expectations and motivation for treatment. The better the family is suited for treatment the better the outcome and vice versa (Beutler & Crago, 1987).

1. *Formulation of the problem and distress:* Usually therapists think of developing "the" formulation of the couple's or family's dynamics and problems, which means, of course, their professional explanation of why the family acts and functions the way it does. So why

should the therapist be concerned with the family's own formulation? For a number of reasons. First, all families, particularly parents and older children, have formed an explanation of the family's concerns. These explanations may be singular or plural; that is, family members have different explanations, and their formulations may either be common knowledge or they may never have been disclosed before. Secondly, the family's formulation may be considerably different from the therapist's. Since treatment goals and plans are based on formulations, the greater the disparity between the therapist's and family's formulations, the more resistance and noncompliance to the treatment plan can be anticipated. Couples and families will collaborate more easily with a therapist when they have achieved a "meeting of the minds." Thus, the therapist should elicit formulations, share his or her own formulation, and then negotiate an acceptable common formulation (Sperry & Carlson, 1991). This may involve considerable discussion and education of family members on family dynamics. Such discussion is central to collaboratively focused treatment. If the family insists on projecting or scapegoating their problems onto the identified patient, an outsider, or an outside influence, they probably are not able to assume the kind of responsibility required to engage in the change process and would rank low in suitability for treatment.

Eliciting the couple's or family's formulation begins with asking, "Why do you think your family isn't working so well?" This question should be posed to each member, without discussion, until all have spoken. Common explanations range from, "It's really because of dad being gone all the time," to "It's because we don't have enough money to make ends meet," to "We're being punished because of that abortion," to "We just don't know how to communicate or respect one another." Then the therapist asks the family to come up with a family formulation they can all accept. The way in which they respond to this task can be diagnostic.

2. *Expectations for treatment:* The therapist assesses the family's or couple's expectations for treatment, beginning with the questions "What were you hoping would be the result of our work together in therapy?" and "What needs to happen for these results to come about?" Unrealistic expectations, particularly those that involve "magic cures" with little or no commitment and involvement from family members, need to be noted and discussed. The family should be queried on their treatment objectives. Do they want symptom relief only, structural changes, divorce, medication, and so on? It is also useful to assess the family's or couple's previous efforts to make

changes in their relationship. The family who has a history of some previous success in making a change is likely to repeat that success and can be so encouraged.

3. *Readiness and motivation for treatment:* Treatment readiness for couple and family therapy has been described by Myers (1992). Myers specifies three criteria for readiness: (1) family's willingness to participate in therapeutic tasks; (2) their ability to engage in the tasks of therapy; and (3) their confidence that therapeutic success is possible. She describes four levels of readiness ranging from high (whereby the family is able, willing, and confident to make a specific change) to low (whereby the family is unable, unwilling, and lacks the confidence to make a specific change). Myers (in press) describes methods for assessing readiness.

In addition to treatment readiness, one must clarify the motivation of family members for change. Usually one or two family members appear more motivated than others. In individual therapy the client with high motivation tends to be self-referred, verbalizes a desire to change, has ego-dystonic symptoms, and is responsive to initial therapeutic tasks and intrasession homework. This compares to the individual with low motivation, who tends to be referred by others, has ego-syntonic symptoms, and verbalizes and shows little desire for change. These same characteristics can be noted in family members. Thus, the therapist will observe family members' verbalizations concerning other family members, themselves, and therapy, noting the degree of congruence between their behavior and their statements. The therapist may ask the family members questions like "What specifically do you want to be different in this situation?" "What role do you see yourself taking?" and "How willing are you to see this change through?"

Matching a Therapeutic Strategy

Rational decisions about matching specific treatment strategies to couples or families are possible based on the comprehensive assessment. The first three dimensions of that assessment—situation/severity, system, and skills—are the basis for matching. Situation/severity is a particularly useful criterion. It can be operationalized in terms of levels of family functioning as described by Weltner (1985) and Schultz (1984), level of distress as described by Worthington (1989), or level of marital conflict as described by Guerin et al. (1987). For example, a family functioning at level two—an under-organized family—would probably be best matched with a structural intervention, whereas a family functioning at level three—an overorganized and resistant family—would probably be best matched with a more strategic intervention.

The extent to which the family's problems appear to be focused on power as compared to boundary or intimacy issues will also suggest different types of intervention or strategies. Boundary problems appear to be best matched with structural strategies, whereas intimacy problems lend themselves to psychodynamic, psychoeducational, behavioral, and communication approaches. Power problems may be best matched with strategic and cognitive-behavioral strategies.

If skill deficits are the prominent basis for family or couple dysfunctioning, psychoeducational and behavioral strategies offer good matches. Similarly, if a couple is recently married and presents with minimal marital conflict, [that is, level I (Guerin et al., 1987)], a psychoeducational approach would likely be the best match.

Often, however, couples or families present with major dysfunctionality in both the systemic and skills dimensions. In such situations, matching will involve two or more strategies—for example, structural and psychoeducational strategies may be indicated for the family with prominent boundary problems and skill deficits in assertiveness and conflict resolution. The therapist must then decide whether to sequence or blend and combine these strategies.

Tailoring the Strategy

As noted earlier, tailoring is the process of "fitting," or customizing, a particular treatment strategy to a particular individual, couple, or family. Currently, there are no standardized or research-based guidelines for tailoring. Nevertheless, Worthington (1992) offers some suggestions for making tailoring decisions. First, decide at which level tailoring will occur. Will it be based on client-system values, requests, cultural identity, or some other variables? Second, decide on the decision rules for tailoring. What are the cultural family deficits, characteristics, and strengths? Third, decide what to do if family members differ on important variables. Fourth, predict what will happen if the clinician does or does not consider important issues or factors when tailoring treatment. Fifth, be realistic. Practical considerations must be weighed against ethical mandates and clinical resources. Tailoring decisions can be based on the comprehensive assessment of dimensions of style and suitability for treatment. The therapist's timing and sequencing of questions, clarifications, and reframes, confrontations, and/or interpretations should be based on an understanding of individual family members' personality styles. Clearly, the couple's or family's readiness for treatment (Myers,

1992) must be considered. Accordingly, the therapist can titrate, or modify, the degree of direction and support he or she provides the couple or family based on their level of readiness.

Implementation, Review, and Revision

The last step of the protocol involves continuing the implementation of the matched strategy or strategies along with continued monitoring of the couple's or family's responses to treatment. Treatment will continually be tailored or fine-tuned based on this ongoing monitoring and assessment.

The preceding pages described the suggested clinical protocol for matching and tailoring treatment of couples and families. Descriptions of clinical applications of this protocol appear in subsequent chapters. An extended case example involving a chronically conflictual dual-career couple is presented in Chapter 7.

Concluding Note

This chapter described the theoretical as well as clinical challenges of individualizing psychotherapeutic treatment for client-systems. It presented several clinical innovations for matching or tailoring treatment for couples and families. It also provided a clinical protocol for both matching and tailoring treatment based on a comprehensive assessment. The current interest in matching and tailoring treatment reflects not only the economic realities of present times but also the maturing of the field of family therapy. The prospects for the future of marital and family therapy are bright (Clarkin, 1992).

References

Beavers, W. (1985). *Successful marriage: A family systems approach to couples therapy*. New York: W. W. Norton.

Beavers, W., Hampson, R., & Hulgus, Y. (1985). Commentary: The Beavers systems approach to family assessment, *Family Process, 24,* 398–405.

Berman, E., & Lief, H. (1975). Marital therapy from a psychiatric perspective: An overview. *American Journal of Psychiatry, 132,* 582–591.

Beutler, L. E. (1983). *Eclectic psychotherapy: A systemic approach*. New York: Pergamon.

Beutler, L. E., & Clarkin, J. F. (1990). *Systematic treatment selection: Toward targeted therapeutic interventions*. New York: Brunner/Mazel.

Beutler, L., & Crago, M. (1987). Strategies and techniques of prescriptive psychotherapeutic intervention. In R. Hales & A. Frances (Eds.), *Psychiatric updates: APA annual review Vol. 6.* (pp. 331–446). Washington, D. C.: American Psychiatric Press.

Carlson, J., & Sperry, L. (Eds.) (1996). *The disordered couple.* New York: Brunner/Mazel.

Clarkin, J. (1992). Tailoring treatment with families and couples: Interview with John F. Clarkin. *Topics in Family Psychology and Counseling, 3*(1), 7–16.

Coleman, S. B. (Ed.) (1985). *Failures in family therapy.* New York: Guilford.

Dinkmeyer, D., & Carlson, J. (1986). TIME for a better marriage. *Journal of Psychotherapy and the Family, 2,* 9–28.

Doherty, W., & Baird, M. (Eds.) (1987). *Family-centered medical care: A clinical casebook.* New York: Guilford.

Fish, R., & Fish, L. (1986). Quid pro quo revisited: The basis of marital therapy. *American Journal of Orthopsychiatry, 56,* 371–384.

Frances, A., Clarkin, J. F., & Perry, S. (1984). *Differential therapeutics in psychiatry: The art and science of treatment selection.* New York: Brunner/Mazel.

Guerin, P., Fay, L., Burden, S., & Kautto, J. (1987). *The evaluation and treatment of marital conflict: A four-stage approach.* New York: Basic Books.

Howard, G. S., Nance, D. W., & Myers, P. (1987). *Adaptive counseling and therapy: A systematic approach to selecting effective treatments.* San Francisco: Jossey-Bass.

Kates, N., Greiff, B., & Hagen, D. (1990). *The psychosocial impact of job loss.* Washington, D. C.: American Psychiatric Press.

Laner, M. (1978). Love's labors lost: A theory of marital dissolution. *Family Coordinator, 25,* 175–181.

Lazarus, A. (1981). *The practice of multimodal therapy.* New York: Guilford.

Lazarus, A. (Ed.) (1985). *The practice of multimodal therapy.* New York: McGraw-Hill.

Levinger, G. (1976). In conclusion: Threads in the fabric. *Journal of Social Issues, 32,* 193–207.

Lorenz, F., Conger, R., Simon, R., & Whitbeck, L. (1991). Economic pressure and marital quality. *Journal of Marriage and the Family, 53,* 375–388.

McGoldrick, M., & Gerson, R. (1985). *Genograms in family assessment.* New York: W. W. Norton.

McGoldrick, M., & Carter, E. (1982). The family life cycle. In F. Walsh (Ed.), *Normal family processes* (pp. 221–249). New York: Guilford.

Myers, P. (1992). Using adaptive counseling and therapy to tailor treatment to couples and families. *Topics in Family Psychology and Counseling, 1*(3), 56–70.

Myers, P. (1995). How therapists ACT: Cases combining major approaches to psychotherapy and the Adaptive Counseling and Therapy model. (Don W. Nance, Ed.) (pp. 105–128). Accelerated Development, Inc., Washington, DC, US; xii.

Nichols, W. (1988). *Marital therapy: An integrative approach.* New York: Guilford.

Olson, D., Portner, J., & Labee, Y. (1985). FACES-III. Family Social Science, University of Minnesota, 290 McNeal Hall, St. Paul, MN 55108.

Olson, D., Sprenkle, D., & Russell, C. (1979). Circumflex model of marital and family systems: I. Cohesion and adaptability dimensions, family types and clinical applications. *Family Process, 18,* 3–28.

Paul, G. (1967). Strategy of outcome research in psychotherapy. *Journal of Consulting Psychology, 31,* 109–118.

Perry, S., Frances, A., & Clarkin, J. (1990). *A DSM-III-R casebook of treatment selection.* New York: Brunner/Mazel.

Schultz, S. (1984). *Family systems therapy: An integration.* New York: Jason Aronson.

Sperry, L. (1986). Contemporary approaches to family therapy: A comparative and meta-analysis. *Individual Psychology, 42,* 591–601.

Sperry, L. (1989). Assessment in marital therapy: A couples-centered biopsychosocial approach. *Individual Psychology, 45,* 446–451.

Sperry, L. (1995). *Handbook of diagnosis and treatment of DSM-IV personality disorders.* New York: Brunner/Mazel

Sperry, L., & Carlson, J. (1991). *Marital therapy: Integrating theory and technique.* Denver: Love Publishing.

Stuart, R. (1980). *Helping couples change: A social learning approach to marital therapy.* New York: Guilford.

Thornton, A. (1977). Children and marital stability. *Journal of Marriage and the Family, 39,* 531–540.

Weltner, J. (1985). Matchmaking: Choosing the appropriate therapy for families at various levels of pathology. In M. Mirkin & S. Koman (Eds.), *Handbook of adolescent and family therapy* (pp. 237–246). New York: Gardner.

Worthington, E. (1989). Matching family treatment to family stressors. In C. Figely (Ed.), *Treating stress in families* (pp. 44–63). New York: Brunner/Mazel.

Worthington, E. (1992). Strategic matching and tailoring of treatment to couples and families. *Topics in Family Psychology and Counseling, 1*(3), 21–32

6

Tailoring Treatment
The Significance of Culture

The therapist who wants to tailor treatment to meet the unique needs of specific families must be aware of all the variables that can add to the complexity of family life. Because the diversity of the families we serve is steadily increasing, culture is clearly among the most important of these variables.

Family therapists will have to work hard to become truly multicultural in their practices. In fact, as Levant (1994) suggests, the field of family psychology as a whole has a great deal of work to do to achieve multiculturalism. He urges family psychologists to:

- Include culturally diverse samples in their research so that the unique characteristics of families from different cultural groups will be better understood.

- Develop more culturally aware approaches to family assessment and intervention.

- Incorporate scientific and professional knowledge about families from different cultural groups into our training programs . . .

- Continue . . . advocacy efforts to eliminate racial and cultural discrimination and its devastating effects on ethno-cultural minorities.

- Recruit members of under-represented groups into the field and into leadership roles. (p. 1)

How can we meet the challenge of developing "culturally aware approaches"? First we need to consider the scope of the term *culture*. If we hope to understand its relevance for families, we need to use a broad definition, such as the following:

125

> [Culture is] the learned and shared knowledge, beliefs, and rules that people use to interpret experience and to generate social behavior; the guiding focus behind the behaviors and material products associated with a group of people. (Monroe, Goldman, & Dube, 1994, p. 27)

When we use this broad definition, we come to realize that ethnicity is but one of the central factors in culture. A number of building blocks can go into the construction of a particular family's cultural heritage. Along with race and ethnicity, a family's culture can be affected by gender, education, sexual orientation, and age of its members, as well as language, social class, income, geographical location, religion, and a myriad of other factors. Family members may hold values and world views that differ from those of the therapist. In fact, cultural differences may occur even among family members themselves. The key to a multicultural perspective is to embrace the reality of cultural diversity, recognizing the significance of culture in family life and working with all clients in accordance with their own cultural contexts.

The multicultural perspective has special repercussions for family therapy because culture deeply affects the most basic meaning that family life holds for each individual. Our effectiveness depends on our ability to understand how families are influenced by the values that underlie their notions of family life, by their experience of oppression, and by the conflicts inherent in acculturation.

The Values Underlying Family Life

As they proceed on the journey toward multiculturalism, many family therapists find that they must stop and reexamine their own assumptions about what the concept of *family* really means. Suppositions that they believe to be universal sometimes turn out, on closer examination, to be culture-bound.

Individuation and Family Unity

The basic definitions of family life vary from culture to culture. Consider, for example, the search for balance between the values of individuation and family unity. What family therapists perceive as enmeshment within a family—or what counselors might view as an individual's tendency toward codependence—may in fact be a cultural manifestation that should be honored.

Inclan and Hernandez (1992) address this issue in an analysis of the concept of codependence as it affects family therapy with Hispanic clients. They point out that although separation, individuation, and clear boundaries are often considered positive goals of therapy, these concepts are not universally accepted across cultures. Therapeutic interventions designed to increase individual autonomy may be "unwittingly defining recovery and normality as the client's and family's ability to incorporate values, beliefs, and behavior that are more congruent with the ways of the Anglo culture than with their own" (p. 247).

If a therapist is unaware of the value placed by Hispanic families on family loyalty, on the preservation of traditions, on interdependence among family members, and on subordination of individual needs to the needs of the family, the therapy may inadvertently undercut firmly held cultural values. Worse yet, the therapist may interpret culturally appropriate behaviors as pathological.

Inclan and Hernandez (1992) warn against therapeutic approaches that emphasize detachment and independence:

> This treatment approach is anchored in the cultural narrative of a Western-Anglo society that highly values individualism, action, mastery, and equality. . . . Anchoring treatment goals and methods to such a social narrative is contrary to Hispanic family values and counterproductive to effective treatment. (p. 251)

This concern is certainly not limited to Hispanic families. In fact, Sue and Sue (1990) suggest that, in comparison with the dominant culture in the United States, "almost all minority groups place greater value on families, historical lineage (reverence of ancestors), interdependence among family members, and submergence of self for the good of the family" (p. 123). The fact that the dominant culture emphasizes individualism means that people whose cultures have a stronger relational dimension may be subjected to undue pressures to conform.

Women, as a cultural group, are also subjected to pressures to conform to changing views of what constitutes healthy behavior. Following advice that emphasized relationships, which was once considered appropriate for women, now leaves them open to criticisms of enmeshment or codependency. As Walters (1993) points out, a woman is now expected to recover from her focus on nurturing others and to concentrate instead on meeting her own needs. Sometimes this new norm places a woman in an untenable position.

> It creates yet another of those ever-present, guilt-producing double binds for women: in your role as the *good* mother, you are expected to be a caretaker, responsible for the behavior of your children, protective, approving, available and self-sacrificing in behalf of your family. But these very same behaviors will get you into trouble. . . . (p. 64)

Unfortunately, some of this trouble can actually stem from family therapy if therapists fail to recognize the effect of gender-role socialization
processes that have their roots in the larger society.

The Extended Family

In addition to exploring cultural differences regarding individuation,
Sue and Sue (1990) also contrast the European-American emphasis
on the nuclear family with the concept of the extended family. They
state that "middle-class white Americans consider the family unit to
be nuclear (husband/wife and children related by blood), while most
minorities define the family unit as an extended one" (p. 120). Ho
(1987) points out that the conceptual framework of the nuclear family
is often misused in services to Native Americans, whose family structures are more likely to be characterized by extended networks that
include several households and active kinship systems. Boyd-Franklin
(1989) states that "many black families have become extended families
in which relatives of a variety of blood ties have been absorbed into a
coherent network of mutual emotional and economic support" (p. 15).
In addition, the Hispanic families described by Inclan and Hernandez
(1992) are defined not just in terms of the nuclear unit but in terms
of an extended kinship system that may include *compadres, comadres,*
and *hijos de crianza* and that is expected to provide support in times
of crisis.

Culturally based definitions of the family unit have important implications for the therapeutic process. Clearly, therapists need to ask family
members how they define *family* before they address any issues related
to boundaries.

Culturally Based Views of Family Life:
The Effect on Family Therapy

Families define themselves within cultural contexts. These contexts
have to be taken into account when therapists assess family systems
and select interventions. Otherwise, family processes that are in fact
normal within a particular culture may inadvertently be pathologized.

Ina (1994) provides an example that demonstrates the difficulties
that can arise when a therapist is unaware of a family's cultural norms.
She describes a young, Japanese-American college student who was
referred to her by a Buddhist minister. The young man was in a state
of deep depression following the intervention of his previous therapist.
He had sought counseling initially because his father, a farmer in rural
California, had announced that he would be leaving the land to his

eldest son. The client, who was the second son, had tried to earn his father's love and felt rejected.

After constructing a genogram, the previous counselor had diagnosed the family as dysfunctional, saying that the family was characterized by men who were authoritarian, remote, and emotionally unavailable and women who were passive and personality-disordered. Boundaries between the parental and sibling subsystems were seen as diffuse. Communication patterns were assessed as triangulated because of the likelihood that one family member would approach another member indirectly by conveying a message through a third party.

Thus, family dynamics that in fact reflected the values of traditional Japanese-American families in this rural area were pathologized by a counselor who was uninformed about the culture. The young man was counseled to state his concerns directly in a public confrontation with his father. When this confrontation took place, the humiliated parent responded with an unremitting silence, refusing to speak to his son. The client, after being excluded from his family, fell into near-suicidal despondency.

Ina, working from a culturally sensitive perspective, helped the client understand the cultural beliefs underlying his father's behavior. The family's indirect communication pattern, far from being pathologized, was recognized as a culturally adaptive tool and used to defuse this conflict. The client's eldest sister acted as an intermediary, taking a conciliatory message back to the father. Through this mechanism, the son was integrated back into the family, and a disaster rooted in cultural illiteracy was averted.

Falicov (1994) presents another example of the kind of problem that can occur when helpers are unaware of cultural norms. She describes a situation in which a young child of Puerto Rican descent was hospitalized with a life-threatening illness. An elderly great-aunt, who was godmother to the child, spent innumerable hours at his bedside, praying, overseeing his treatment, and pampering him. The health care providers, exasperated with the aunt's constant "interference" and mystified by the fact that she was present more frequently than the child's parents, asked for a psychiatric consultation. The psychiatrist, who was unschooled in Latino culture, interpreted the aunt's behavior as a reaction formation that was based on her resentment at being forced to spend her spare time at the hospital in place of the child's mother. The hospital staff discouraged the aunt's participation.

What messages can we receive from these two examples? The counselor described by Ina was unaware of the risk involved in encouraging a client to exert a brand of individualism that was not accepted as a value in his traditional family. The health care providers described by

Falicov did not understand that the family's definition of a *family* was much broader than their own. According to Falicov, the family's cultural values of strong kinship bonds, shared parenting, and three-generation involvement were misinterpreted by people whose own cultural values emphasized leisure, autonomy, and freedom from parenting in old age. Falicov does say that this event, which took place some years ago, would be less likely to occur today. Although we may hope that such exaggerated ethnocentrism is a relic of the past, many helpers still fail to recognize the degree to which assumptions about the nature of family life differ among families and across cultures. Family therapists who are aware of cultural factors use their knowledge not to make generalized assumptions about various ethnic groups but to guide their exploration of each family's world view.

The Experience of Oppression

Just as family therapists need to be sensitive to cultural differences in the values underlying family life, they also need to be aware of differences related to the experience of oppression. *Oppression* can be defined as "that state or condition within an ordered society . . . where one segment of the society has differentially and involuntarily limited access to all the available opportunities, resources, and benefits of that particular society" (Wilson, 1987, p. 19). Groups are targeted for oppression on the basis of such characteristics as ethnic and racial status, gender, and religion. The process of oppression is insidious because targeted people must face a lethal combination of overt bigotry, covert discrimination, and a socialization process that encourages internalization of negative self-views.

How could this process fail to affect the dynamics of family interactions? Consider, for example, the effect of racism on the family life of African Americans.

> The experience of being black in this country is almost a daily process of pulling out the arrows that racism hurls at us. The added burden that African-American families and couples must carry is to create an emotional atmosphere in which the arrows can be pulled out. . . . Unfortunately, many of the African-American families that we treat in family or couples therapy have redirected these daily arrows at each other. We cannot begin to address the anger and pain in these families unless we are willing to look at the racism that exists for them in society and in our field. (Boyd-Franklin, 1993, p. 55)

To be effective as family therapists, then, we need to be active in encouraging intense exploration of the effect of racism.

Addressing Racism Directly

Boyd-Franklin points out that African-American clients sometimes avoid talking about their experiences of racism even when these issues are foremost in their minds. "They know that many therapists will try to talk them out of what they are feeling because they do not understand the need for African-American individuals and families to vent their rage about situations in which there is an undercurrent of racism" (Boyd-Franklin, 1993, p. 56). When therapists are reluctant to address racism head-on, they impede the therapeutic process. As A. J. Franklin says (1993):

> Once the pervasive impact of racism is acknowledged as a force in a black family's experience, the family can move on to confront other issues. But if the impact of racism is ignored, it's unlikely that therapy will go anywhere. (p. 36)

"Healthy Paranoia"

Racism and other oppressions are also relevant to family therapy because of their influence on the family's willingness to participate. People who have had to deal with a lifetime of racism and discrimination have many reasons to be suspicious of therapists and therapy (Boyd-Franklin, 1989; Willis, 1988). They may perceive extensive history-taking as an invasion of privacy, designed to place destructive labels on them. Negative experiences with the welfare system and other social and governmental agencies may have made distrust an appropriate response. There is no way for clients to be certain that the agency providing family counseling is different and that confidentiality will be maintained. Family members may have been socialized from early childhood to distrust people who press for personal information. The referral for therapy may have come from the courts or from other systems that have agendas going beyond the well-being of the family. Grier and Cobbs (1968) coined the term "healthy cultural paranoia" to describe the intense suspiciousness that may be the only route to survival in the context of racism. In the face of this reality, we should not be surprised by "minorities' help-seeking behaviors that include under-utilization of family therapists who generally are monolinguistic, middle-class, and ethnocentric in family problem diagnosis and treatment" (Ho, 1987, p. 14).

Oppression: The Effect on Family Therapy

Wilson (1987) says that "empowerment is the antidote of oppression" (p. 20). Therapy can lead toward empowerment when the therapist exhibits a belief in clients' potential ability to cope with life problems;

when problems are perceived as coming from a political, social, and economic context; when clients learn to understand and work with power dynamics; and when the therapist uses skill-building strategies to help clients gain control over their environments (McWhirter, 1991). Empowerment-oriented family therapy rests on the assumption that clients who recognize the role of oppression in their lives are most likely to be able to move from the morass of self-blame to the solid ground of self-management.

Of course, exploring the experience of oppression is not an alternative to taking personal responsibility. Instead, it lays the groundwork that makes other therapeutic tasks possible. Consider, for example, an African-American family described by Franklin (1993). The family was seen in therapy primarily because of the adolescent son's behavior problems in school. The father was upset because the teacher and the school psychologist both seemed reluctant to deal with him, the father. He was angered by his son's treatment in school, which he viewed as racist.

Some of the son's problems were, in fact, due to his own behavior. Yet, the racism experienced by both father and son was real. As the therapist, Franklin knew that he could not discount the family's accurate observation of institutionalized racism. He allowed time for family members, particularly the father, to express their sense that racism was a central problem in this situation. Once the issue of racism had been explored, the family was ready to move on and help the adolescent take more responsibility for his own actions. As Franklin puts it, "therapy provided an opportunity to explore the crossroads where family dynamics and racism met" (Franklin, 1993, p. 36).

Cultural Values and Conflict

The concept of *world view* is another important theme running through the current literature on multicultural counseling (Carter 1991; Ho, 1987; Lewis, 1994; Sue & Sue, 1990). Cultural diversity creates differences in values that are so basic as to constitute different world views. For instance, Carter (1991), extending the work of Kluckhohn and Strodtbeck (1961), explains that cultures vary in terms of their orientations toward the following factors: human nature, person and nature, time sense, activity, and social relations.

In terms of *human nature*, cultures vary widely, with some teaching that people are born with evil inclinations that must be controlled and others inculcating in their members a belief that people are basically good.

The differences among cultures are even more apparent when we consider the relationship between *person and nature*. Some cultures believe in the subjugation of humans to nature and suggest that people cannot expect to control natural forces. Other cultures, in contrast, are built on the assumption that humankind can gain mastery over nature. An alternate world view suggests that people can achieve partnership and harmony with nature.

Time sense is also central to cultural world views, with some cultures valuing the traditions of the past and others focusing on planning for the future.

Closely associated with time sense is the orientation toward *activity*. Cultures that focus on *being* emphasize spontaneous self-expression, whereas those that focus on *doing* emphasize achievements that are measurable by external criteria.

Finally, orientations toward *social relations* run the gamut from an acceptance of clearly established lines of authority, to an emphasis on collective decision making, to an assumption that individuality and autonomy are more important than group goals.

On the basis of a review of numerous studies, Carter (1991) points out that "in general, these researchers have found significant differences between the dominant white middle-class value orientation and those of the cultural and ethnic groups with which they were compared" (p. 167). The value system of white middle-class Americans is characterized "by a belief in mastery over nature, future time, doing-oriented activity, and individual relationships" (p. 165). Studies of Latin cultures, Native American cultures, Asian cultures, African cultures, and Mediterranean cultures have pointed toward major value differences in all these categories.

The fact that world views are so diverse has important implications for cross-cultural family counseling in that therapists have to see their own values in perspective. Again and again, they will face situations in which their values and those of the families they are treating differ so greatly that the goals, the assumptions, and the processes of therapy will be affected.

> Middle-class therapists, no matter what their ethnic origins, have been socialized in terms of mainstream values. The therapist will be future-oriented, expecting clients to be motivated and to keep appointments punc-tually. He or she will also expect families to be willing to work on therapeu-tic tasks (doing), over reasonable periods of time (future), with the prospect of change before them (mastery-over-nature) . . . and clients will be expected to separate themselves from enmeshment in the family structure and to develop increased autonomy (individual). (Spiegel, 1982, p. 46)

Each therapist will have to respond with openness, adhering to his or her own value system but recognizing that it is but one choice among many. "The therapist's beliefs, like those of the family, are only a 'comment on' the cultural context where they were learned, rather than the truth" (Schwartzman, 1983, p. 144).

Responding to these deep cultural differences is especially complex because the therapist can never assume that a client's value system necessarily coincides with his or her ethnic background. Adding to this complexity is the fact that many family systems are characterized by internal conflicts brought about by differences in acculturation among family members.

Conflicting World Views

Each individual and each family is affected by multiple cultural contexts. Within the United States, people may be influenced both by the traditional values of their families of origin and by the norms of the dominant culture. In their discussion of Hispanics in the United States, Szapocznik, Scopetta, Ceballos, and Santisteban (1994) say that much of the literature about this group is preoccupied with understanding the culture of origin while, in fact, no individual is purely a product of this idealized culture of origin.

> A Hispanic family in America, even in a very Hispanic region like Little Havana, is exposed to a complex melange of cultural influences which includes the culture of origin that exists in the living memories, values and behaviors of the older members of the family. . . . This cultural melange also includes the hybrid culture in which the children are immersed both in school and with acculturating peers. (p. 23)

This culturally pluralistic environment often leads to intensified generational conflict within families, with young people becoming acculturated into the mainstream while their parents try to maintain traditional values. Sometimes this situation culminates in a struggle wherein the adolescents strive for autonomy while the elders seek family connectedness.

Szapocznik and Kurtines (1993) describe the conflicts they saw in clinical observations of Cuban refugees families in the 1970s:

> The impact of a culturally diverse environment on these families resulted in the emergence of conflict-laden intergenerational acculturational differences in which parents and youths developed different cultural alliances (Hispanic and American, respectively). These intergenerationally related cultural differences were added to the usual intergenerational conflicts that occur in families with adolescents to produce a much compounded and exacerbated intergenerational *and* intercultural conflict. As a consequence, parents became unable to properly manage youngsters who made strong claims for autonomy and who no longer accepted their parents' traditional Cuban ways. (p. 403)

Szapocznik and his colleagues (1993) developed bicultural effectiveness training to work with these families. This strategy involves placing the cultural conflict itself in the role of identified patient and helping the family to develop a transcultural perspective. "Parents are encouraged to accept and understand the value of certain aspects of the American culture represented by their child, and the adolescents are encouraged to accept and understand the value of certain aspects of the Hispanic culture represented by their parents" (p. 404).

Cultural Conflict Within the Family: The Effect on Therapy

Individual problems and family issues sometimes become clearer when they are reframed in terms of cultural conflict. Consider, for example, the case of Silvia.

Silvia, a 22-year-old woman, had been living on her own since the age of 16. She left home at that time in the midst of an intense conflict with her father.

Silvia was an honors student in high school. She had wanted to continue her education, but her parents told her they would not be able to send her to college because they needed to save their money in case her older brother, Carlos, decided to go. In fact, Carlos had never shown any interest in higher education. Silvia felt that, no matter what she did, she could never win her father's approval.

Silvia's father, who had moved to Chicago from Mexico as a teenager, complained that Silvia was trying to turn her back on her family and her culture. Although he recognized that she was doing well in school, he criticized her lack of fluency in Spanish and her interest in "running around" with her friends in the evenings.

Once Silvia realized that she would not be able to go to college, she gave up on school altogether, moving out and spending her time with a group of young people who had always succeeded in shocking her parents. After 18 months of living on her own, Silvia grew tired of waking up in too many strange places with no memory of what drugs she had ingested the night before; she decided to return to the straight life. She finished her G.E.D. and got a clerical job. She soon established a strong relationship with Brent, an executive with her company. Brent asked her to marry him, but somehow Silvia was unable to make this commitment, although she was sure she loved him. She said that she was so paralyzed in her own depression that she could not make any decisions.

The main source of her depression had to do with her family of origin. She had tried to reconnect with her family, but they said they could not forgive her for all that she had put them through when she left home. She thought that her mother might have forgiven her but that her father would not allow it. She had been able to forge some connections with her aunt, uncle, and cousins but said that being with them made her feel all the more lonely for her parents.

Another source of her depression was that she had not disclosed to Brent any of the things that had happened to her in the 18 months after she left home. She feared that he would leave her and that he would be right to do so. She did not believe that she deserved to have a happy relationship with someone like Brent.

Silvia ran into an old friend from her "wild days" and began to experiment with heroin. She was still involved with Brent, who could not understand the changes she was going through and asked her to enter couples counseling with him. She felt that she was on the edge of an abyss and that this therapy was her one last hope.

Although some therapists might seek the reasons for Silvia's drug use and depression within herself or in her relationship with Brent, those with a multicultural perspective would recognize the salience of the cultural conflict within her family of origin. Silvia's attempts to be completely acculturated into the dominant Anglo culture ran the gamut from her monolingualism (English only) to her choice of a non-Hispanic mate. Even her drug use was a sign of her acculturation.

Despite her acculturation, however, Silvia could not come to terms with a life style that others might call independent. Her separation from her family was a pain that was at the very core of her being. In essence, both she and her father were bicultural beings, each trying to maintain a hold on one of their cultures at the expense of the other. Her culturally aware therapist knew that Silvia and Brent could not move on in their lives until her need for connection with her family of origin was addressed. Gradually, with the help of other members of the extended family, an accord was reached.

Strategies for Tailoring Family Therapy

As the previous chapter indicated, "matching" and "tailoring" treatment are quite different. When it comes to multiculturalism, family therapists sometimes wish that they could use a simple matching strategy: learn about various ethnic groups and then match the treatment to the family's ethnicity. In fact, however, multiculturalism involves tailoring, not matching. The therapist must address the specific needs of the particular family, while taking cultural factors into account. Thus, the therapist has to be knowledgeable enough to be sensitive to cultural norms and values without assuming that any generalization can possibly apply to all members of a group. As Berg and Miller (1992) point out, the therapist has to be able to "balance consideration of the impact of culture on clients' world view with how clients personally experience ethnic and cultural influences" (p. 363).

Hardy (1989) helps to clarify the issue of balance by putting it in a historical perspective. First, family therapists were trained according to the "theoretical myth of sameness" (TMOS), a belief system based on the assumption that all families were the same and that context could safely be ignored. A more contemporary view focuses on the difference between minority and non-minority families, but ignores differences within groups.

> Unless special topic areas give acute attention to the differences within any one group, be it women, gays or lesbians, or ethnic minorities, the inevitable consequence is a perpetuation of the epistemological error (TMOS) which these areas have been designed to rectify. Can there be a family therapy model that is effective for and applicable to *all* Hispanics? Is it possible for feminist family therapy to address the needs of all women given the vast number of gender-related permutations that may be a function of the interaction between race, ethnicity, religion, social class, etc.? Can we assume that a given technique or therapeutic principle that applies to *this* Hispanic family or *this* woman can be applied globally to all Hispanics or women? (p. 21)

Cultural knowledge should serve as "a background from which the figure emerges" (Sue & Sue, 1990, p. 48). The process of tailoring begins, of course, with appropriate assessment.

Culture-Aware Family Assessment

McGoldrick (1982) points out that "the language and customs of a culture will influence whether or not a symptom is labeled as a problem" (p. 7). Solomon (1992) also emphasizes cultural differences in the expression of symptomatology and in the meanings of various behaviors. She gives an example of a Ghanian woman whose mother had recently died. The woman, who was living in America, was unable to return to Ghana for the funeral. The women reported seeing visions of her mother and hearing her mother's voice constantly in her head, telling her what to do. These symptoms led to a diagnosis of schizophrenia, triggered by traumatic life changes.

Solomon says that the diagnostic interview included no questions regarding the client's spiritual beliefs or the grieving process in her culture, although "normal grieving in some cultures includes elements that Western culture might view as psychotic (for example, seeing the dead and communicating with them as they were in life or as transformed into birds, animals, or spirits)" (p. 373). If the assessment had been sensitive to culture, the problem would have been seen in terms of depression or bereavement, rather than schizophrenia.

The point of taking culture into account is not to make stereotypical generalizations but to enhance the possibilities for understanding the particular family. Some of the following questions might need to be asked:

- If the therapist has difficulty understanding the family, might the therapist's own culturally biased assumptions and values be standing in the way?

- Are there aspects of the family's world view that might help to explain individual behaviors or family dynamics?

- To what degree are the family members embedded in a traditional culture or acculturated into the dominant society?

- What differences in cultural identity exist among the family members themselves?

- How do the members define the boundaries of their family? Do they have an extended or multi-generational network that constitutes their family system?

- How do such cultural variables as gender, ethnicity, religion, and economic class interact to affect the family's values and concerns?

- How does this family view the balance between individual and family priorities?

- In what ways does oppression play a role in the life of this family?

If we consider again the case of Silvia, described earlier, we can see how important such a culturally sensitive assessment process really is. The dynamics of Silvia's family make sense only when we consider carefully the alternate world views represented by Silvia and her parents and when we recognize the depth of intra-familial differences in cultural identity. The interaction of ethnicity and gender role is also important in this case, with gender stereotyping playing an important role in limiting Silvia's perception of the options open to her.

Empowerment Strategies

Ho (1987) recognizes that "racism and poverty dominate the lives of many ethnic minorities" (p. 14). Consider, for example, the effect of oppression on the African-American community. Because of the history of virulent racism and the prevalence of the "deficit view" of black families, Boyd-Franklin (1989) emphasizes that empowerment should be seen as the most important goal of family therapy with African Americans. Implicit in Boyd-Franklin's interpretation of the empowerment process are two basic needs: building a positive black identity and mobilizing the family's ability to interact effectively with outside systems.

People who have been subjected to oppression are often completely disempowered by this process. Instead of recognizing the social, political, and economic context of their difficulties, they may be mired in self-blame. In place of self-worth and self-efficacy, they may be caught in a cycle of victimization and helplessness. Far from having access to support systems, they may feel isolated and alone.

The practical implication of this reality is that therapy with families who are part of oppressed minority groups should be focused on empowerment. Specific empowerment strategies include reframing issues to recognize and focus on family strengths; directly addressing racism, sexism, and other oppressions; and building skills and supports for navigating through hazardous environments. The therapist must redefine the meaning of systems theory, which "can be expanded to include society at large and problems such as prejudice, poverty, gender and ethnic minority issues" (Sue, 1994, p. 20). Family issues can be reconceptualized if the following *empowerment questions* are addressed:

1. *How can the family's issues or problems be redefined in an empowering way? What strengths and competencies can be identified and encouraged?*

   The value of these questions lies in the necessity of helping family members and the family as a whole to recognize their potential for strength. Oppression is insidious because external discrimination is combined with socialization processes that bring about internalized oppression; victims learn to accept the negative views of themselves that have been inculcated by the mainstream society. As we have seen in some of the examples presented earlier in this chapter, the characteristics of families are often pathologized when they differ from those of the dominant culture. The therapist's ability to view families as having adaptive strengths, rather than as being inherently dysfunctional, makes the first step toward empowerment possible.

2. *How has this family been affected by oppression?*

   Exploring this issue with family members can help to lay the groundwork for empowerment both by bringing about a release from self-blame and by readying the family to move toward consideration of the changes for which they can take responsibility. A key issue here is that the therapist must recognize how the family has been affected by economic, legal, and political systems in order to discuss the subject of oppression with the family.

3. *What therapeutic strategies can be used to overcome oppression-based barriers to healthy functioning?*

Beginning with a recognition of the role of oppression helps widen the range of possibilities considered by the therapist. Additionally, this issue brings to the foreground the idea that the therapeutic strategies selected must be sensitive to the world view of the client family. The therapist avoids the possibility that the therapy itself may play a role in the family's oppression.

4. *What positive environmental resources might be available to this family?*

The isolation of disempowerment can be addressed by helping the family identify potential sources of positive support in the broader environment. Moreover, this question points the therapist toward an acknowledgment of the important role of informal helping networks available in many minority communities.

Returning once more to Silvia's family, we can see the utility of addressing the empowerment questions. First, the strengths of Silvia and her family of origin would be recognized. As an individual, Silvia has many strengths, including courage, intelligence, and a willingness to connect with others. Although some therapists might focus on the problems in her family life, an empowerment-oriented helper would focus instead on the deep caring that has made complete separation impossible. An clear-headed exploration of the role of oppression in this case might also open new doors. Silvia has faced oppression as a woman; one aspect of therapy should focus on what she and her family view as the meaning of being male or female in traditional and contemporary cultures. Internalized oppression might also be playing a role in this situation. Is Silvia's urgent desire to be completely acculturated based on an assumption that the dominant culture is superior? Could her feeling that she does not deserve "someone like Brent" relate to her awareness of their class differences? As Silvia develops a more integrated cultural identity, will she relate differently to Brent and to her parents? Clearly, these questions take the therapy down a road that would have been bypassed if a less contextual approach had been taken.

Summary

A family's culture is affected by race, ethnicity, age, language, social class, income, geographical location, education, religion, gender, sexual orientation, and many other variables. Meeting the needs of a specific family requires that the tailoring process take these cultural factors into account.

When family therapists embark on the difficult work of becoming aware of culture, they often learn that their notion of what characterizes a healthy family is not universal. Cultural heritage affects such values as the desired balance between individuation and family unity. Families in various cultures also differ in terms of their definitions of the family unit and its boundaries.

The experience of oppression must also be recognized as a condition with a major effect on family life. Racism and other oppressions may need to be addressed directly before family members are ready to deal with other issues.

Family therapists also are learning that differences in world view, whether between the family and the therapist or among family members themselves, have to be explored. In fact, conflicting cultural values may sometimes be found to be at the heart of turmoil that seems incomprehensible to people who overlook the salience of culture.

Each of these issues has implications for therapeutic strategies, pointing up the need for culture-aware family assessment and for case conceptualizations aimed toward a goal of empowerment.

References

Berg, I. K., & Miller, S. (1992). Working with Asian-American clients: One person at a time. *Families in Society: The Journal of Contemporary Human Services, 73*, 356–363.

Boyd-Franklin, N. (1989). *Black families in therapy: A multisystems approach.* New York: Guilford.

Boyd-Franklin, N. (July/August, 1993). Pulling out the arrows. *Family Networker,* 54–56.

Carter, R. T. (1991). Cultural values: A review of empirical research and implications for counseling. *Journal of Counseling & Development, 70*, 164–173.

Falicov, C. (1994). *Cultural change on a global scale: Crossing cultural borders.* Paper presented at the 1994 Annual Convention, American Association of Marriage and Family Therapy, Chicago.

Franklin, A. J. (July/August, 1993). The invisibility syndrome. *Family Networker,* 33–39.

Grier, W., & Cobbs, P. (1968). *Black rage.* New York: Basic Books.

Hardy, K. V. (1989). The theoretical myth of sameness: A critical issue in family therapy training and treatment. *Journal of Psychology and the Family, 6*(1–2), 17–33.

Ho, M. K. (1987). *Family therapy with ethnic minorities.* Newbury Park, CA: Sage.

Ina, S. (1994). *Culturally sensitive family therapy.* Paper presented at the American Counseling Association Forum on Racism and Sexism: Promoting Dignity and Development through Diversity. National conference of the American Counseling Association. Minneapolis, April 24–27.

Inclan, J., & Hernandez, M. (1992). Cross-cultural perspectives and codependence: The case of poor Hispanics. *American Journal of Orthopsychiatry, 62*(2), 245–255.

Kluckhohn, F. R., & Strodtbeck, F. L. (1961). *Variations in value orientations.* Evanston, IL: Row, Patterson & Co.

Levant, R. F. (1994). Diversity, the division, and the gathering storm. *The Family Psychologist. 10*(2), 1, 6–7.

Lewis, J. A. (1994). Issues of gender and culture in substance abuse treatment. In J. A. Lewis (Ed.), *Addictions: Concepts and strategies for treatment* (pp. 37–43). Gaithersburg, MD: Aspen.

McGoldrick, M. (1982). Ethnicity and family therapy: An overview. In M. McGoldrick, J. K. Peace, & J. Giordano (Eds.), *Ethnicity and family therapy* (pp. 3–30). New York: Guilford.

McWhirter, E. H. (1991). Empowerment in counseling. *Journal of Counseling and Development, 69,* 222–227.

Monroe, A., Goldman, R., & Dube, C. (1994). *Race, culture and ethnicity: Addressing alcohol and other drug problems* (instructor's guide). Providence: Brown University Center for Alcohol and Addiction Studies.

Schwartzman, J. (1983). Family ethnography: A tool for clinicians. In C. J. Falicov (Ed.), *Cultural perspective in family therapy* (pp. 137–149). Gaithersburg, MD: Aspen.

Solomon, A. (1992). Clinical diagnosis among diverse populations: A multicultural perspective. *Families in Society, 72,* 371–377.

Spiegel, J. (1982). An ecological model of ethnic families. In M. McGoldrick, J. K. Peace, & J. Giordano (Eds.), *Ethnicity and family therapy* (pp. 31–51). New York: Guilford.

Sue, D. (spring, 1994). Incorporating cultural diversity in family therapy. *The Family Psychologist, 10*(2), 19–21.

Sue, D. W., & Sue, D. (1990). *Counseling the culturally different: Theory and practice.* New York: John Wiley & Sons.

Szapocznik, J., & Kurtines, W. M. (1993). Family psychology and cultural diversity: Opportunities for theory, research, and applications. *American Psychologist, 48,* 400–407.

Szapocznik, J., Scopetta, M. A., Ceballos, A., & Santisteban, D. (spring, 1994). Understanding, supporting and empowering families: From micro-analysis to macrointervention. *Family Psychologist, 10*(2), 23–27.

Walters, M. (March/April, 1993). The codependent Cinderella and Iron John. *The Family Networker,* 60–65.

Willis, J. T. (1988). An effective counseling model for treating the black family. *Family Therapy, 15*(2), 185–194.

Wilson, M. (spring, 1987). Classnotes on the psychology of oppression and social change. *The Family Psychologist, 20*(2), 18–19.

7

Tailoring Treatment
Families under Stress

In situations of extreme stress, families need to call on all available resources. Of course, families with some experience of healthy functioning have the best chance of dealing successfully with new problems. Even these families, however, may find that their usual ways of operating need to change in response to serious pressures.

Froma Walsh, in an interview conducted by Carlson (1992), said that healthy families are diverse but that they do share some of the ways in which they function. How does a healthy family operate? One of the behavioral characteristics that is usually mentioned in this context is the kind of clear and open communication that makes it possible for family members to address and solve problems together. Walsh also emphasizes balance: balance between connectedness and separateness, between cohesion and individual responsibility, between stability and flexibility. Although healthy families have clear, predictable structures, they are able to change when necessary.

A family under severe stress needs these adaptive characteristics more than ever. When faced with difficult challenges, families certainly need to communicate directly so they can find fresh solutions to pressing problems. They need to pull together without losing sight of individual needs and goals. They need to adapt to new stressors by making systemic changes that empower them to meet and overcome seemingly insurmountable burdens.

In reality, however, families under stress often lose the balance that they need most. Instead of communicating openly they may depend on avoidance as their primary coping strategy. Instead of seeking intimacy, they may choose the extremes of either distance and isolation or overprotection. Instead of making second-order changes, they may seek refuge in a rigid adherence to systems that no longer work for them.

When working with families under stress, therapists have to focus on ways to help family members mobilize whatever resources they have at their command. Sometimes the therapist will find that the family's unhealthy transactions preceded or exacerbated the current stressor. Often, the therapist will find that the family's coping mechanisms and interaction patterns were simply overwhelmed by pressing demands. Tailoring treatment involves both assessing the family's ability to function effectively and taking into account the realities inherent in the particular type of stressor involved. Consider, for example, the special needs of families dealing with each of the following stressors: addiction, illness and/or disability, and family violence or abuse.

Families and Addiction

There is no doubt that tailoring treatment to the needs of an addiction-affected family requires at least some degree of focus on the nature and extent of drug use. As Lewis, Piercy, Sprenkle, and Trepper (1991) point out in their discussion of family approaches with adolescent substance abusers, "while changes in cognitions, affective expression or interaction patterns may be interesting and useful, our goal clearly is to eradicate, or at least diminish, adolescent substance abuse."

Despite this concern with the individual's drug or alcohol use, however, the therapist's systemic focus must still remain at the forefront. When an individual abuses alcohol or other drugs, his or her entire family is placed under severe ongoing stress. Parental addiction may leave children without stable supervision. Young people's substance abuse may leave parents feeling guilty, powerless, and fearful for their children's future. Couples may adapt to one member's addiction by creating imbalances in power and responsibility. Over time, families often get caught in rigid patterns of interaction that are adaptive to drug use but are not associated with general family well-being. Attempts to keep the problem a secret may lead the family system to develop impermeable boundaries that prevent members from seeking the help and support · they need.

When a family member is addicted to alcohol or other drugs, this factor tends to become central to the system's functioning. According to Kaufman (1985) substance abuse is both a "systems-maintaining and systems-maintained device."

> Drinking behavior interrupts normal family tasks, causes conflict, shifts
> roles, and demands adjustive and adaptive responses from family members
> who do not know how to appropriately respond. A converse dynamic also
> occurs: marital and family styles, rules, and conflict may evoke, support,
> and maintain alcoholism as a symptom of family system dysfunction or
> as a coping mechanism to deal with family anxiety. (pp. 30–31)

Alcohol abuse is "systems-maintaining" in the sense that it provides
the family with a way to sustain its customary patterns of interaction.
For instance, Steinglass, Bennett, Wolin, and Reiss (1987) studied a number of couples in which one member abused alcohol. They found that, in
most cases, alcohol-related behaviors served a systemic purpose by helping the family to cope, at least temporarily, with problems in daily living.
Whether the problems being faced were internal or external, the families
believed they could cope with them only when alcohol was present. When
problems arose and tensions mounted, intoxication would emerge as a
response that allowed the system to become restabilized.

Just as addictive behaviors maintain systems in their steady states,
they are also "systems-maintained." Families develop consistent ways to
adapt to the presence of alcohol or other drugs within the system. Over
time, of course, these patterns of interaction become deeply entrenched.
Family members see few alternatives and continue carrying out behaviors that allow the substance use of the identified patient to continue.
For instance, other family members often relieve the addict from carrying out normal responsibilities, possibly by picking up the slack through
their own overresponsibility (Bepko & Krestan, 1985). Although this
pattern may allow the family unit to survive intact, it also allows—even
encourages—the substance use to continue unabated.

The addictions specialist and the family therapist perceive this situation very differently. Substance abuse treatment providers try to recognize the effect of systemic thinking but tend to view the addiction as the
single root cause of the family's problems. Conversely, family-systems
therapists try to recognize the effect of the physiology of the addictive
process but may view the alcoholic or addict simply as the identified
symptom-bearer in the family rather than as the primary focus of attention. A rapprochement between these two viewpoints depends on the
ability of all helpers to focus both on the health of the individual and
on the functioning of the entire system. An important aspect of this effort
is to take into account the family's situation at the time of the intervention. The appropriateness of a therapeutic strategy depends on the stage
in the development and resolution of the addiction-related problem
(Lewis, Dana, & Blevins, 1994). The goals and methods used depend on
whether the drug use is currently active, whether the behavior is in the
process of alteration, or whether behavior change has been established.

Stage Models

Bepko and Krestan (1985) suggest that there are three stages in addiction-related family treatment, each differing from the others in terms of immediate goals and appropriate strategies. The first stage, attainment of sobriety, involves unbalancing the system so that healthy change is possible. In the second stage, adjustment to sobriety, the family needs to work on stabilizing the system. In the third stage, long-term maintenance of sobriety, the system can be rebalanced in a new configuration.

Schlesinger and Horberg (1988) also identify three stages but describe them in terms of a journey through several "regions." In the first region, "exasperation," family members feel overwhelmed because their lives are characterized by helplessness, shame, and chaos. Individually, each person may feel that his or her own needs are unmet and that his or her own behaviors are unacceptable. In the region that Schlesinger and Horberg call "effort" family members begin to view their escape from chaos as a possibility. They work toward improving their lives and begin to feel a sense of satisfaction about their efforts. Finally, in the region of "empowerment," family members feel a sense of purpose and meaning. They begin to feel that they are competent as individuals and as a family unit. Mutual commitment becomes a possibility at last.

Usher (1991) identifies four phases of the recovery process for families affected by alcohol. In the phase of treatment initiation, the family becomes engaged in treatment. The second phase, learning, brings the development of the new skills that are needed once alcohol is no longer a central part of the system. The third phase, reorganization, facilitates the process of maintaining the abstinence of the alcohol-abusing family member. During consolidation, the alcoholic is securely abstinent and the family is ready to create a new form of organization.

Each of these models helps to make clear the fact that systems interventions must fit the family's stage of readiness. One set of strategies is needed to help family members make initial changes in the systems that support alcohol and drug use. Still another set of strategies is needed to help families cope with the stress that accompanies the abrupt changes associated with individual recovery.

Making Initial Systemic Changes

Not all family members are ready for change at the same time. Family therapy should be available to those family members who want to change their patterns of interaction even if the drug or alcohol abuser is not ready to take part. The key factor associated with success at this point is that family members explore the possibility of changing their customary roles. Family members may need help in making the choice between two difficult alternatives: (1) actively confronting the substance abuser in an effort to press him or her into treatment or (2) disengaging from an unhealthy focus on substance use as the central factor in family life.

Family members sometimes gather together to confront the individual substance abuser as a group. The focus of this kind of intervention is usually to convince the individual that his or her substance use is problematic and to press the individual into treatment. Ideally, the individual comes to accept the idea that his or her drinking or drug use is the source of the family's problems.

> For families in pain, the appeal of this approach, with its promise of treatment as a potential "happy ending," is obvious. Unfortunately, however, it is in the very simplicity of the intervention that its shortcomings lie. The overriding purpose of the intervention is to make a convincing case that alcohol (or another drug) is the root cause of the problems affecting the individual and the family and to present treatment as an immediately available solution. Thus, the approach oversimplifies problem attribution, conceptualizing issues in linear, cause-and-effect terms. (Lewis, 1991, p. 43)

Such an intervention should be approached with caution. First, the emphasis on the single cause of the family's pain overlooks the systemic nature of most problems. Second, the intervention assumes that the individual will face consequences if he or she refuses treatment. In fact, the intervenors need to be prepared for the possible failure of the intervention to meet their goals. What might be the consequences for them and for the family as a whole if the identified patient refuses treatment? Third, the results of even a successful intervention will be short-lived if the family fails to make systemic changes.

A valid option to the confrontation is to help those family members who are ready to change begin the process on their own. These family members can be encouraged to improve their own lives, working toward goals that focus on their own growth rather than on the drinking or drug use behavior (Schlesinger & Horberg, 1988). If family members can interrupt rigid patterns of interaction and move away from accepting responsibility for others' behavior, they may decrease the degree to which the system makes continued drug use likely. Even if this outcome is not achieved, the family members who have been involved in the process can benefit. Ackerman (1983) says that family members can move from a reactive mode to an active one. Instead of being dominated by reactions to the addict's behavior, family members can focus on meeting other needs.

Adjusting to Early Recovery

Families with a long history of transactional patterns that are based on the presence of a member's addiction frequently face crises when the individual's substance use subsides. Behaviors that have been reasonably adaptive to the presence of an addict are no longer appropriate when the identified patient moves out of his or her role. Families with newly abstinent members now need coping skills that are outside their usual repertoires. The sudden need for change often comes as a shock, especially because substance use has previously replaced problem-solving and conflict-resolution skills. In addition, families are often disappointed to find that problems they have always attributed to substance use alone continue to exist.

Usher, Jay, and Glass (1982) call this situation the "crisis of abstinence." They say that, although some families resolve the crisis successfully and make meaningful systemic changes, many respond to the crisis by splitting up or by reintroducing alcohol into the system. The way that alcohol and other drugs are "reintroduced" is through family members' return to previous patterns of interaction that can establish the familiar equilibrium.

How can family therapy address a family's needs during this crucial juncture? Bepko and Krestan (1985) say that the most important things to do at this point are to keep the system calm, to defuse conflicts, to address individual issues, and to encourage members to focus on their individual needs. They suggest that the therapist work with the family to make minor structural changes that can give the system time to adjust. Family members can go through a process of negotiation, working out compromises so that individual needs are addressed. Later, after a period of stabilization, the family may be ready to make the more basic systemic changes that serve to rebalance the system.

There is a great deal of evidence indicating that couples counseling is especially effective in early recovery (O'Farrell, 1992). For instance, Wetchler, Nelson, McCollum, Trepper, and Lewis (1994) have developed a program of systemic couples therapy for drug-abusing women. Their model calls for an assessment process that includes defining the problem, identifying interpersonal sequences surrounding substance abuse, and examining multigenerational patterns. Components of the behavior change process include helping the couple learn to negotiate and altering dysfunctional couple sequences. Wetchler and his colleagues have learned that the sequence of behaviors culminating in an individual's drug-use behavior can be interrupted most effectively when couples learn to notice them in their earliest stages.

Applying Couples Therapy

The context of understanding within which addiction-related problems are viewed should include attention to the balance between family members in terms of the power and responsibility in the relationship. Among families affected by addiction, the years of drug or alcohol use often affect this balance because of impairment in the user's ability to carry out his or her responsibilities. Balance also enters the picture again as we consider the symmetry between separateness and connectedness. Among families affected by addiction, issues regarding boundaries are common, at least in part because of attempts to keep the alcohol or drug problem a secret from the outside world. The therapist also needs to attend to the larger systems within which the family operates. Addictive behaviors take place within a social context that may exacerbate the risk for problem development and resolution. With this understanding as a backdrop for action, the therapist can help the couple negotiate new behavioral patterns.

Consider the potential effect of couples counseling in the cases that follow.

The Case of Ruth and Jack   Ruth and Jack, a young African-American couple, had lived together for over 6 years before Jack was arrested for selling a small amount of cocaine. Even in their own neighborhood, Jack had never been considered a major supplier. In fact, he had become involved initially only because he and Ruth had been unable to secure other employment despite their education and skills. His arrest, and subsequent imprisonment, came about because he was caught up in a larger undercover operation. Still, Jack's involvement in the sale of cocaine had been the couple's main source of income. Although they were both users, they were able to live comfortably.

When Jack went to prison, Ruth had to find a way to support herself. (During her years with Jack, she had left it up to him to take care of their financial well-being and to decide what kind of life style they would have.) She was not sure how to take care of the family business on her own because Jack's main suppliers were gone. She was prepared to go out on the street but was now more frightened of that life than she had been 6 years ago. Before she succeeded in gathering her courage, a neighbor suggested that she take a job temporarily cleaning rooms in a newly opened hotel. Ruth did get the job and, during the time Jack was away, stayed with the job and was promoted to housekeeper. Her current managerial job is quite demanding.

Now Jack has returned home. During his time away, Jack had become connected with a group of men who helped him get in touch with the religious and spiritual nature that had been buried during his years of drug use. Now, on probation and adamant about abstaining from drugs, Jack is hoping to find a career. In the meantime, they are both living on Ruth's salary.

When he first came home, both Ruth and Jack felt optimistic about their new life. It seemed miraculous that both of them were turning their lives around at the same time. Both of them were intent on living the straight life. Yet, some problems have arisen. Jack expected that their new lives would be a healthier, drug-free duplication of what their existence had been before. He expected that he would still be the main decision maker in the relationship and that Ruth would devote her attention to him. He felt that she should be happy to spend all her time with him after having gone through a painful separation. Ruth finds Jack's attitude unrealistic and feels that it is impossible to live up to his expectations. Her job is demanding and time-consuming, but Jack wants her to spend more time with him, to entertain his friends, and to take better care of the apartment. Also, she has become accustomed to making decisions on her own. Time after time, conflicts arise about money, about the apartment, about Jack's unemployment, and about the nature of the relationship. Twice, Ruth has left after one of these arguments and gone out to get high with one of her friends. When she returned, Jack was furious with her for using. The conflict became even more severe.

Conceptualizing the Situation of Ruth and Jack   A therapist working with this couple would recognize that the reestablishment of customary interactions would create a relapse risk for both Ruth and Jack. Their former pattern left a major role to be played by cocaine; falling into this old pattern is as easy as it is dangerous.

One aspect of the couple's established pattern involves the balance of power in their relationship. Although their life may seem non-traditional to some people, Ruth and Jack have lived according to a conservative view of gender roles. Before the crisis of his imprisonment, Jack was both the primary breadwinner and the primary power holder in the relationship. Ruth's newfound economic power and the drain her job places on her time, make it difficult for her to return to her previous role. Jack's ideal, that the relationship could be a drug-free equivalent of what it was before, is easy to understand. Yet, this notion reflects a ubiquitous problem among recovering families. Family members often assume that the removal of the substance is all they need. In fact, an unchanged system clearly increases the likelihood that the drug will be reintroduced.

The balance between separation and connection is also relevant in this case. During Jack's absence, Ruth began to recognize herself as a separate entity. Again, Jack's reluctance to recognize these new boundaries is understandable but needs to be addressed in therapy. The fragile balance that Ruth and Jack seek is affected not just by their own attitudes and behaviors but by their cultural milieu. The racism that has limited their career opportunities and the gender stereotypes that have limited their social roles both need to be addressed by the therapist.

Within the context of these systemic factors, the therapist can help Ruth and Jack make concrete changes in their interactions. Once they learn to recognize the signs of impending conflict, they can negotiate alternatives that prevent the disastrous endings of their previous friction.

The Case of Steve and Tim   Steve and Tim were first introduced by a mutual friend at a bar that serves as the focal point of social life in the gay community. After seeing each other for more than a year, they moved in together. They have lived for almost 2 years in an apartment close to the place where they first met. From the beginning, they have had an active social life, meeting their group of close friends at the bar or socializing over drinks at home.

Four months ago, Steve lost the job he had held as a paralegal in a large law firm. The late nights of drinking and socializing had taken their toll and he found himself arriving at work either hungover or very late. (This has been less of a problem for Tim, who is a psychotherapist and has more flexible hours.) Steve sometimes met Tim for lunch at the bar. He was fired when one of the attorneys complained about smelling alcohol on his breath.

Steve has been seeing an addictions counselor and has been working hard at maintaining abstinence. He has been attending AA meetings and enjoys them. He hopes to find a new job and to get his life back to what it was before.

Surprisingly, however, he and Tim have begun to have arguments for the first time in their relationship. Tim says that Steve has become fanatical about AA. He complains that Steve won't talk about anything else and that their social life has become non-existent. He does not want Steve to drink but does suggest that Steve could go to the bar or have their friends over and drink soft drinks while the others drink beer or wine. Steve does want his life with Tim to get back to normal, but he is afraid to be around alcohol. Tim says that he will simply go to the bar on his own, but that idea makes Steve feel jealous and abandoned.

Conceptualizing the Situation of Steve and Tim   Tim, like Jack, would like his relationship to be an alcohol-free duplication of the past.

In fact, this ideal would be very difficult to achieve. At least in the earliest stages of recovery, Tim would find it problematic to spend a great deal of time surrounded by drinkers. Yet, it is not realistic for Tim to expect the people around him—even Steve—to make drastic changes in their lifestyles. Oppression plays a role here, too. For many members of the gay community, bars have provided the most comfortable opportunity for socializing. Within this context, the therapist would help Steve and Tim negotiate short-term compromises that could allow each some separateness while maintaining the customary closeness and trust in the relationship.

Families' Responses to Illness and Disability

Few problems are more stressful to a family than the illness of one of its members. The family's customary coping style may be inadequate, resulting in a situation in which resources are stretched to the breaking point.

> Serious illness not only takes over the patient's life, it also greedily expands to consume the energy and resources of the patient's family. Far from being tightly confined inside the individual's skin, serious illness invades the entire network of connections around the sick person. For some families, this crisis offers opportunities for emotional as well as physical healing. For others, the illness ravages everything in its path. (McDaniel, Hepworth, & Doherty, 1993, pp. 20–21)

As is the case with addiction-related problems, the process of tailoring treatment for families affected by illness must balance a focus on the individual's health and a focus on the family's general level of functioning. As Steinglass and Horan (1988) point out, "interventions have to respect both the psychological health of the family and support of the patient's medical treatment" (p. 139). Sometimes the treatment that seems most appropriate for the individual's needs, such as home dialysis, may be stressful and demanding for the family. In other instances strategies that seem to be appropriate for the family system may leave the needs of the medical patient unattended. The characteristics of the specific illness or disability also have a major effect on the nature of family stress and on the kinds of coping strategies that will be needed. "The task of adapting to the illness varies with the nature of the illness and its treatment, the extent to which it disables or threatens the life of the patient, the patient's role in the family, the family's prior experience and attitudes about illness and the family's developmental stage" (Koch-Hattem, 1987, p. 33).

Nature of the Illness or Disability

Rolland (1994) has designed a topology of illness that emphasizes the varying effects of health-related problems in terms of their onset, course, likely outcome, degree of incapacitation, and degree of predictability. Each of these factors affects the kind and degree of challenge the family must meet. Moreover, families vary in terms of the degree to which their structures and styles tend to be successful in coping with particular types of illness.

Onset   Whether the onset of an illness is acute or gradual affects the kind of readjustment a family must make. A condition with an acute onset, such as a stroke, requires that the family mobilize quickly, using crisis management skills and making rapid adjustments. A gradual-onset health problem, such as Alzheimer's, may require the same degree of problem solving and restructuring but allows these changes to take place over a longer period of time.

> Some families are better equipped than others to cope with rapid change. Families able to tolerate highly charged affective states, exchange clearly defined roles flexibly, solve problems efficiently, and utilize outside resources effectively have an advantage in managing acute-onset illnesses. Other families' style of coping may be more suited to gradual change. (Rolland, 1994, p. 23)

One cannot assume that it is possible distinguish between functional and dysfunctional family styles for coping with illness. The same family that shows a high degree of success in responding to crises may be overwhelmed when called on to deal with illnesses that are characterized by long-term, steady deterioration.

Course   Illnesses may also be characterized as progressive, constant, or relapsing/episodic. A "progressive" illness may require a family to reorganize itself again and again over time as the disability reaches new stages. The family with flexibility at its core is most likely to be successful in managing these changes, but even then the need to restructure can be so overwhelming that therapy aimed at deeper changes may be needed. Illnesses that Rolland categorizes as "constant" become stable after the initial event; the family may need help to make a major adaptation but can assume that the new structure will suffice for a long period of time. Illnesses that are subject to relapses or episodes of disability bring their own special challenges because families have to reorganize for periods of health and relapse. Because these episodes are unpredictable, families cannot always prepare for change and must be on guard to deal with unexpected crises. Therapeutic needs will change over time as the family is buffeted by change.

Outcome   Rolland posits a continuum from illnesses that do not affect life span to illnesses that shorten life span to illnesses that are fatal. Family therapy needs differ according to the expected outcome of the illness. When the illness is expected to be fatal, families often need help dealing with anticipatory loss and its associated conflict between the desire for intimacy with the ill member and a need to let go. Illnesses that shorten life span or that are characterized by uncertainty about the possibility of sudden death have very complex effects on family life. Rolland (1994) says that in families grappling with these kinds of illnesses issues of mortality are "less prominent but more insidious in day to day living." Uncertainty makes varying interpretations and expectations of the situation possible. Family members may opt for overprotectiveness, for distancing, or for unpredictable swings between opposite behavioral poles.

Incapacitation   Of course, some illnesses and disabilities bring with them impairments that have a major effect on family life. Families are differentially affected according to the nature of the incapacitation (for example, impairments in mental functioning, sensation, movement, or energy) and the extent of the disability.

Degree of Uncertainty/Predictability   Realigned topology places degree of certainty in the role of a metacharacteristic that affects all of the other categories. Illnesses vary in the predictability of their course, outcome, degree of incapacitation, and rate of progression. Uncertainty brings heightened stress.

> Families coping with highly unpredictable diseases, such as multiple sclerosis, often state that these ambiguities are the hardest aspects to accept and master. The more uncertain the course and outcome, the more a family must make decisions with flexible contingencies built into their planning. (Rolland, 1994, p. 33)

Just as families are affected by the uncontrollable course of the family member's illness, they are also affected by the sociocultural context within which illness is viewed.

Sociocultural Context of Disability

Kirshbaum (1994) makes the important point that families' responses to disabling conditions are colored by the tendency of the broader systems to pathologize disabilities. Certainly, society as a whole is oppressive toward disabled individuals. Of particular concern is the fact that the medical care system itself is not immune to oppressive attitudes. Health care providers may inadvertently place such a strong focus on individual and family deficits that they miss the importance of empowerment. Moreover, the family is especially vulnerable to these negative messages just at the times when they most need to be proactive in their adaptations.

> The cumulative effect of such pervasive and repetitive negative social messages is that we construct a personal framework of meaning regarding disability. This frame can, in turn, have a profound effect on individual family members' self-esteem, sense of defeat, and depletion. It can narrow our families' sense of the range of what we can do together, of who we can be together. (Kirshbaum, 1994, p. 9)

When families respond to disability or illness in ways that seem dysfunctional, they may in fact be responding not just to their own internal structures but also to external stigmatization. Distancing within the family is sometimes a result of the dehumanizing stance of the culture at large. Overprotectiveness may be a response to an onslaught of conflicting advice gleaned from health and social systems. Kirshbaum suggests that the process of therapy should focus on reframing the meanings inherent in the disability. Connections with the community of disabled persons enhance the process of depathologizing health-related problems.

> The adult disability culture is inherently a reframe or a complex of reframes. . . . People in disability traditions can experience profound shifts in meaning from contacts with individuals with long-term disability experience and disability community involvement. . . . Being involved in the adult disability community is likely to expose one to a cultural perspective that values disability. (Kirshbaum, 1994, p. 10)

Similarly, recent years have seen the parents of disabled children take strong political action that is associated with their own success in overcoming deficit-focused beliefs.

Family Treatment Goals and Strategies

When therapists build their practices on a recognition of the effect of oppression, they are more able to help families develop the kind of positive reframe suggested by Kirshbaum. McDaniel, Hepworth, and Doherty (1993) state that, even when the illness in question is fatal, a major goal of therapy for families dealing with medical problems must be to increase the family's "sense of agency."

> This means increasing their involvement and personal choices in managing their illness. There cannot be many experiences, short of war, incarceration

or mass disaster, that so deplete feelings of personal competence and self-determination as being both very sick and caught in the tentacles of the modern medical health care system. A medical family therapist can help families maintain or reacquire the habit of making personal choices about medical decisions and take back aspects of their lives that they have sacrificed to the illness. (p. 28)

Helping families work together toward this kind of empowerment requires an emphasis on open communication. In fact, McDaniel and her colleagues (1993) suggest that an equally important goal of family therapy involves enhancing the communion found in emotional bonds.

> Family members may be stuck together in a tight clump of single-minded preoccupation with the illness and its costs, while at the same time feeling deeply isolated from one another. Their love and concern for one another can become fused with guilt, anguish, resentment, and depression that completely distort the quality of family life. By communion, we mean a restoration, where possible, of human connections within the family and between the family and the community, connections based on qualities of affection, humor, friendliness, common interests and mutual respect that may have given way in the collective isolation imposed by illness. (p. 62)

Rolland (1994) also emphasizes the role of the family therapist in opening up communication within the family. He suggests that, in the couple relationship, members be encouraged to "revise their closeness to include rather than avoid issues of incapacitation and threatened loss" (p. 237). Among the subjects he suggests for discussion are the demands of the illness over time, the couple's beliefs about the factors that caused the disorder and might affect its course, ways to live with loss, priorities for the relationship, patient and caregiver roles, and ways to maintain balance and mutuality in the relationship. For families with children, he suggests open, age-appropriate communication about all of the health issues being faced.

> Levels of personal disclosure that may have been functional before a disorder appeared often become inadequate. Discussions about living with threatened loss may represent new territory. (Rolland, 1994, p. 238)

Underlying all these discussions is the need to "find a place for the illness within the family while at the same time ensuring that the illness is kept in its place" (Steinglass & Horan, 1988, p. 139). Somewhere between the extremes of denying or overemphasizing the illness lies a functional balance.

The Case of the Peterson Family By the time Jim and Julie Peterson had reached their late 30s, they had come to view their lives as stable and predictable. Their two children, Linda and Scott, were weathering early adolescence without anything more than the standard degree of conflict. Although Jim's professional work as an architect was very demanding, it was also lucrative. Julie was glad that she had been able to stay home with the children when they were younger. She was now working part-time as a designer.

The Petersons barely noticed the subtle symptoms of Jim's illness at first. It was only when the symptoms became impossible to ignore that he sought a medical diagnosis and realized that he had multiple sclerosis. Even after the diagnosis, Jim and Julie had difficulty taking in the reality of the situation. Jim had long periods of time when he was free of symptoms and could almost forget that he had M.S. At first, the adult Petersons thought they could postpone discussing the illness with the children.

In time, however, the family members became conscious of changes in their lives. Julie knew that she had to think about some kind of career plan for herself but felt helpless about moving her life in a new direction. Linda's grades dropped, and she began to spend long hours alone in her room. Scott's teachers reported that he was acting out in school. The solid structure of their family life seemed to be crumbling, even though Jim was still functioning well.

The need for major adaptation became pressing when Jim's health no longer allowed him to depend on his ability to perform effectively at work. Now, he cannot always predict whether he will be able to finish a project. Although his work is still excellent, he and the family have begun to realize that their traditional roles are changing. Jim's work can no longer be the only source of support for the family. Julie will have to make her work more central to her life, even to the extent of securing a job with family health insurance that will cover pre-existing conditions. The children will have to adapt by taking on more adult responsibilities than they are used to.

Conceptualizing the Case of the Petersons   The Peterson family has virtually had to reinvent itself in response to the illness of one member. Family members who saw their solid stability and their success in carrying out traditional roles as sources of pride must now learn to practice and value flexibility. Clearly, each family member must accept new roles and responsibilities. Even then, however, the new structure that has been created may have to be dismantled and rebuilt again and again as Jim's physical abilities and the needs of the family change. Within the context of this constant renewal, the family will have to "put the illness in its place," making sure that the roles of parent and child remain intact despite their transformations.

The importance of open communication about health-related issues is clear in the case of the Petersons. The parents' assumption that silence could protect their children was quickly proven to be inaccurate. Open family discussions about the nature of this new stressor and the best ways of coping with it will be crucial to the Petersons' adjustment. These family members will have to use every possible resource and coping skill at their command.

Violence and Abuse

The need to tailor therapy in accordance with the stressor affecting a specific family becomes especially salient in cases of violence or abuse. Many therapists question the use of conjoint therapy at all when abuse is present in a family. Systems thinking is often also called into question because the concept of circularity ignores power differences and fails to provide a mechanism for focusing on the individual responsibility of the perpetrator.

> When applied to problems such as battering, rape, and incest, circular causality subtly removes responsibility for his behavior from the man while implying that the woman is co-responsible. . . . Similarly, systemic notions of neutrality emphasize that all parts of the system contribute *equally* to the production and maintenance of problems/dysfunction, and render totally invisible differences in power and influence between family members. (Avis, 1988, p. 17)

One way to address this issue is to view family systems through a lens that takes in the larger systems within which families operate. Although it is always important for family therapists to focus on socio-cultural factors, it is even more vital to keep these factors in the forefront when dealing with violence and abuse. The feminist critique of family systems theory has been especially useful in this regard because it emphasizes the effect of the patriarchal culture on all women and men.

> A feminist critique shakes the very precepts upon which our epistemology is based; it challenges the notion that men and women are equal participants in the relational dance; it challenges the idea that there is no villain and no victim. A feminist perspective demands that we take seriously the consequences of living in a patriarchal culture: marriage is not just an interactional scene, but a political institution reflective of the patriarchal culture in which it is immersed. (Braverman, 1988, p. 6)

Brooks (1992) offers a perspective from the viewpoint of men's studies that also highlights the salience of culture. According to Brooks, "one of the most serious errors in the treatment of violent men is to ignore the cultural context in which this violence takes place" (p. 29). Therapists often assume that individual abusers have not been success- fully socialized against violence and that they need to be taught to com- ply to society's normative behavior. In fact, men are socialized toward violence as a solution for problems. Brooks suggests, therefore, that vio- lence is the product of such factors as the message that violence is manly and the pressure to maintain a role of sole leadership in the family.

In addition to the urgent need for a broad cultural perspective, fam- ily therapists dealing with violence and abuse must also make special adaptations in therapeutic goals. Ensuring the safety of the victim and changing the behavior of the perpetrator must provide the central focus of the therapeutic process. For example, Brooks (1990) presents a model for treating spousal abuse in which the male perpetrator and the vulner- able woman are first treated separately. The therapist works to enhance the woman's empowerment and to support the man's positive efforts toward change. Conjoint therapy is begun only when three conditions have been met: "the woman's empowerment should be secure; the hus- band should be committed to her continued empowerment and to an egalitarian marital relationship; both parties independently, without coercion, choose to pursue the therapy" (Brooks, 1990, p. 61).

As these critiques of conventional therapy make clear, tailoring treatment for situations involving violence requires several special adap- tations, including: (1) acknowledging and addressing the role of the larger culture in encouraging violent and abuse behavior: (2) recogniz- ing the need to keep the safety of the vulnerable woman or child as the most important goal of treatment; and (3) accepting a focus on individ- ual responsibility, even at the expense of the pure notion of circularity. These adaptations are necessary both for situations of wife abuse and for intrafamilial sexual abuse.

Wife Abuse

Carden (1994), in her overview of the literature related to the sources of wife abuse, recognizes the differences among various perspectives.

> The sociopolitical response to the question "Why does he do it?" has been: He does it because cultural norms support his belief that (a) violence is an acceptable and effective method of resolving interpersonal conflict, (b) he is entitled to dominate and expected to control his wife, (c) it will get him what he wants, and (d) he can get away with it. (p. 552)

Psychological perspectives, in contrast, emphasize the effect of the perpetrator's developmental experience as well as the possible role of dysfunctional transactions. Differences in perspective lead in turn to differences in treatment. According to Carden, the sociopolitical perspective implies the use of social control strategies that hold the batterer accountable for his violence, while psychological perspectives use either cognitive-behavioral interventions such as anger management training or conjoint therapies emphasizing such skills as conflict resolution.

Carden recommends an integrative perspective that takes into account the combined influences of cultural, intrapsychic, and interpersonal variables. She cites, for example, the work of Dutton (1985), who suggests that the violent behavior of an individual man will be affected by variables within four layers of experience: (1) individual experience; (2) the microsystem of the family; (3) the exosystemic layer, which is made up of such systems as work, religious affiliation, social setting, and neighborhood; and (4) the macrosystem of society's rules and norms. The approach she describes uses an array of treatment options dedicated to three general goals: "(1) the safety and well-being of victims; (2) the empowerment of men to live emotionally enriched, cognitively aware, violence-free lives; and (3) the prevention of the intergenerational transmission of violence." Her treatment program includes psychoeducational strategies addressing issues within each of Dutton's ecological layers, group work confronting gender-role issues, and finally conjoint therapy in a separate or group milieu.

Sexual Abuse of Children

Barrett, Trepper, and Fish (1990) use an equally well-integrated approach for the treatment of intrafamilial sexual abuse of children. They accept as valid the feminist critique of the application of family systems therapies for treating sexual abuse. Although Barrett and her colleagues recognize the peril of overlooking sociopolitical factors, ignoring power differentials, and allowing vulnerable family members to shoulder part of the blame for the perpetrator's behavior, they suggest that family therapy can provide the context for addressing these concerns. "Protection of the incest victim, while at the same time empowering her to defend herself, is best done through a gender-sensitive, family systems approach" (Barrett et al., 1990, p. 164).

For Barrett, Trepper, and Fish, the child is the primary concern and the cessation of abuse the first goal of treatment. With this caveat always in mind, they use systemic approaches to try to equalize power in the family. Their goal for the offender is not only to end his denial but also to help him become engaged in a nurturing role as a parent and in an appropriate sexual relationship with a partner of an appropriate age.

The Multiple Systems Model (Trepper & Barrett, 1986) recognizes that abuse results from a combination of external, family, and internal systems.

> This does not supplant the fact that the ultimate responsibility for the abuse rests with the offender who after all is the older of the two and is responsible for the well-being of his children. It merely recognizes that responsibility is not cause and that to fully understand the cause of incest, so that we may effectively intervene, we must accept that complex interactions among various systems make a family more or less vulnerable to the development of incest. (p. 130)

Differentiating between responsibility and cause, Trepper and Barrett say that attributing blame is not enough; other contributing factors must be addressed if long-term change is to take place.

Although they are aware of the complexities of using this modality, Trepper and Barrett use conjoint treatment, along with individual therapy and dealing with larger social systems, as one of their methods. They suggest that this approach is practical for several reasons. First, the victim often does have contact with the offender and this contact may keep her in a powerless position if she does not have the opportunity to confront the perpetrator in a safe environment. Second, families often do intend to remain together and need conjoint meetings to discuss their future plans. Finally, discovery of the abuse throws the entire family into a crisis that should be addressed in therapy.

Treating Adult Survivors of Early Abuse

Of course, the early effects of abuse follow the individual throughout the life span. Many women survivors are plagued with such ongoing symptoms as depression, anxiety, guilt, self-blame, and problems with relationships and sexuality (Ratican, 1992). Often, women have a history of repeated experiences of re-victimization in childhood, adolescence, and adulthood. Addiction-related problems are very common (Barrett & Trepper, 1991). Family therapists may be especially helpful to such individuals because of their ability to view the problems from a systemic perspective. Even when the client is being seen individually, the family perspective remains an underpinning of the therapy.

Whether or not the individual remembers the experience of abuse, she or he may be unaware of its connection to current problems. The creation of a safe environment for bringing these issues to the surface makes it possible for the survivor to decide when she or he is ready to begin exploring them. Individual interventions may be combined with group procedures that actually give some female clients the first experience they have ever had in making connections with other women.

The Case of Mary   Mary appeared at a hospital emergency room complaining of severe abdominal pain. She was admitted to the hospital detoxification unit because she began showing signs of withdrawal from alcohol and because it was suspected that she was also addicted to barbiturates. She admitted that she had been using tranquilizers and, occasionally, sleeping pills for some time. Mary was kept in the hospital until she was medically stabilized and then referred to a non-medical substance abuse treatment facility.

Mary is a divorced, 28-year-old woman of Irish and German descent. She has three children, ages 6, 8, and 10. She says that she has some experience doing secretarial work but has been unemployed for several years. She has no income other than what she gets in public assistance but says that a legal aid attorney has been trying to get some of the child-support money owed to her by her former husband, Carl. She is not optimistic about obtaining this money, since her ex-husband has a long-term problem with heroin addiction. She has not seen him for some time but has no reason to expect that there has been any change in his condition since their marriage ended 5 years ago.

Mary has had very little contact with her family of origin since her marriage at the age of 18. Her parents disliked Carl but insisted that she marry him when she became pregnant at 17. Mary says that her father is an alcoholic and that she and her mother have never been close. She also says that several times in recent years she has thought about visiting her family. Each time, however, she became so anxious that she went on a binge and became too ill to go.

Now, she feels uncertain about her future. She says she wants to change because she is a bad mother and wants to take better care of her children. She says that if she didn't feel responsible for them she would have no reason to live. She wishes she could get her life together but says she is unable to find employment. She has not been able to work because of a lack of child care. Now that the children are in school, she could work but believes that her career history is too spotty for her to be employable.

Mary says that she has no social life, although she does drink with a group of women. She sees these acquaintances regularly but does not feel close to them and reports that she does not trust them. She believes that she "gets along better" with men, but in fact she has had several bad experiences. Since her divorce, one man moved in with her but left because of impatience with her children. Another left when neighbors heard him beating her and called the police. Her drinking and drug use began during her marriage, when her husband wanted her to keep him company, but she says that her heaviest use began at the time of their break-up.

Conceptualizing the Case of Mary   The chance that there was abuse in Mary's background shows up in subtle ways. Her experience of repeated victimization, her attempts to find salvation in a relationship with a man, her escape into drugs and alcohol, her difficulty in forming trusting relationships, her extreme anxiety at the thought of visiting her family of origin: all of these factors indicate the possibility of early abuse. The therapist's role is to walk a narrow line, giving Mary the opportunity to explore her history and believing her if she does describe abuse but avoiding placing even the slightest pressure on her to delve into areas that she is not ready to consider. Both Mary and her children certainly have an improved outlook for success if Mary's substance abuse is interrupted. The therapist must recognize, however, that slips are likely to occur even if Mary sincerely desires abstinence. Throughout her adult life, drug and alcohol use has formed her primary coping strategy for dealing with the anxiety and depression that might otherwise have over-whelmed her. Moving toward health will have to be a gradual process that recognizes the client's fragility. At the same time, Mary's recovery depends on her ability to move from the morass of self-blame to the high ground of empowerment.

Summary

Families dealing with highly stressful situations need effective coping mechanisms to meet pressing demands that might otherwise overwhelm them. In fact, however, families under severe stress sometimes lack the ability to adapt effectively, or they lose sight of the strategies that worked for them in the past. In these circumstances, tailoring treatment involves both assessing the family' general functionality and recognizing the effect of the specific stressor. In this chapter, we have examined three examples of serious family stressors: addiction, illness, and violence or abuse.

   In the case of addiction, the therapist should balance attention to the individual's drug use with a focus on dynamics within the family. When working with addiction-related family issues, the therapist needs to fit his or her strategies to the stage in the development or solution of the problem. To make initial changes, family members will need help in disengaging from their focus on substance use as the central factor in the family's life. In the stage of early recovery, family members will have to be prepared for the fact that they are entering a point of crisis when their usual ways of interacting are no longer effective. It may be because of the urgent need for systemic change at this point that couple counseling is among the most effective treatments available for substance abuse.

Families affected by illness or disability may also be faced with the need to make major systemic changes. Tailoring treatment involves taking into account not only the way the family functions but also the nature of the specific illness or disability. The demands on the family differ drastically in accord with the onset, course, outcome, degree of incapacitation, and degree of uncertainty that characterize the illness. Among the general goals for working with health-related issues are increasing the family's "sense of agency," enhancing the family's ability to communicate openly, and finding an appropriate balance between denying and overemphasizing the illness.

Tailoring treatment for families dealing with violence or abuse also brings unique concerns to the surface. In response to feminist critiques of systemic approaches for dealing with abuse, family therapists have learned to take into account the culpability of a culture that condones violence and domination. When violence or abuse is an issue, therapy must be adapted to acknowledge the role of cultural factors, to recognize that the safety of the victim is the most important goal, and to keep the responsibility for violence focused on the perpetrator.

References

Ackerman, R. J. (1983). *Children of alcoholics: A guidebook for educators, therapists, and parents* (2nd ed.). Holmes Beach, FL: Learning Publications, Inc.

Avis, J. M. (1988). Deepening awareness: A private study guide to feminism and family therapy. In L. Braverman (Ed.), *A guide to feminist family therapy*. New York: Harrington Park Press.

Barrett, M. J., & Trepper, T. S. (1991). Treating women drug abusers who were victims of childhood sexual abuse. In C. Bepko (Ed.), *Feminism and addiction* (pp. 127–145). New York: Haworth Press.

Barrett, M. J., Trepper, T. S., & Fish, L. S. (1990). Feminist-informed family therapy for the treatment of intrafamily child sexual abuse. *Journal of Family Psychology, 4,* 151–166.

Bepko, C., & Krestan, J. A. (1985). *The responsibility trap: A blueprint for treating the alcoholic family*. New York: The Free Press.

Braverman, L. (1988). *A guide to feminist family therapy*. New York: Harrington Park Press.

Brooks, G. W. (1990). Traditional men in marital and family therapy. In M. Bograd (Ed.), *Feminist approaches for men in family therapy* (pp. 51–74). New York: Harrington Park Press.

Brooks, G. R. (1992). Gender-sensitive family therapy in a violent culture. *Topics in Family Psychology and Counseling, 1*(4), 24–36.

Carden, A. (1994). Wife abuse and the wife abuser: Review and recommendations. *The Counseling Psychologist, 22,* 539–582.

Carlson, J. (1992). Interview: Froma Walsh. *Topics in family psychology and counseling, 1*(1), 1–5.

Dutton, D. G. (1985). An ecologically nested theory of male violence toward intimates. *International Journal of Women's Studies, 8*(4), 404–413.

Kaufman, E. (1985). *Substance abuse and family therapy.* New York: Grune and Stratton.

Kirshbaum, M. (1994). Family context and disability culture reframing: Through the looking class. *The Family Psychologist, 10*(4), 8–12.

Koch-Hattem, A. (1987). Families and chronic illness. In D. Rosenthal (Ed.), *Family stress* (pp. 33–49). Gaithersburg, MD: Aspen.

Lewis, J. A. (1991). Change and the alcohol-affected family: Limitations of the "intervention." *The Family Psychologist, 7*(2), 43–44.

Lewis, J. A. (1992). Treating the alcohol-affected family. In L. L'Abate, J. E. Farrar, & D. A. Serritella (Eds.), *Handbook of differential treatments for addictions* (pp. 61–83). Boston: Allyn and Bacon.

Lewis, J. A., Dana, R. Q., & Blevins, G. A. (1994). *Substance abuse counseling: An individualized approach* (2nd ed.). Monterey, CA: Brooks/Cole.

Lewis, R. A., Piercy, F. P., Sprenkle, D. H., & Trepper, T. S. (1991). The Purdue brief family therapy model for adolescent substance abusers. In T. C. Todd & M. D. Selekman (Eds.), *Family therapy approaches with adolescent substance abusers* (pp. 29–48). Boston: Allyn & Bacon.

McDaniel, S. H., Hepworth, J., & Doherty, W. J. (Jan/Feb, 1993). A new prescription for family health care. *Family Networker, 17*(2), 18–29, 62–63.

O'Farrell, T. J. (1992). Families and alcohol problems: An overview of treatment research. *Journal of Family Psychology, 5,* 339–359.

Ratican, K. L. (1992). Sexual abuse survivors: Identifying symptoms and special treatment considerations. *Journal of Counseling & Development, 71,* 33–38.

Rolland, J. S. (1994). *Families, illness, and disability: An integrative treatment model.* New York: Basic Books.

Schlesinger, S. E., & Horberg, L. K. (1988). *Taking charge: How families climb out of the chaos of addiction . . . and flourish.* New York: Simon & Schuster.

Steinglass, P., Bennett, L. A., Wolin, S. J., & Reiss, D. (1987). *The alcoholic family.* New York: Basic Books.

Steinglass, P., & Horan, M. E. (1988). Families and chronic medical illness. *Journal of Psychotherapy and the Family, 3*(3), 127–142.

Trepper, T. S., & Barrett, M. J. (1986). *Treating incest: A multiple systems perspective.* New York: Haworth.

Usher, M. L. (1991). From identification to consolidation: A treatment model for couples and families complicated by alcoholism. *Family Dynamics of Addiction, 1*(2), 45–48.

Usher, M. L., Jay, J., & Glass, D. R. (1982). Family therapy as a treatment modality for alcoholism. *Journal of Studies on Alcohol, 43,* 927–938.

Wetchler, J. L., Nelson, T. S., McCollum, E. E., Trepper, T. S., & Lewis, R. A. (1994). Couple-focused therapy for substance-abusing women. In J. A. Lewis (Ed.), *Addictions: Concepts and strategies for treatment.* Gaithersburg, MD: Aspen.

8

Tailoring Treatment
Work-Family Concerns

Family therapists and corporate leaders are responding to the changing portrait of the American family sketched in Chapters 1 and 3. Corporate America is recognizing that pro-family policies and family life programs not only build worker loyalty but also reduce turnover as well as operating costs. In short, it is good business to respond positively to work-family concerns (Rosen, 1991). Presumably, as more corporations become more family-friendly, work-family conflicts and stressors should lessen. However, this major shift in the corporation function may take a decade or more. In the meantime, marital and family therapists can provide important therapeutic and consultative interventions to the variety of work-centered families.

This chapter overviews both therapeutic and consultative strategies focused on work-family concerns. Since more is known about working with dual-career couples and families, the majority of the chapter is devoted to this family type. However, because there is considerable overlap between the concerns of dual-earner and dual-career couples, much of the information and strategies should be applicable to dual-earner couples also. Strategies unique to the working, single-parent family are also briefly described.

Therapeutic Interventions with Dual-Career Couples

Therapeutic interventions involving dual-career couples and families can take two forms: prevention or treatment. The preventive form involves educating individuals regarding potential problems and challenges that spouses in a dual-career relationship face. The purpose of this type of intervention is consciousness raising and skill acquisition. Individuals are provided the opportunity to learn about day-to-day realities of the dual-career life style; to examine their personal values, attitudes, and life goals in terms of the concept of equity; and to assess their receptivity to making the attitude and behavior changes needed to accommodate the dual-career life style.

A number of such preventive, psychoeducational workshops have been developed and are typically aimed at undergraduates. Some of these are described in the professional literature (Amatea & Cross, 1983; Kahnweiler & Kahnweiler, 1980). Follow-up studies have indicated that participation in such programs helps prepare individuals for involvement in dual-career relationships (Amatea & Clark, 1984).

Most therapists have had experience working with dual-career couples who are experiencing difficulties, and most marital and family therapists focus their energy at the treatment intervention level. Several types of treatment interventions are described in this section. These include psychoeducational, interpersonal, psychodynamic, and integrated intervention group and consultative strategies. Before turning to these strategies, however, we must consider factors that can help or hinder the therapeutic situation, as well as some general treatment goals.

Therapeutic Facilitating and Biasing Factors

Providing effective treatment to dual-career couples may be impossible if the therapist has inadequate knowledge of or holds negative or unrealistic attitudes about this relational pattern. Clinicians need to protect against intrusion of their own biases into the treatment process. They must examine whether their own value system is incompatible with the assumptions underlying the dual-career lifestyle. This may be easier for a female therapist who, having a career herself, may be more easily attuned to the multiple problems and challenges faced by dual-career couples. However, her own marital and family experiences may leave her with certain biases and unresolved conflicts that could limit therapeutic effectiveness (Rice, 1979). Therapists who are ambivalent or opposed to women pursuing careers, to men engaging in family chores, or to changes in traditional gender roles may find it impossible to understand and effectively counsel individuals or couples in dual-career relationships. The dual-career spouse who detects therapist bias about role stereotypes is likely to withdraw, feel threatened, or be pessimistic about being understood (Goldenberg & Goldenberg, 1984).

Particularly crucial to effective therapeutic interventions is the recognition that the experiences of men in dual-career relationships are different from women's experiences. Because the gender-role socialization of men and women differ dramatically, the areas they experience as problematic and the factors contributing to problem areas can be markedly different. For example, the traditional structuring of professional careers has presented an obstacle for men's full involvement in family life, while the traditional division of labor in the home has presented obstacles to women who wish to become more involved in professional careers. These differences surface in the day-to-day conflicts of dual-career couples. Thus, while men may struggle with esteem issues such as perceived loss of power, loss of prestige, and involvement with "women's work" within the family, women may struggle with esteem issues regarding role conflict, redefinition, the roles of wife and mother, and expectations of spouse's involvement in family work (Gilbert & Rachlin, 1987).

Common Themes Across Different Treatment Strategies

From her comparative review of marital therapy literature, Stoltz-Loike (1992) notes six underlying themes related to effective dual-career couple functioning: (1) couples must establish boundaries between themselves and others; (2) spouses must be able to express supportiveness, both emotional and physical, to each other; (3) effective couple relations depend on mastering and using basic communication skills; (4) effective couple relations depend on mastering and using conflict-resolution skills; (5) dysfunctional couple patterns can be framed as problems in need of solutions; (6) effective couple relations involve the process of change that couples tend to fear and resist. The obvious implication is that therapist-guided change can greatly enhance the functioning of dual-career couples.

Psychoeducational Strategies

Generally speaking, family therapists should be able to provide dual-career couples with accurate information, link them with appropriate social supports, and intervene with strategies and techniques appropriate to the dual-career couple's unique needs. A generic five-step intervention protocol has been described by Jordan, Cobb, and McCully (1989) that is representative of the psychoeducational approach. The steps include (1) goals and values clarification; (2) communication training, (3) negotiation and contracting skills training, (4) time management techniques, and (5) stress-management techniques.

First, the couple's role expectations are assessed with regard to career, marriage, parenting, and personal life. The therapist assists the couple in identifying discrepancies between expectations and reality so that mutually satisfying goals can be established.

Second, since successful communication patterns at work may not generalize to parental and marital relationships, deficits in communication skills are assessed. Particular attention is given to communication issues of power and control. The couple is assisted in practicing such skills as active listening, clarification, "I" statements, feedback, request making and self-expression, and positive aspects of non-verbal communications.

Third, when the couple can communicate their needs directly and positively, they have the prerequisite for negotiating areas of conflict through the use of formal and informal contracts. Contracting can help spouses overcome resentments caused by unmet needs or inequitable division of household duties. The issue of equity is, of course, a cornerstone of treatment with dual-career couples. Fourth, time management involves setting priorities and scheduling tasks. The couple is assisted in establishing their career, family, and personal priorities so that realistic decisions about scheduling can be made.

The final step of the protocol is stress management. Even though realistic goals, priorities, and effective time management, communication, and conflict-resolution skills can greatly reduce stressors for the dual-career couple, additional stress reduction skills are needed. The couple is counseled on rules for low stress living that include deep relaxation, breath control, exercise, sensible eating, hobbies, guarding personal freedom, and so on.

Again, these five areas represent the traditional relational skills that most psychoeducational and behavioral marital therapists deem essential for effective and satisfying marital functioning. Furthermore, they have particular value with dual-career couples.

Interpersonal-Systems Strategies

Goldenberg and Goldenberg (1984) believe that effective therapy with dual-career couples can best be achieved within an interpersonal systems perspective. They note that the relationship between dual-career spouses is too complex and interdependent for individual psychotherapeutic interventions to succeed. Goldenberg (1986) maintains that successful treatment needs to involve the spouses conjointly and be highly focused. Frequently, the conjoint sessions are the first time that one spouse has had to attend to the other spouse's agenda. They may see that their relationship system needs reorganizing. Sometimes a first session will create dramatic changes from this new vision of the relationship.

From his relationship-systems perspective, Goldenberg (1986) emphasizes the importance of social and professional networks. He contends that dual-career couples function better if they are not in social isolation. Thus, it is important for them to develop a network of friends and professional colleagues with whom they can share experiences. Feedback provided from being with other couples is useful since it highlights how couples can work out differences. Similarly, a professional support network of individuals or a group of colleagues is most helpful for discussing and venting workplace problems and frustrations. Without a professional support network, the temptation is to dump the day's accumulated stresses and complaints on one's spouse.

Goldenberg (1986) believes that the clinician must continuously maintain a systems perspective and continually view issues, stresses, and problems in light of a non-traditional, rather than traditional, view of marriage. This can be particularly challenging for a therapist who is in a traditional marital relationship. Similarly, the therapist must understand that each developmental lifestyle is important and take care not to identify with the person whose life stage is closest to the therapist's own. For example, if the husband has had an ongoing career, the therapist needs to be reminded that the wife also deserves a turn, even if it comes later in life, is periodically interrupted, and is achieved in a less than orderly or orthodox manner.

Like most other writers on treating dual-career couples, Goldenberg believes that the essential goal of therapy is to achieve or restore a sense of relationship equity, and assist the couple in nourishing their relationship. Since therapeutic impasses are common in conjoint therapy of dual-career couples, Goldenberg (1986) uses the following two therapeutic exercises. In the first, the couple is encouraged to reverse positions emotionally and honestly attempt to offer arguments as though they were the other partner. In the second, the couple is asked to imagine themselves as 15 to 20 years older and construct an autobiography noting what has happened to their relationship and to their careers, as well as dealing with the matter of children. This exercise helps couples foresee the issues of balance of family and career. The therapist's role is to focus each spouse on the other's agenda. As a result, each spouse can become more sensitive to the fact that more is happening in their relationship than his or her own individual unhappiness.

Psychodynamic Strategies

While psychoeducational and systemic strategies aim to teach relational and coping skills or the achievment of adaptive solutions, these approaches tend to be of limited use in helping dual-career couples work through resistance to change or the developmental blocks that lead to relational and therapeutic impasses. Therapeutically confronting these resistances and impasses may require exploring issues from early in each spouse's development (Glickhauf-Hughes, Hughes, & Wells, 1986).

Confronting and resolving the unfinished developmental business of one or both spouses is often part of the process of becoming a mature, dual-career couple (Hall & Hall, 1979). Glickhauf-Hughes et al. (1986) consider the developmental issues that underlie six common conflict areas for dual-career couples. Three of these will be briefly considered here: power conflicts, competition, and commitment.

Glickhauf-Hughes et al. contend that power conflicts often reflect each spouse's childhood experience that others cannot be counted on to meet their needs. As adults they are likely to develop a look-out-for-number-one attitude. In addition, when parents are insensitive to their children's needs and frustration level, these children will likely become adults who have difficulty tolerating the frustration of unmet needs. Thus, compromise with a spouse may be both difficult and painful since it is associated with loss rather than mutual gain. Equity is often proposed as the corrective solution for resolving power conflicts or struggles. But this solution requires several things. First, each spouse must keep one's needs in mind; second, each must develop the ability to tolerate the frustration of not getting one's needs met immediately; and third, each spouse must view the other's requests as legitimate and not as attempts at control or domination. In terms of Erikson's stages of psychosocial development, the resolution of power conflicts by equity is difficult if either or both spouses have insufficiently mastered the developmental tasks of trust and autonomy.

Another common conflict of dual-career couples is competition. The opposite of competition is cooperation or collaboration. Collaboration requires the capacity to separate one's own feelings from the spouse's feelings and behavior, the ability to sustain and augment self-esteem via encouragement, and an acceptance of competitive feelings, both within oneself and in one's spouse. The developmental obstacle that can impede a couple's resolving conflicts about competition results from insufficient mastery of the tasks of autonomy and initiative by one or both spouses.

A third common conflict involves commitment. Since many dual-career spouses value success, achievement, and independence and respond more to external rather than internal validation, these individuals find it easy to "hedge their bet" about relationships and thus place a higher priority on personal attainment and satisfaction. To commit oneself to another requires the ability to be intimate, to develop an internal reward system, and to make the spousal relationship a priority. The developmental tasks that must be mastered involve industry and intimacy.

Essentially then, Glickhauf-Hughes et al. proposes that psychodynamic intervention strategies are necessary when problem solving and communication training are not working because of resistances and impasses secondary to more basic developmental issues. They state "when therapists who work with dual-career couples find that 'I' messages are not working, it may be time to take the emphasis off the message and place it back upon the 'I'" (p. 262).

A related strategy is described by Rice (1979). He proposes a psychoanalytically oriented approach to therapy with dual-career couples, focusing on intrapsychic dynamics. Rice notes that, generally speaking, dual-career couples have special difficulty with interpersonal commitment. In part, this is because of anxiety over the possibility that they might fail at marriage, since there is no guarantee of success. It is also a by-product of the personality pattern dynamics that typify spouses in dual-career relationships. Three styles or themes are common among those adopting a dual-career lifestyle: (1) the need for achievement; (2) strong narcissistic and/or self-esteem enhancement needs; and (3) difficulty forming and sustaining interpersonal commitment. Besides the high need for achievement, dual-career spouses tend to rely heavily on extrinsic rewards such as promotions and their spouse's recognition of their efforts. Their narcissistic vulnerability to self-esteem injury through dependency, frustration, and fear of failure is heightened when they do not receive these expected recognitions. Accordingly, they may react by lashing out at the spouse or using the "silent treatment." Or one spouse may distort the other's intentions, become less trusting and unwilling to take risks, and thus feel justified by limiting his or her commitment to the relationship.

As a result, concern arises about whether certain aspects of the relationship such as career opportunities or shared home responsibilities are working out fairly for both spouses. Partners also get into difficulty when other important aspects of their relationship are perceived as inequitable. Given these dynamics, the increasing stress and conflicts between family and work demands, and the fact that many dual-career couples have had few or no role models for being a dual-career couple, it is often difficult for these couples to work out their relationship problems satisfactorily on their own.

Because individuals in dual-career relationships are usually intelligent, verbal, and successful individuals used to solving problems with cognitive analysis, they frequently resort to the defenses of intellectualization, rationalization, and isolation of affect when faced with conflict. So it is not surprising that strong feelings are viewed by both spouses as obstacles to problem-solving efforts. Often such couples have undeveloped skills of identifying and sharing feelings.

Rice notes three common problem areas that dual-career couples contend with in marital therapy: issues about children, time management, and relationship with others. These three problem areas often involve manifestations of underlying power struggles between the spouses.

Treatment Goal and Strategies

The guiding principle in therapy with dual-career couples is, for Rice, to help them achieve or restore a sense of equity in the marital relationship. Unlike individual psychodynamically oriented psychotherapy, psychodynamically oriented marital therapy is much shorter, averaging nine to ten treatment sessions. The marital therapist must be rather active, particularly in the early sessions. Rice (1979) suggests a general treatment strategy for working with the dual-career couple in marital therapy that is characterized by the following points:

1. A stronger relationship bonding between the couple than between the therapist and the couple or between the therapist and either spouse.

2. The need for a mutually agreed-on definition of what problem or problems will be the critical focus of therapy and the therapist's respect for the couple's definition.

3. The need for a higher therapist activity level than in individual psychodynamic psychotherapy and subsequently the likelihood that treatment will be much briefer than individual therapy.

4. Anticipation of a strong, early dyadic resistance by the couple to the therapist's intervention. This may be lessened by use of a co-therapist.

5. The necessity of combining a psychodynamic formulation of the conflict areas with behavioral and gestalt techniques for modifying these conflicts.

6. The necessity for the therapist not to collude with the couple in seeking premature, verbal solutions to problems with strong affective components.

Rice repeatedly emphasizes that, given the couple's preference for verbalization and cognitive solutions to problems, the therapist must quickly tune into the affective substrata of their interaction and relate to them on that level. This is necessary to disrupt the couple's "set" and to reorient their response styles to both affective and cognitive material. Since the process of dynamic therapy tends to be inherently anxiety-arousing at times, it is particularly important that the therapist not use defenses similar to the couple's to face his or her own anxiety as treatment unfolds. The dissolving of old, familiar defenses and behavior leaves the spouses feeling literally defenseless and anxious until new, more effective coping skills and patterns are learned. Thus, a major therapeutic effort is to assist the couple in separating out and accounting for both the "tasks" component and the "feeling" component in problem solving. As an example, Rice notes that the most creatively and equitably arranged time schedule will not work for long if the husband continues to feel very strongly that his wife should pursue her career only if it does not result in any inconvenience for him. In short, the therapist's failure to take the affective substrata into account will eventually undermine the most carefully arrived at solutions to marital problems.

Rice describes various therapeutic tasks, particularly in the early and middle phases of therapy. These will be briefly summarized in the following paragraphs.

The early phase of treatment involves two specific tasks. The first has already been mentioned—that is, helping to balance cognitive and affective communication so that both modes are valued by the couple. Specific behavioral exercises in listening, empathic responding, and providing supportive verbal feedback are particularly useful. These can be demonstrated in early sessions and then practiced by the couple between sessions. This focus on the affective component is an essential prelude to helping each spouse directly share feelings regarding perceived inequities in the relationship. Early resistance to change will be evidenced during this time.

A second important task in the early phase is the elaboration of the couple's marital contract. Rice suggests a procedure based on Sager (1976) in which the spouses are helped to articulate their initial contract or expectations of one another at the time of their marriage. This is followed by an elaboration of the present contract from each spouse's perspective. Usually, current marital difficulties reflect the disparity between these contracts or expectations. The goal is to focus on these expectations and goal disparities in each spouse's separate, individual contract and work with the couple toward developing a single, mutually acceptable contract.

Once the initial resistance to changing behaviors and communication patterns begins to decrease and acceptance of the affective component in the couple's communication is evidenced, therapy moves into the middle phase. This phase is characterized by the working through of core marital problems. These usually include competition between the spouses, power issues, and difficulties in arranging support networks for the relationship. Standard marital therapy strategies and techniques are used to restore trust, respect, and the perception of equity to the relationship. Rice (1979) provides considerable case material to illustrate these techniques, as well as an extended case study describing each of the fourteen sessions of a completed therapy.

Finally, Rice details characteristics of dual-career couples who respond positively and negatively to treatment. Couples who have shown a positive response are characterized by one or more of the following: (1) freedom from rigid gender role behaviors; (2) new behaviors; (3) willingness to share power as an alternative to competition; (4) valuing the sharing of feelings; and (5) appreciating the spouse's right to self-fulfillment and the willingness to make appropriate sacrifices.

Couples who have not shown substantial improvement are characterized by one or more of the following: (1) inflexible and rigid gender-role stereotyping behavior; (2) unwillingness to risk and try new solutions in the relationship; (3) inability to separate from their families of origin and participate more fully in the dual-career mode; (4) tendency to escape into their respective careers rather than working on balancing career and marital satisfaction; and (5) inability to share power and reduce competitiveness.

Integrative Strategies

Stoltz-Loike (1992) describes what she calls an integrated approach to counseling dual-career couples. She believes that dual-career couples do not represent a variant of traditional couples in which the career responsibilities of the woman are simply attached to her family role and the man's family commitment is formed by his career role. Thus, she advocates that an integrated approach is essential to effectively address the unique demands of dual-career couples who present for consultation. The integrated approach is based on several assumptions: (1) a family has a variety of responsibilities that must be performed and must be comfortably divided depending on the skills, talents, and preferences of the family members; (2) attitudes toward responsibilities need to be communicated, and conflicts need to be discussed and resolved;

(3) since dual-career couples typically have few role models for balancing career and family roles, therapists must provide such information and modeling. This may include dual-career couples and groups that can facilitate functional modeling in being an effective dual-career couple; (4) since types of conflicts and ways of resolving them change throughout the couple's life span, communication, negotiation, and problem solving need to be viewed as ongoing processes; (5) because of individual differences, gender concerns, and personal needs, effective solutions to a couple's family and career conflicts will vary, and the therapist must be cognizant of tailored interventions; (6) a spouse must balance his or her own family and work responsibilities with those of the other spouse; and (7) solutions to dual-career couple issues must be made within the larger context of each spouse's life within a specific corporate and community setting. Thus, the therapist must comprehensively assess the couple's life space and circumstances.

The integrated approach has a distinctive goal, focus, and strategy. The goal of treatment is to achieve balance and negotiate family and career equity. The focus is on helping couples recognize how family and career concerns and role conflicts evolve over the course of the life span and how both rewards and challenges differ over time. Strategies are drawn from life-span development counseling, marital and family therapy, career counseling, and gender counseling to deal with the unique problems.

Since dual-career couples have overlapping roles and responsibilities, reducing the overlap and balancing responsibilities in order to achieve equity is only possible when a couple has mastered the basic relationship skills of communication, negotiation, conflict resolution, and life-span success. Stoltz-Loike believes that the therapist's primary responsibility is to train spouses in these skills and reinforce their acquisition. She notes that successful dual-career couples are characterized by mutual respect for achievement at home and performance in the workplace, as well as deep commitment to personal and spousal accomplishments. Furthermore, the sense of equity associated with both spouse's achievement enriches their couple and family relationship while enhancing career productivity.

Stoltz-Loike's book (1992) offers a wide range of assessment devices for such areas as family and career status and priorities, perceived balance between family and career, couple communication, gender sensitivity, conflict-resolution style, definition of career and family success, and couple goals and career stepladders.

The second section of Stolz-Loike's book describes and illustrates a variety of strategies for skill training and therapeutic interventions regarding communication and negotiation, conflict resolution, gender sensitivity, and life-span success. Stoltz-Loike notes that developing success goals as a couple depends on the commitment of each spouse to his or her own achievement, as well as that of his or her partner. Life-span success is achieved when both can benefit according to their own standards, rather than when one spouse's self-defined success overshadows or obviates the other's ability to achieve. Basically, life-span success is reached by pursuing a series of short-term goals that represent distinct achievements and lead to long-term objectives. Each of these goals can be achieved in various ways, even amid the time-outs or workloads that occur for any number of reasons.

Unlike Rice's more traditional clinical approach, the integrated approach has been used in a variety of settings: in the clinical setting with one or both spouses in a dual-career relationship; in groups of dual-career couples in a clinical setting; in groups of dual-career couples in a corporate setting; or in a seminar program or series in a corporate setting. It appears that the integrated approach as described in Stoltz-Loike's book is primarily a psychoeducational approach focused to couples with Level I conflicts in Guerin's schema (Guerin et al., 1987). Nevertheless, the comprehensiveness of this approach also lends itself to work with couples at Level II, whereby psychoeducational interventions are used concurrently with structural, strategic, cognitive, and dynamic intervention methods.

Group Strategies

Group treatments, which involve either homogeneous or heterogenous formats, have become increasingly available and useful in working with couples. Traditional group therapy is heterogeneous, including individuals or couples with a wide variety of presentations and concerns, and it tends to be ongoing and long term. Homogeneous groups, in contrast, provide a structural social network for individuals or couples with a common presentation or concern. These groups tend to be shorter and time-limited and can have either a dynamic or interpersonal, or psychoeducational, focus. Furthermore, these groups vary in their use of different therapeutic group factors, yet they rely heavily on cohesiveness and universality, as well as imparting information. Groups specifically for dual-career couples are, of course, homogeneous groups and tend to have a psychoeducational format.

The following description by Prochaska and Prochaska (1982) illustrates a typical group format. A six-session format with 90-minute sessions is advertised. Prospective couples are told they can share their experiences and learn a variety of new coping skills to help each other with the typical conflicts arising in balancing a career, marriage, and family. Usually the group comprises five to six couples at differing stages in the life cycle, which is important for providing role modeling and anticipatory experiences for couples who have not faced some of the dilemmas yet to come. Because of the therapy's psychoeducational focus, a variety of methods—including group discussion, minilectures, handouts, role playing, and structured and experiential exercises—are used.

The first session focuses on eliciting the issues and concerns of each couple and their learning needs. The goal of this session is to create a relaxed atmosphere that will foster therapeutic group factors of cohesiveness and universality.

The second session introduces the concept of equity in dual-career relationships. Equity is distinguished from equality. Problem solving-skills that are oriented toward equitable alternatives to the demands facing dual-career couples are described and discussed.

The third session centers on children—the effect dual-career relationships have on them and vice versa. Usually one or more of the couples are in various stages of deciding whether or when to have children, and they are trying to anticipate the ways in which their lives will change. Usually in this session skills are taught for implementing weekly family meetings in which equitable rules and decisions are arrived at by a process of consensus. This forum provides an opportunity for families to change and grow as the needs of the family group and individuals change.

The fourth session focuses on time issues. Time-management concepts and skills are presented, including "time borrowing" whereby someone outside the family is hired to perform time-consuming tasks. Empathy training exercises in dyads and triads also occur in this session.

The fifth session focuses on styles and methods of conflict resolution. Role playing with prompt cards is used to address typical dual-career conflict issues.

The sixth and last session emphasizes role flexibility. A group dinner is planned the session before so that each member can contribute in a unique and novel way. Typically, one or more of the men who usually never cook prepare the meal, while the woman or women who usually take total responsibility for the meal relax and read the newspaper. The dinner discussion centers on feelings of being out of role and the advantages to the couple of increasing their flexibility. Also discussed are termination issues that include intense termination feelings. It is not unusual for groups to decide to continue to meet monthly as a support group to further discuss issues of mutual concern.

Consultation Interventions

Dual-career couple intervention includes assisting individuals in resolving conflict between career and relational demands, assisting couples in resolving internal and external strains on relationship, and assisting employers in understanding and more effectively responding to the needs of dual-career couples in the workplace.

As marital and family therapists become more involved as consultants to organizations, they can affect the organization and workplace in a number of ways, by (1) providing on-site clinical services and/or case consultation for Employee Assistance Programs (EAP) personnel (Sperry, 1993); (2) conducting psychoeducational or skills-building workshops within the organization; and (3) consulting with top leadership regarding a wide variety of work-family policies and procedures. This section will briefly focus on the last two activities.

Therapist/consultants are usually retained by corporations as external consultants, while some may serve as internal consultants. Internal consultants serve as salaried employees, while external consultants tend to work on a fee-for-service basis (Stringer, 1985).

Psychoeducational Workshops

In the role of consultant, the marital and family therapist can provide a variety of presentations on topics related to the work-centered family. These can include time management, stress reduction, lifestyle management, communication and negotiation skills, stress and sexuality, women's health issues and work, and balancing career, family, and personal life. The presentations can be one time lectures, an ongoing formal seminar, or part of a more informal brown bag luncheon.

There are several ways of organizing these presentations. They may be open to all employees or to certain segments. Stoltz-Loike (1992) describes seminars focused on female issues in dual-career and dual-earner relationships, as well as seminars that are directed at both spouses. Avis (1986) describes a marriage enrichment program for dual-career couples that emphasizes the topics of renegotiating roles and responsibilities, structuring and managing time, meeting emotional needs, dealing with competition, and sharing control and power. This program consists of seven 2½-hour weekly sessions. Long (1984) describes a training seminar for top managers to assist them in identifying issues common to dual-career marriages, helping these couples resolve career and family concerns, and clarifying and developing the organization's policies and practices with regard to these couples.

That these seminars and workshops are beneficial is beyond question. That they may not be reaching those most at risk is another matter. King and Winnett (1986) report data suggesting that clerical and other hourly workers have as great or greater need than professional workers for stress management and conflict resolution training. Typically, however, it is the professional worker who is targeted for such programs. These researchers further noted that men in dual-earner marriages appear to be less interested in attending such training programs than men in dual-career marriages.

There are now many excellent resources for training seminars and workshops. Stoltz-Loike (1992) provides a number of simple inventories that are useful in group formats involving individuals or couples. Michaels and McCarty's book (1992) is one of a number of recent trade publications that can be suggested or assigned as reading for participants.

Consulting on Work-Family Issues

Marital and family therapists/consultants also can have significant effect on work-family functioning through consulting on policy and programming matters. Sekaran (1986), an expert in organizational management, is among a growing number of management consultants who advise corporations on changing corporate policies to accommodate the needs and concerns of work-centered families. She particularly emphasizes changes in hiring practices, parental leave, flexible work scheduling, and child-care assistance. She provides an extended discussion on such policy matters in her book *Dual-Career Families: Contemporary Organizational and Counseling Issues.*

Vanderkolk and Young (1991) focus most of their work regarding examples of policy and programming changes on work-family matters that corporations have already successfully implemented. They also provide a number of worksheets, surveys, and strategies to aid in overcoming management's resistance to such changes. They point out that these changes not only result in increased worker satisfaction and productivity but are also cost-effective and necessary for a corporation to maintain its competitive edge in a changing world economy.

Therapist/consultants will find much value and advice in both of the preceding books. An extended section of the Stoltz-Loike (1992) book is entitled "Corporate Response to Dual-Career Couples" in which she describes the needed policy changes that corporations must make to become more family friendly. She describes policies and programming for child care and eldercare, flexible scheduling, leave policies, recruitment and retention, relocation, and the type of corporate climate or culture that is consistent with such family-friendly policies. A professional therapist and consultant, Stoltz-Loike believes that clinicians have a unique opportunity to consult on the development and implementation of various family-friendly programs and that both internal relational dynamics and external sources of corporate stress must be addressed for the concerns of dual-career couples to be effectively resolved.

Sekaran (1986) also argues that both internal and external sources of dual-career couple stress must be addressed. Sperry (1993) contends that clinically trained individuals with knowledge and experience in family systems theory are much better suited to consult with organizations on work-family issues than non-clinically trained management consultants. Cole (1992) also indicates that business and management consultants are trained to approach organizational issues from a linear and rational perspective, while family therapists are trained to think systemically and circularly. Cole notes that an increasing number of marital and family therapists are being called on to serve as consultants on work and family interactions. Reportedly, Nova University's School of Social and Systems Studies has begun a Family Systems Business Program not only to consult with work organizations on family issues but also to formally train graduate students on work-family issues.

In addition to the dual-career couple, Chapter 2 described another kind of work-related couple: the family business couple—either the two-person career couple, wherein the female spouse typically supports the business-owner husband, or the dual-earner couple, wherein both spouses work for the same corporation as employee-owners. Clinical work or consultation with either type of family business couple is relatively straightforward for the therapist trained in systemic family therapy. The full range of family dynamics is perhaps more clearly evidenced in this type of work-centered couple than in others. Family myths, rules, roles, boundaries, power and intimacy issues, and triangulation pervade the business communication and decisions of this couple. Not surprisingly, the need for conflict resolution and problem solving is commonplace, as are restructuring of boundaries and resolution of multigenerational concerns. Although Levinson (1983) opined that family business couples are particularly difficult to work with in therapy and in consultation, recent developments in systems interventions are changing this perception. Jaffe's (1990) recent book on using family systems interventions with family business couples offers useful aids to the therapist/consultant working with these couples.

A Protocol for Matching/Tailoring Treatment with Dual-Career Couples

The protocol proposed here is simple, perhaps deceptively simple. It involves four steps:

1. Comprehensive assessment
2. Matching to a therapeutic strategy and treatment format
3. Tailoring the chosen strategy
4. Implementation, review, and revision of matching/tailoring efforts

Assessment

The assessment format outline in Chapter 3 is slightly modified with dual-career couples. In addition to situation/severity, system, skill, style, and suitability for treatment, the dimensions of support network and synchronism/asynchronism are added. As described by Sekaran and Hall (1989), *synchronism* is a condition under which an individual's or a couple's experience is "on" schedule in relationship to some "timetable" of development, while *asynchronism* refers to being "off" schedule. These timetables are defined by the family, the couple, and the work organization. For instance, couples who marry and have children late are usually considered out of sync with social norms, also called family *asynchronism*. If one spouse's career started later than the other, or if the progress of one was slower than the other, this would illustrate *couple asynchronism*. But when an individual is not promoted to a managerial level by the age of 40, that individual is considered behind schedule and subsequently may never receive such a promotion. This is called *organizational asynchronism*. Among dual-career couples, the more types of levels of asynchronism, the more stress the couple is likely to experience (Sekaran & Hall, 1989). Assessing the dual-career couple's career and family timing and synchronism/asynchronism is thus useful in formulating a matched/tailored treatment plan.

Matching a Therapeutic Strategy and Treatment Format to the Couple

Clinical experience with dual-career couples suggests that matching a couple with a therapeutic strategy should be based on the dimensions of situation/severity, system, support network, and skills. As noted in Chapter 4, situation/severity can be operationalized by level of marital discord (Guerin et al., 1987), level of functioning (Weltner, 1985), or level of distress (Worthington, 1989).

Using level of marital conflict is particularly helpful. As described in Chapter 4, the first level of marital conflict involves couples who demonstrate preclinical or minimal degree of marital conflict. Such conflict has lasted for less than 6 months, and most often the couples are newlyweds. Level two consists of couples who are experiencing significant marital conflict lasting longer than 6 months. Although their communication patterns remain open and adequate, criticism and projection have increased. Level-three couples present with severe marital conflict. Often this conflict is greater than 6 months duration, and projection is intense. Levels of anxiety and emotional arousal are high, as are the intensity and polarization of surrounding triangles. Communication is closed with marked conflict, the level of criticism is high, and blaming is common. Finally, couples at level four are characterized by communication that is closed, poor or nonexistent information exchange, high levels of criticism and blaming, and an absence of self-disclosure activity. In the vast majority of level-four cases, attempts to keep the marriage from dissolution appeared doomed.

For instance, if the dual-career couple is recently married with level-one conflict, a psychoeducational intervention strategy would likely be indicated, particularly if the couple also displays skill deficits in one or more areas like communication, negotiation, conflict resolution, time and stress management, or goal clarification. A consultative intervention might also be a good match. In contrast, with a couple presenting with level-two or level-three conflict, an interpersonal or psychodynamic intervention might be a better match than a psychoeducational one. However, psychoeducational input might be selectively used at some point in the course of treatment.

A second consideration at the matching stage of the protocol is treatment format. Whether individual, conjoint couple, or couples group therapy format is indicated depends on a number of factors including the nature of the presenting problem situation and systemic factors. The situation/severity and systems dimensions can provide useful information with regard to matching. Generally speaking, the individual format is indicated if a single spouse is experiencing difficulty adjusting to or coping with stress within the career-relationship. In contrast, the conjoint format tends to be more appropriate if the issue affects the dynamic within the relationship, particularly when issues of equality/power, boundaries, and intimacy are prominent. The couples group format is helpful if the stressors are largely external to the couple—that is, from the workplace—and/or the couple's concerns reflect level-one marital conflict (Guerin et al., 1987).

Usually decisions about matching treatment are made before, during, or after the first session. However, tailoring decisions tend to be made at various points throughtout the course of treatment. This is because tailoring involves a fine tuning or fitting of the matched treatment strategy to the couple's unique needs, expectations, and treatment readiness.

Tailoring the Chosen Therapeutic Strategy

Once a therapeutic strategy and treatment format match has been made, the therapist can focus on tailoring treatment to the couple's unique needs and expectations. Clinical experience suggests that tailoring be based on the dimensions of style, synchronism, and suitability for treatment.

The style dimension will reflect the intrapsychic dynamic of each spouse. As Rice (1979) observes, narcissistic features are often prominent in both spouses in dual-career marriages. Obsessive compulsive features may be noted in the achievement focus and workaholic patterns of one or both spouses. Irrespective of the therapeutic strategy used, the effective therapist will reconfigure treatment mindful of these individual dynamics. In other words, the therapist's questions, clarifications, confrontations, reframes, and/or interpretations will be tailored to "fit" that couple or spouse. Lazarus' BASIC ID model (1981) is likewise valuable in tailoring interventions to dual-career couples, particularly because of its emphasis on specifying specific interventions with specific treatment methods.

The therapist will also consider the dimension of synchronism/ asynchronism in tailoring a specific therapeutic strategy. Therapist sensitivity to family, couple, and/or workplace asynchronism can aid in both reducing stress and empowering one or both spouses.

Finally, the dimension of suitability for treatment is valuable in decisions regarding tailoring. Spousal expectations for treatment and their treatment readiness are the major considerations. If one or both spouse's treatment expectations are unrealistic or conflicting, the therapist must address them in the initial sessions. Not to do so is to risk premature termination, which is not uncommon with dual-career couples. Similarly, the couple's level of readiness (Myers, 1992) is an important consideration in tailoring a particular treatment strategy. To maximize treatment efficacy, the therapist needs to adapt how much direction and how much support he or she provides the couple. For the couple with low task readiness, the therapist who responds in a highly supportive or delegating style will be out of sync with that couple, while being quite in sync with a couple high in task readiness.

Implementation, Review, and Revision of Matching/Tailoring

In this last step of this protocol, the therapist continues the therapeutic intervention(s) while monitoring response and outcomes. Usually the therapeutic strategy remains the same, while treatment goals may need to be modified and tailoring of the chosen therapeutic strategies continues. However, it may be necessary to change the strategy or even the treatment format. For instance, although treatment may begin in a conjoint format, it may be useful or necessary to switch or to add individual sessions for one or both spouses.

Case Example of Matching/Tailoring with a Dual-Career Couple

The following case illustrates the matching/tailoring process with a dual-career couple experiencing moderately severe marital discord. Given the chronicity of the couple's discord, successful outcome following 21 sessions is likely due to the tailored nature of the treatment. By the careful blending and sequencing of interpersonal, psychoeducational, and dynamic strategies with a conjoint treatment format, the couple was aided in redirecting and reclarifying their relationship.

Dale and Claire Justen have been married 6 years and have a 3-year-old son. They presented for therapy after a particularly vitriolic disagreement in which Dale had pushed Claire into a wall. Although this was the first such incident, both were shaken sufficiently to seek professional help.

Dale, 43, is chief financial officer for a national fast-food chain. Claire is 40 and a junior partner in a high visibility corporate law firm. She had worked full-time for 6 years in her firm before her son was born. She then took a 3-month maternity leave and returned to her job on a 20 hour a week basis. She hoped to be made a full partner in the firm 6 months ago but was told she would not even be considered until she returned to full-time status. This greatly distressed her because she felt strongly about spending "enough" time with her son, at least until he began first grade. She felt some guilt about working at all during her son's "most formative years," as her mother continued to remind her.

Both Claire and Dale come from traditional families in which their mothers were full-time homemakers and their fathers were the sole breadwinners. Claire and Dale were also the first generation of their respective families to attend college. Both began careers immediately and were quite successful. They met about 2 years before their marriage and discussed their desire to balance a family while continuing their careers. Things never quite worked out that way after the baby was born. Claire ended up assuming nearly total responsibility for child care. When the child was 2½, Claire and Dale decided the child would change from half-time to full-time day care so that Claire could return to her career full time. But Dale never seemed to be free to drop off or pick up the child from the day-care site, and he was always too tired to help with household chores or spend time alone with Claire. For 3 weeks she attempted to juggle her work and home responsibilities before dropping back to 20 hours a week, much to the consternation of the senior partners and Dale, but to the delight of her mother. Dale insisted that they needed a full-time income from her to meet their increasing expenses since they had recently purchased a ski lodge condo.

These events served to fuel an already chronic incendiary relationship marked by periods of sharp verbal exchange followed by the same "cold shoulder" treatment or "stonewalling" (Gottman, 1994) that they had noted in their parents' relationships. Although they have never seriously considered separation or divorce—"our religion doesn't permit it"—they noted a decline in sexual relations since the baby was born to a point in the last year when Dale complained that he had "lost all interest, because I'm too tired and stressed out."

Dale's corporation was recently involved in a hostile takeover and he has spent considerable time and effort making the merger work. It has been considerably stressful for him because of the increasing travel demands and the fact that he has much less time to play golf and ski with his buddies.

Since Claire had moved when Dale was transferred right after they were married, she left behind the support network she had been a part of since college. Except for one unmarried woman in the firm, Claire has not had or taken the time to develop other friendships.

After two sessions of comprehensive assessment had been completed, issues of inequality of power, gender stereotyping, and inhibited sexual desire were prominent. Results of FACES-III (Olson, Portner, & Labee, 1985) confirmed the therapist's impression of low marital cohesion and adaptability with unclear boundaries. The negative effect of Claire's mother was obvious to the couple. The Millon Clinical Multiaxial Inventory-II (MCMI-II) showed elevations on narcissistic and obsessive-compulsive scales for Dale and histrionic elevations for Claire. Although both were quite successful in their careers, skills of communication, negotiation, encouragement, conflict resolution, and empathy were not evident in their relationship, although the time management skills seemed adequate. While Dale's support network was adequate, Claire's was not. There was considerable couple and career asynchronism for Claire, which she experienced as a moderate stressor.

Because of the chronicity of their presenting concerns, the couple met criteria for level-three marital discord (Guerin et al., 1987). Blaming and projection were common and reflected both their hostility and increasing hopelessness (Gottman, 1994). Their different personality styles, lack of relational skills, and power, boundary, and intimacy issues led to their ongoing conflict and inability to resolve their differences. Given their relatively strong motivation to make changes and commitment to stay together, their prognosis appeared favorable. Relevant goals were mutually negotiated to increase the likelihood the couple would assume ownership and be more motivated and adherent to the treatment process. The treatment goals were:

1. Reduce the present level of conflict and distress

2. Establish clearer boundaries regarding careers and families of origin

3. Establish a more equitable relationship and increased gender-sensitivity

4. Develop more effective relationship skills of communication, conflict resolution, negotiation, empathy, encouragement, and time management

5. Increase the understanding of individual and couple dynamics

6. Assist Claire in better understanding and resolving her career and family asynchronism

These six goals were stated in the developmental order in which they would be addressed therapeutically; that is, symptom relief and boundary restructuring would be a prerequisite for working on equity and gender sensitivity along with skill-building, which would be followed by insight and awareness. (L'Abate [1986] advocates such a sequential process of marital and family interventions.) Based on the assessment dimensions of situation/severity, systems, skills, and support network, three therapeutic strategies were matched. The interpersonal-systems strategy would be employed to achieve the first three goals. A psychoeducational strategy was planned for the fourth goal, while a psychodynamic strategy was envisioned for the fifth and sixth goals.

Tailoring treatment was based on the dimensions of style, synchronism, and suitability for treatment. Since the couple had high levels of task readiness, commitment to the marriage, and motivation for treatment, it would be assumed that the therapist would easily form a therapeutic alliance. Anticipating the alliance would be collaborative and the therapist would probably encounter minimal resistance on symptom reduction, boundary issues, and skill training, an active, albeit support-ive, therapist style would be well tolerated.

Tailoring with regard to the psychoeducational strategy would be manifested by considerable in-session modeling of effective communi-cation, conflict resolution, and negotiation skills given the couple's incendiary style, family history, and limited success in this area. It would be inappropriate to simply prescribe workbook exercises to learn these skills as would be possible with some other couples. For this reason, the use of a co-therapist would be indicated in this case. Both therapists could model and enact potentially conflictual situations for the couple to observe, discuss, and then role play. Similarly, because both spouses reflect cultural gender stereotyping in which histrionic behavior in females has been considered feminine while obsessive-compulsive behavior in males tends to be rewarded professionally, more androgy-nous co-therapist interaction could greatly enhance efforts to increase gender sensitivity.

Because of Dale's empathic deficits, reflective of his narcissistic per-sonality style, the therapist would use mirroring as well as empathy training. However, the therapist's use of encouragement through refram-ing and stroking would be necessary for both spouses given their narcis-sistic and histrionic styles.

As anticipated, the treatment process eventually became a collabora-tive endeavor, but not until they were able to reduce their hurtful, incen-diary communications and establish reasonable boundaries involving their job and family demands. Surprisingly, they responded quickly to skill-building tasks and other psychoeducational interventions. By the eighth session they have met the first four treatment goals and had stabi-lized their relational system. The next twelve sessions were primarily focused on individual and family-of-origin dynamics that Claire and Dale brought to their marriage. During this time relapse prevention strategies were introduced. The last session reviewed their progress and current level of functioning. Both agreed they were less stressed and much hap-pier about their relationship and career. Dale recognized the need for additional work on issues of entitlement and blame. Subsequently, he continued for six additional individual sessions with the therapist.

Therapeutic Intervention with the Single, Working Parent

Therapeutic work with the working single parent who has child custody can be considerably challenging. In addition to the unique system stres-sors of the single-parent family, the therapist must account for the job component and its unique stresses and challenges for the single parent. This section briefly describes some treatment strategies and resources.

Initially, the therapist must remain mindful of the psychological presence of the absent parent, as this individual probably exerts considerable influence on the therapist-family dynamics. The therapist must assess the manner in which single parenthood occurred, including the ages of children and the stage of the marriage in which the death, divorce, or desertion occurred.

Second, the therapist will assess the family structure, including boundaries and coalitions, particularly observing for the presence of a parentified child. Assessment also includes the type of work, stressors, child care plan, and the type and quality of support network the working parent has both on and off the job. Particularly, attention should be focused on the relationship the working parent has with job supervisors and on work-family policies and programs at the place of employment such as schedule flexibility, child care, leave, absenteeism, and personal time.

Third, the therapist begins to assist the family in thinking of themselves in systems terms, as this can facilitate later intervention aimed at changes in both family structure and work relations. Generally, the therapist begins with strengthening the executive function of the parent and restructuring the system so that the child or children assume some responsibility for supportive tasks. Since support systems are critical to the single-parent family, the therapist encourages the working parent to develop and/or strengthen support on the job, in the community, and from relatives if possible.

Fourth, often single parents will need to develop parenting skills to remediate specific family concerns. The working single parent may also need to develop a number of additional self-management and self-care skills to better cope with day-to-day realities.

Fifth, the "fit" between the working single parent and her or his job may need attention. A poor fit may be the source of considerable stress because of role ambiguity, role conflict, role overload, or spill-over into the family. The therapist's knowledge of career counseling methods and strategies can be quite useful in such situations. Although Burden (1986) ruled that single female parent employees functioned at high levels, she believes they do so at great expense to their physical and psychological well-being. Thus, the therapist must assist the working parent in inventorying her work-family stressors and personal and corporate coping resources and deciding on whether more self-management or self-care skills must be acquired or whether a job change might be indicated.

Although there are few resources focused on working with single parents, what is available is excellent. Morawetz and Walker's *Brief*

Therapy with Single-Parent Families (1984) is a general treatment of the topic and is an indispensable guide for the therapist. Morawetz and Walker describe the most common therapeutic interventions, as well as their use during the four stages that single-parent families go through after loss of the other parent: (1) the aftermath; (2) regrouping and realignment; (3) reestablishment of a social life; and (4) successful separation of parent and child.

Michaels and McCarty (1992) focus more specifically on the working single parent. They suggest eight critical areas that should be considered: (1) evaluating and re-evaluating job and career; (2) building effective support networks; (3) dealing with depression; (4) acquiring needed life-management skills (that is, delegating, planning, priorities, and so on); (5) developing self-care skills; (6) finding and keeping appropriate child care; (7) getting sufficient sleep; and (8) financial planning.

Concluding Note

This chapter has reviewed a wide variety of treatment strategies germane to work-family problems and concerns, particularly those of the dual-career couple and the working, single-parent family. The detailed case example illustrated a method of matching and tailoring treatment based on a comprehensive, integrative assessment. The reader should note that the published literature on counseling and consulting with families and couples on work-family issues is steadily increasing but is relatively small in comparison with general marital and family therapy literature. As those who teach, supervise, research, and practice family therapy continue to respond to the changing portrait of the American family, particularly regarding the work-family connection, our therapeutic expertise should correspondingly increase.

References

Amatea, C., & Clark, J. (1984). A dual-career workshop for college couples: Effects of an intervention. *Journal of College Student Personnel, 25*(3), 271–272.

Amatea, E., & Cross, E. (1983). Coupling and careers: A workshop for dual-career couples at the launching stages. *Personnel and Guidance Journal, 62*(1), 48–52.

Avis, J. (1986). An enrichment program for dual-career couples. Journal of Psychotherapy and the Family, *2*(1), 29–45.

Burden, D. (1986). Single parents and the work setting: The impact of multiple job and homelife responsibilities. *Family Relations, 35,* 37–43.

Cole, P. (1992). Family systems business: A merger at last. *Family Therapy News, 23*(2), 29.

Gilbert, L., & Rachlin, V. (1987). Mental health and psychological functioning of dual-career families. *The Counseling Psychologist, 15*(1), 7–49.

Glickhauf-Hughes, C., Hughes, G., & Wells, M. (1986). A developmental approach to treating dual-career couples. *American Journal of Family Therapy, 14*(3), 254–263.

Goldenberg, H. (1986). Treating contemporary couples in dual-career relationships. *Family Therapy Today, 1,* 1–7.

Goldenberg, I., & Goldenberg, H. (1984). Treating the dual-career couple. *American Journal of Family Therapy, 12,* 29–37.

Gottman, J. (1994). *Why marriages succeed or fail.* New York: Simon & Shuster.

Guerin, P., Fay, L., Burden, S., & Kuetto, J. (1987). *The evaluation and treatment of marital conflict: A four stage approach.* New York: Basic Books.

Hall, F., & Hall, D. (1979). *The two-career couple.* Reading, MA: Addison-Wesley.

Jaffe, D. (1990). *Working with the ones you love: Conflict resolution and problem solving strategies for a successful family business.* Berkeley, CA: Conari Press.

Jordan, C., Cobb, N., & McCully, R. (1989). Clinical issues of the dual-career couple. *Social Work, 34*(1), 29–32.

Kahnweiler, J., & Kahnweiler, W. (1980). A dual-career family workshop for college undergraduates. *Vocational Guidance Quarterly, 28,* 225–230.

King, A., & Winnett, R. (1986). Tailoring stress-reduction strategies to populations at risk: Comparison between women from dual-career and dual-worker families. *Family and Community Health, 9*(3), 42–50.

L'Abate, L. (1986). *Systematic family therapy.* New York: Brunner/Mazel.

Lazarus, A. (1981). *The practice of multimodal therapy.* New York: McGraw-Hill.

Levinson, H. (1983). Consulting with family business: What to look for, what to look out for. *Organizational Dynamics,* Summer, 71–80.

Long, R. (1984). Designing a dual-career marriage seminar. *Training and Development Journal, 38*(10), 87–91.

Michaels, B., & McCarty, E. (1992). *Solving the work/family puzzle.* Homewood, IL: Business One Irwin.

Morawetz, A., & Walker, G. (1984). *Brief therapy with single-parent families.* New York: Brunner/Mazel.

Myers, P. (1992). Using adaptive counseling and therapy to tailor treatment to couples and families. *Topics in Family Psychology and Counseling, 1*(3), 56–70.

Olson, D., Portner, J., & Labee, Y. (1985). *FACES-III.* Family Social Sciences, University of Minnesota, 290 McNeal Hall, St. Paul, MN 55108.

Prochaska, J., & Prochaska, J. (1982). Dual-career families are a new challenge for spouses and agencies. *Social Casework, 63,* 118–120.

Rice, D. (1979). *Dual-career marriage: Conflict and treatment.* New York: Free Press.

Rosen, R. (1991). *The healthy company.* Los Angeles: Jeremy Tarcher.

Sager, C. (1976). *Marriage contracts and couples therapy.* New York: Brunner/Mazel.

Sekaran, U. (1986). *Dual-career families.* San Francisco: Jossey-Bass.

Sekaran, U., & Hall, D. (1989). Asynchronism in dual-career and family linkages. In M. Arthur, D. Hall, & B. Lawrence (Eds.), *Handbook of career theory* (pp. 159–180). Cambridge: Cambridge University Press.

Sperry, L. (1993). *Psychiatric Consultation in the Workplace.* Washington, DC: American Psychiatric Press.

Stoltz-Loike, M. (1992). *Dual-career couples: New Perspectives in counseling.* Alexandria, VA: American Association for Counseling and Development.

Stringer, D. (1985). Counseling dual-career couples. In D. W. Myers (Ed.), *Employee problem prevention and counseling* (pp. 191–206). Westport, CT: Quorum Books.

Vanderkolk, B., & Young, A. (1991). *The work and family revolution.* New York: Facts on File.

Weltner, J. (1985). Matchmaking: Choosing the appropriate therapy for families at various levels of pathology. In M. Mirkin & S. Koman (Eds.), *Handbook of adolescents and family therapy* (pp. 237–246). New York: Gardner.

Worthington, E. (1989). Matching family treatment to family stressors. In C. Figley (Ed.), *Treating stress in families* (pp. 44–63). New York: Brunner/Mazel.

9

Treatment Adherence and Relapse Prevention
Ensuring Therapeutic Results

Therapists are traditionally trained to identify, diagnose, and remediate the full spectrum of psychopathology (Sperry & Carlson, 1993). Although therapists are initially successful in helping couples and families improve their status, follow-up research shows that seldom do these gains maintain themselves (Gottman, 1994b; Jacobson, 1989; Jacobson, Schmaling, & Holtzworth-Munroe, 1987; Sperry & Carlson, 1990). The degree to which a couple or family follow through with (adhere to) the planned treatment change process is very low. Failure to adhere is a major obstacle to successful change, although therapists often deny or are very surprised that it is so common.

Therapists have had extensive training in frontloading the helping process by putting all their resources into identification, diagnosis, and remediation and very little into treatment adherence and relapse prevention. It is necessary for therapists to have a clear conception not only of how to help distressed couples and families learn to function more effectively but also of how to maintain those gains once they are reached. It is becoming increasingly obvious that termination should not imply an end to treatment as much as it does a change in treatment intensity.

A great challenge for the therapist is to gain the ability to predict therapeutic success and maintenance. Some treatments seem to be likely to have long-term effectiveness while others are probably temporary at best. What can therapists do to change the therapeutic conditions in order to increase long term treatment success and prevent a return or relapse to previous levels of dysfunction? How long do effects last after successful intervention? What percentage of couples/families

195

relapse after a successful intervention? What distinguishes those who maintain treatment gains from those who relapse? What causes or creates relapse? Can relapse be prevented or minimized? This chapter will answer these and other questions in describing how treatment adherence and relapse prevention principles can be used with couples and families. It is hoped that the professional community will begin to understand the importance of these concepts as both research and clinical issues.

Treatment Adherence

No one set of adherence enhancement procedures will be successful across populations. More than 20 years ago, Epstein and Masek (1978) catalogued more than 30 different techniques designed to increase medical patient adherence. Examples of these techniques that we have found helpful are as follows:

1. Provide specific appointment times

2. Use reminders (mail, telephone)

3. Elicit and discuss reasons for previously missed appointments

4. Involve family/couple in planning and implementation of treatment program

5. Tailor treatment plan

6. Simplify treatment directives

7. Use psychoeducation and check for comprehension

8. Anticipate side effects

9. Process any negative feedback

10. Teach self-management skills

11. Use graduated regimen implementation

12. Involve significant others

13. Use role playing and paradoxical techniques when appropriate

14. Use a combination of approaches rather than single strategies

We have found it is essential to diagnose and assess each instance of non-adherence and to be flexible and tailor procedures to the specific circumstances and characteristics of the family/couple. For example, a couple came back after 1 week indicating that the assigned homework of conducting a daily 10-minute dialogue was completed on only one day. The couple was asked to discuss their understanding as to why the assignment was not completed. After each person gave his or her explanation, a more detailed assignment was developed. A specific time was established, and a modified plan to meet every other day was agreed to. The couple was willing to conduct the activity; however, they needed assistance in changing present behavioral patterns.

Treatment Adherence Guidelines

As we have previously discussed, the therapist needs to begin the treatment process with a comprehensive assessment. The therapist not only needs to diagnose the family's/couple's clinical condition but also needs to diagnose or assess the chances and reasons for non-adherence. The therapist must assess the family's adherence history, relationship beliefs, expectations, and possible barriers or obstacles to adherence.

Once this has taken place, the following guidelines (adapted from Meichenbaum & Turk, 1987) will be useful.

1. Anticipate Non-Adherence

Therapists need to begin to think about adherence at the beginning of treatment, often when information is provided by the referral source. The therapist must carefully weigh all data provided, especially those about treatment, length of problem, locus of responsibility, and extent of problem. Many clients are confused and misinformed about the process of marriage and family therapy (that is, who does what). It is usually helpful to begin therapy by asking:

a.   Why have they come to treatment?

b.   What have they heard or been told about treatment?

c.   What do they expect to happen during treatment?

d.   What will be different after treatment?

The therapist also needs to assess factors that may facilitate or impede treatment such as rapport, readiness to learn or change, and willingness to accept responsibility.

Specifically, therapists need to assess factors such as:

a.   The family's expectation for treatment (if treatment is successful, how will you know? What will be different?)

b. The beliefs and misconceptions about the cause, severity, and symptoms of the problem (would you each give your explanation of the problem and describe how you believe it can be changed?)

c. The goals of treatment (what do you want to accomplish in therapy?)

d. The family's commitment to treatment (that is, how badly do they want to change?) (on a scale of 1 to 10 with 1 being low and 10 high, how important is it to you that change occurs?)

e. The present level of skills

f. The sense of helplessness and hopelessness versus resourcefulness and self-efficacy (how optimistic are you that the situation can be changed?—give a ranking on the 1 to 10 scale; have you ever brought about change in other aspects of your or your family's life?)

g. Educational or physical limitations

h. The life circumstances that may affect adherence (that is, limited time, limited financial resources) (what are some things that might get in the way of successful change?)

The preceding information is usually gathered directly using questions similar to the examples or indirectly in the initial interview. The information is used in tailoring the approach to deal with possible adherence problems. The therapist who anticipates non-adherence can usually make the corrections necessary to maximize treatment adherence.

2. Consider Treatment from the Family's Perspective

The therapist should not assume that his or her perceptions of events is the same as the family's. Families come into treatment with certain attitudes, beliefs, expectations, and resources. The therapist should *join* the family (Minuchin, 1974). In this process the therapist adjusts to the communication style and perceptions of the family members.

There are aspects of personality style conviction that guide a family's/couple's behaviors and habits. These beliefs form an explanatory model that aids the family in making sense of problems and events: how they respond, how they describe events, and how they cope with situations. This model also gives insight into the family's expectation for treatment, the outcome and level of participation. The therapist needs to understand the family's explanatory model in order to develop a lasting intervention.

Additionally, the therapist must realize that families have other commitments, demands, and life circumstances that may make the problem easier to maintain/support than its solutions. Families live and have their problems supported within a social network. It *cannot be assumed* that just because someone has a problem and brings it to a therapist that they will adhere to change.

3. Facilitate a Collaborative Relationship That Is Based on Negotiation

A wise therapist knows how to avoid resistance by involving the family in the decisional process regarding their treatment: "an acceptable treatment plan that is carried out appropriately is much better than an ideal one that is ignored. The therapist must be willing to negotiate within reason.

The therapist needs to use the family's words, ideas, and explanatory model in developing a treatment plan. The plan must flow from the family, using statements such as "It sounds like you all want to . . ." or "It looks like you want . . . to happen in this way . . ." "You all seem to be in touch with the need to . . ."

4. Be Family-Oriented (Understand the Family's Views/Explanatory Model)

What are the family's views, expectations, and knowledge concerning the problem and treatment? Do they believe they can successfully adhere to the treatment? Do they believe the treatment will actually work? How important do they feel the treatment is? What barriers does the family envision that will prevent or impede successful treatment? What does the family believe can be done to make adherence easier?

It is important to listen not only to what the family says but also to what they fail to say. The failure of the family to answer certain questions usually indicates that they are not collaborating and will not follow the treatment plan.

5. Tailor Treatment

As we have discussed throughout this book, there is no standard treatment for any couple or family. In considering a set of treatment recommendations, the therapist must consider, adjust, and modify treament to fit each family.

As a general rule, treatment plans should be effective, simple, convenient, produce the fewest side effects, and require the least interference with normal daily activities. Whenever possible, connect adherence behaviors to normal daily routines such as meals, bedtime, time of awakening, and so on. Families will need assistance in integrating new demands on their daily routines. For example, a suggestion of talking for 10 minutes each night at bedtime is more likely to be adhered to than talking during the day.

6. Enlist Family Support

Generally it is useful to make sure that family and other significant people understand the treatment plan and goals in order to be allies. Therapists need to keep asking questions such as "tell me again what you believe needs to be done and what exactly you are working on."

7. Provide a System of Continuity and Accessibility

Families need to know that the therapist views the treatment process as lifelong and is therefore accessible at various stages in the family life cycle. The therapist needs to be an ally who is accessible, nonjudgmental, respectful, and sincere in the willingness to cooperate with them. The open-ended therapy model (Lebow, 1995) sees families making use of treatment at various times in the life cycle.

8. Don't Give Up

Many therapists write off non-adherence to system resistance. This allows them to blame the family or couple and excuse themselves of any responsibility. However, skilled therapists must navigate the waters of resistance and develop tailored treatment plans. A well-designed plan will create cooperation and treatment adherence. It is this challenge that makes working with couples and families so rewarding.

What Is Relapse Prevention (RP)?

Relapse prevention (RP) is a self-control program designed to teach couples and families who are trying to change their behavior how to anticipate and cope with the problem of relapse. In a very real sense, relapse refers to a breakdown or failure in a system's attempt to change or modify behaviors and adhere to treatment. Traditionally, based on the principles of social-learning theory (Bandura, 1977), RP is a psychoeducational program that combines behavioral skill-training procedures and cognitive intervention techniques with systems thinking.

The RP model was initially developed as a behavioral maintenance program for use in the treatment of addictive behaviors (Marlatt & Gordon, 1985). In the case of addiction, the typical goals of treatment are either to refrain totally from performing a target behavior (for example, to abstain from drug use) or to impose regulatory limits or controls over the occurrence of a behavior (for instance, to use diet as a means of controlling food intake).

The concept of RP has become a central focus of research and practice in health psychology and behavioral medicine. Because non-adherence, previously called non-compliance, with treatment is so high, ranging from 30–80% (Sperry, 1986), clinicians have sought ways to reverse this phenomenon. At the most general level, relapse is a return of a problem behavior following a problem-free period. The recent *Webster's New Collegiate Dictionary* refers to relapse as both an outcome and a process. The *outcome* is reflected in the use of the term "relapse" to denote "a recurrence of symptoms of a disease after a period of improvement," and the *process* is captured in the phrase "the act or instance of backsliding, worsening, or subsiding." The process implies that something has occurred that may or may not lead to a full relapse.

Whether the process or outcome definition of relapse is chosen has obvious implications for the conceptualization, prevention, and treatment of relapse. Viewing relapse as a process and not an outcome implies that there are choice points in the process where the therapist and family can intervene (Ludgate, 1995). Marlatt and Gordon (1985) distinguish between "lapse" and "relapse," arguing that a lapse implies a temporary state of affairs that might under some circumstances lead to a relapse. How a family responds to an initial lapse will determine whether a full relapse will occur. It is generally conceded that the prediction and prevention of relapses is desirable because the continuation of behavioral problems may reduce a family's quality of life and place limitations on their successful pursuit of goals. The understanding of relapse and the RP program can be used to ensure treatment adherence.

RP Research

Unfortunately, most research studies have been designed to measure outcome of treatment rather than long-term maintenance or effectiveness. Identification of RP properties I treatment is usually post hoc rather than a part of the original research plans. However, there is some research that can be useful in helping to understand the importance of RP.

Research by Bogner and Zielenbach-Coenen (1984) demonstrated that lengthening the intervals between the final therapy sessions does facilitate a couple's ability to benefit from marital therapy initially and in the long term.

Whisman (1991) investigated the effectiveness of booster sessions on RP. This research used two mandatory booster sessions at 3 and 6 months after therapy and three optional sessions during the same 6-month period. The results were not statistically significant. However, these findings seem to suggest that booster sessions deserve further attention and refinement; however, they do not unequivocally support booster sessions' efficacy. Whisman, however, outlined several ways the efficacy of booster sessions could have been improved, including using an experienced therapist, improving the booster session content, scheduling additional booster sessions during the first 3 post-therapy months, and extending the length of the maintenance component.

Truax and Jacobson (1992) felt that although no treatment differences can be supported at this time by research, there appears to be some treatment characteristics that emerge. These characteristics seem to support the use of matched and tailored treatment. The use of the traditional one-size-fits-all therapy does not seem to be supported by long-term maintenance assessments. Following are the treatment characteristics that emerged in their research:

1. Flexibility in Treatment Content

Despite many common themes in couples and families, each couple and family is unique. The treatment must therefore be carefully tailored. The content of therapy may focus on thoughts, behavior, feelings, past, present, future, and so forth.

2. Flexibility in Treatment Format

Therapists need to structure the length and spacing of sessions according to the interaction and the purpose of the therapy. For example, traditional 1-hour weekly sessions seldom work during the initial sessions of family therapy or when skill-training is needed.

3. Identifying and Modifying Salient Behaviors (Overt, Emotional, Cognitive)

It is important to gather a complete picture of the couple's functioning. Often therapists and families stop treatment after the presenting problem disappears only to resume treatment after a short passage of time.

4. Focusing on Reasonably Changeable Behaviors

Many behavioral changes may temporarily improve couple or family satisfaction, but it is unlikely they all can be maintained. It is important to focus on behaviors that can be maintained. For example, if a couple is guided to an interaction that leads to increased understanding and a spontaneous hug, this interaction is more likely to be repeated.

5. Effectively Generalizing from Therapy to the Client's World

This is perhaps the greatest challenge to relapse prevention. In addition to the tailoring ideas discussed in this book, the therapist must be able to design interventions that facilitate generalization from the therapeutic environment to the daily life of the couple or family. Several steps have been recommended by Truax and Jacobson (1992) to improve generalization:

a. Maximizing the couple's natural reinforcement potential

b. Assigning homework throughout therapy

c. Lengthening intervals between final sessions

d. Including booster sessions

e. Predicting stressful life events (p. 315)

Why Couples/Families Relapse

Essentially couples and families relapse because they are supposed to. Seldom does behavior permanently change, so that former behaviors never occur. However, relapse has often been seen as synonymous with treatment failure, a return to a previous behavior after a period of gain or change, and it is often viewed as an end state. This all-or-nothing perception fails to take into account that relapse is a common component of effective change. Mistakes and lapses are "human" and common in the change process. By allowing room in the treatment process for mistakes to occur (relapses), it is possible to avoid what has been called the "oscillation effect," whereby a system is either in control or out of control. When relapse is expected and planned for, the affective and cognitive reactions to slips become significantly less intense, and the treatment program can be quickly reinstated. The length of the relapse period often depends on the personal expectations of the system involved. So rather than a relapse being a dead end, it becomes a fork in the road with one path moving toward the old patterns and the other to new ones.

Many people believe that quitting a pattern of behavior has to be all or nothing. Once a mistake has occurred they believe it is for all time and that intervention did not work. Many attribute the cause of relapse to a personal or family weakness or failure, such as the lack of will power, weakness of character, or problematic family composition, rather than to the difficulty of the tasks and the predictability of slips occuring during the course of change. The belief that "total control is the only control" needs to be challenged. People need to be taught how to view change on a continuum of where they are to where they hope to be.

Therapists must be aware that the combination of high-risk situations and no coping responses and negative expectancies increases the likelihood that relapse will occur. High-risk situations pose a threat to the system's sense of self-control and increases the risk of potential relapse. The three most common high-risk categories associated with a high relapse rate (Marlatt & Gordon, 1985) are (1) negative emotional state, (2) interpersonal conflict, and (3) social pressure. To this list we might add (4) highly charged anniversary dates. It is often helpful to work with couples and families to plan responses to these challenging situations. Simple discussion and the ability to be aware of high-risk situations are simple yet effective procedures.

If couples and families are taught a coping response in these high-risk situations, the likelihood of relapse can be decreased. This results in the development of a feeling of control or mastery similar to the concept of self-efficacy (Bandura, 1977). The family thereby develops feelings of confidence and knowledge that they can handle life's problems. Bandura's research indicates that if someone is successful in coping in one situation, this increases the likelihood that he or she will be successful in another.

The family's belief or expectation that relapse will occur seems to be a powerful predictor of relapse. Thus successful relapse prevention needs to address the belief structure of the family. Negative expectancies must be replaced with positive ones that serve as compelling goals. It is important to offer a new story or metaphor for the family that will prevent relapse (O'Hanlon, 1994).

Relapse Prevention

RP is an intervention consisting of specific skills and cognitive strategies that prepare clients in advance to cope with inevitable slips or relapse in compliance to a change program (Marlatt & Gordon, 1985). Although the early work on RP was developed in alcohol and drug treatment programs in which relapse and return to addictive substances is very high, RP principles have been applied to smoking cessation, pain control, weight management, sleep disorders, exercise adherence, and other health-promotion areas (Lewis, Sperry, & Carlson, 1993). With the possible exceptions of Jacobson and Holtzworth-Munroe (1986) and Truax and Jacobson (1992), RP has not been introduced into the family therapy literature.

Daley (1989) describes five different RP models, of which Marlatt and Gordon's (1985) is the most well known and researched. This cognitive-behavioral model emphasizes the following points:

- Identification of individual high-risk situations

- Development of coping skills for high-risk situations

- Practice in coping with potential lapses

- Development of cognitive coping strategies for use immediately after relapse

Marlatt notes that the majority of relapse in adults occurs in response to stressful situations involving conflict or social pressure. He stresses that reframing the relapse as a mistake rather than a factual error or moral shortcoming is an important preventive measure that can help the individual get back on track and learn from the experience. RP helps the individual apply the brakes so that once a slip occurs it does not escalate into a full-blown relapse.

Wilson (1992) identified several different types of RP strategies that have been developed and evaluated to varying degrees with different types of problem behaviors. The techniques include:

1. Booster sessions

2. Treatment programs with RP strategies integrated into the initial treatment

3. Procedures that require minimal therapist contact such as periodic reminder letters (White & Epston, 1990), telephone calls, or the provision of therapy-related reading materials.

Problem behaviors are explained as a series of acquired habit patterns that are governed by cognitive and experiential processes in which antecedent events, beliefs and expectations, previous learning history, and behavioral consequences play important roles. The maintenance stage of intervention must be considered as a period in which there is an opportunity for new learning to occur as the family is faced with situations, events, moods, and beliefs that might increase the risk of reinstatement of previous ineffective behavioral patterns.

According to Wilson (1992), relapse may occur because of a failure at any one of a number of points from initial treatment to maintenance; an effective treatment may not necessarily lead to perceived control or enhanced self-efficacy. Clients may fail to recognize and respond appropriately to high-risk situations. They may fail to develop adequate coping responses and may still have negative outcome expectancies about the use of effective strategies in future situations. Clients may use ineffective responses, or they may have positive expectancies about the effects of old coping strategies that in reality have failed in the past. They may also make incorrect attributions about the causes of lapse.

A major component of the RP program is the identification of high-risk situations for self-monitoring, self-efficacy ratings, and detailed analysis of past relapse episodes. The aim of these activities is to increase the therapist's knowledge of the factors that might lead to relapse and to increase the family's awareness of how these factors operate.

Throughout family therapy, generalizations from therapy to daily life are facilitated through the use of weekly homework assignments and easing out of therapist reinforcement by increasingly drawing attention to natural reinforcers within the family. By tailoring treatment, the therapist can use homework assignments that are unique to each family. To increase the likelihood that families will continue active problem solving, the therapist must find a format that incorporates the family's natural problem-solving style. For example, some families can be initially instructed to note problems for family meetings by jotting them down on an agenda that is kept in an accessible place in the home. Other families, however, may find it uncomfortable to wait and need to solve problems on the spot. Thus it is important for the therapist to identify procedures that a family can easily use. Again, the success of therapy seems to be related to the careful analysis and tailoring of treatment.

Change in Treatment Focus

Traditional therapy strategies are much more effective at reducing negative behaviors than at increasing positive ones. Research continues to show that the differences between distressed and non-distressed families is that distressed families engage in more negative behaviors, while non-distressed families exhibit more positive behaviors. Although these findings are not surprising, they do suggest that a simple reduction of negative behaviors without an increase in positive ones is probably not sufficient to help distressed couples and families to be genuinely happy.

Researchers (Baucom & Hoffman, 1986; Gottman, 1994a; Truax & Jacobson, 1992) believe that therapeutic durability can be improved by identification and creation of positive intimate experiences. Unfortunately, most therapy seems to be focused on the elimination of negative behaviors. This has the effect of making couples/families into better friends but not necessarily better lovers.

The communication skills taught are generally aimed at problem solving. Thus, a number of destructive communications that interfere with the process often tend to be emphasized. To have meaning, many positive communications must be spontaneous, emerging from the person's internal thoughts and feelings about the partner or the topic (Baucom & Hoffman, 1986, p. 600).

Therefore, by changing the treatment focus to increasing positive behaviors, couples can learn to define progress based on realistic goals. It may be wise to help couples and families use the problem-solving process as a way to become more intimate with one another rather than to solve the problems themselves (which are often not reasonably solvable).

To determine an operational definition of intimacy and positive communication is difficult. Generally they refer to knowing and being known by another person. Skinner (1974) indicated that the extent to which someone is known is synonymous to the extent to which his or her behavior can be predicted. Therefore, a primary goal of intimate interventions is to help family members create a context with which they will be likely to get into contact with the reinforcing feelings of the mutual knowledge of one another. Therefore the goals are to increase expression of internal experiences and to encourage this expression. This involves family members learning how to express as well as to accept emotions. Truax and Jacobson (1992) feel that specific interventions are needed to help couples increase their intimate behaviors:

> Specific interventions include (1) providing directives about how to behave more intimately; (2) making suggestions about how to express internal experiences that may have never been aired; (3) reminding the couple of the positive feelings derived from their behavioral differences; (4) emphasizing behavioral sequences that exemplify how the relationship benefits from their differences; (5) pointing out that behavioral differences are a result of different learning histories rather than something each does to the other; (6) educating the couple on how expressing and listening to one another's internal experiences will be mutually reinforcing; and (7) helping the couple understand that the interactions that promote intimacy may have more reinforcement potential than actually solving the problem (pp. 298–299).

In addition, if marital and family success is based on huge individual compromises and changes, relapse is much more likely. A focus on marriage and family satisfaction to the exclusion of individual well-being may also obscure potentially important differences. It is perhaps most important to help couples learn to appreciate differences than to make large behavioral changes.

Whisman (1991) conducted research that seems to support the notion that a couple's/family's ability to maintain therapeutic gains may well be affected by the discrepancy between their satisfaction levels. Thus one must focus attention on reasonable and maintainable behavioral changes. Unfortunately, therapists often bite off more than they can chew. When families attempt to resolve conflicts that are not solvable, they may become more deeply entrenched in hopelessness. It is often more helpful for the therapist to first focus on helping family members understand one another's internal experiences without rushing to a conclusion. Therapists need to pay special attention to behaviors that are naturally reinforcing both in and out of sessions for families.

A typical response to relapse is to increase the number of treatment interventions in order to create a more comprehensive broad-based package. This response seems to be based on the belief that "more is better"; the more treatment components, therefore, the longer the results will last. However, evidence suggests that the more techniques and procedures applied, the more difficult it becomes to maintain compliance. In addition, it seems that most intervention techniques are aimed at *initial* behavior change and not at the *maintenance* of the changed behavior. One of the main differences between initial and maintenance procedures is that initial techniques are usually administered by the therapist, while the maintenance procedures are mostly self-administered. (An obvious exception to this distinction is the use of "booster sessions" which will be described later.)

Open-Ended Family Therapy

A useful perspective for therapists is to think in terms of treating couples and families over a lifetime. The likelihood of one set of meetings putting a permanent end to problems throughout the life span is not great. It's much more helpful to view problems as occurring at different points in the life span and seeing couple/family therapy as a resource that can be used to resolve these difficulties. The therapist therefore becomes a resource, similar to the family medical practitioner. Regarding therapy in this way establishes a direct manner of dealing with the deterioration that seems to occur after successful marital and family therapy.

At the beginning of therapy, the therapist presents the notion of termination with an open-ended viewpoint. The therapist discusses the benefits of having a planned termination; however, he or she also discusses the value of ongoing involvement. Working toward termination occurs throughout the therapeutic meetings.

Lebow (1995) highlights ten tasks that are central to ending most family therapy.

1. *Tracking progress in therapy to determine the appropriateness of ending.* This task involves regular assessment of how the family/couple is progressing toward treatment goals.

2. *Reviewing the course of treatment.* The therapist provides time for the family/couple to review the changes and events that occurred in the treatment process.

3. *Emphasizing the gains made and the client's role in these gains.* Often clients do not fully understand the extent of change nor their role in how change occurred. It is important to help the couple and family realize the sense of competence and confidence that can occur by understanding one's role in successful change.

4. *Abstracting what has been learned from treatment and how it may be applied later.* The therapist helps the family and couple understand the behavioral, affective, and cognitive skills that have been developed and how they may be used as future problems occur.

5. *Internalizing the therapist.* The family/couple needs to learn how to have the therapist remain with the family, not as an active member or participant in the family but as an internalized member. Family members are often encouraged to develop skills by imagining what the therapist would say or suggest they do at a particular moment.

6. *Regarding the ending through the lens of other endings in life.* Therapists should develop an understanding of each family's and family member's unique history of endings. Some families have a difficult time with endings, while others find them comfortable.

7. *Saying good-bye with an opportunity to express gratitude and exchange feelings.*

8. *Discussing the conditions for returning to treatment.* Booster sessions may be used to promote the durability of change. These sessions are scheduled at regular intervals to renew skills and insights.

9. *Referring.* Sometimes ending work with one therapist opens the door to future work with another, such as moving on to some form

of self-help group or educational class. In some cases, the ending of treatment with one therapist occurs when a referral is made to another professional who has different skills.

10. *Defining post-treatment availability.*

Steps to RP

RP has many potential applications for marital and family therapy. One of the most obvious involves providing therapy with families in maintenance (that is, open-ended treatment) whereby the therapists will not only predict relapses but preventively intervene by preparing the family for them. There are five steps that can facilitate RP:

1. Create a treatment alliance
2. Tailor treatment
3. Learn to manage stress
4. Increase and maintain positive to negative interaction ratio
5. Provide skill training

1. Create a Treatment Alliance

Effective intervention involves engaging couples/families in the therapy process, helping them to actively and collaboratively participate through complying with homework assignments. Success seems to be based on the couple's/family's level of involvement in and adherence to therapy. Researchers consistently discover that the level of client involvement is related to therapy outcome (Holtzworth-Munroe, Jacobson, DeKlyen, & Whisman, 1989). Active collaboration in the tasks appropriate to the treatment process may be conceptualized as treatment alliance.

2. Tailor Treatment

It appears that a high level of involvement needs to be sustained in the family and marriage relationship to produce effective long-term therapeutic change. How can this level of involvement be maintained to produce permanent change? As you have learned from this book, the ability to engage a family effectively in the therapeutic process depends largely on the therapist's ability to provide highly structured treatments that are tailored to the needs of particular families. In addition, as we also mentioned, matching intervention strategies to a particular family is an often neglected area of treatment. However, it is not surprising that the "one size fits all" family therapies are not as durable as those than can directly address each couple's or family's specific concerns. The ability to match and tailor treatment according to how particular families conceptualize their distress will greatly increase the maintenance of positive behaviors.

Although many therapists advocate the ideas of matching and tailoring in theory, practice shows that therapists tend to treat all clients with basically the same methods and approaches. The therapists act as if their ideas and intervention strategies are good for everyone. However, Jacobson, Schmaling, and Holtzworth-Munroe (1987) reported that individual tailoring of treatment plans and resultant idiographic flexibility can significantly reduce relapse.

3. Manage Stress

Another important consideration is the need to predict external stressors on the family. These stressors are often related to stages of marriage and family life and are predictable. Research indicates that booster sessions and training in stress management (Sperry & Carlson, 1993) can be very helpful in this area. However, one should remember that just the use of booster sessions alone does not appear to be enough to prevent relapse. The therapist should initiate RP programming in the early stages of therapy and maintain it throughout treatment rather than wait for a relapse problem to occur.

4. Increase and Maintain Positive to Negative Interaction Ratio

Gottman (1994a; 1994b) in his extensive research has concluded that the ratio of positive to negative interactions needed to maintain a marriage in good shape can be quantified. He found that satisfied couples, no matter how bad their marriages stacked up against the ideal, were those that maintained a 5-to-1 ratio of positive to negative moments. The good moments of mutual pleasure, passion, humor, support, kindness, and generosity outweigh the bad moments of complaint, criticism, anger, disgust, contempt, defensiveness, and coldness.

5. Skill Training

Perhaps the most important determinant of relapse is whether or not effective skill training has occurred and whether or not these strategies were tailored to the family's needs in advance of stressful situations.

To have strong, effective, and healthy marriages, for example, couples must also have effective marriage skills (Dinkmeyer & Carlson, 1984). The following six skills are among the most important to be acquired; they form the basis for all relationships within the family:

1. Making the relationship a priority

2. Communicating regularly

3. Practicing encouragement

4. Having marriage meetings and choices

5. Setting up negotiations, rules, and conflict resolution

6. Having regular fun

Couples who learn and practice these skills are able to create and maintain successful relationships.

Carlson and Dinkmeyer (1991) also identify the following traits that contribute to emotional and psychological intimacy in satisfying family relationships:

1. Understanding oneself and being willing to share feelings, thoughts, and beliefs in a sensitive manner

2. Flexibility and responsibility

3. Acceptance of self and partner

4. Permanence of the relationship

5. Trust

6. Ability to live in the present

7. Ability to negotiate

8. Sharing of positive feelings

Perhaps the greatest challenge in promoting relapse prevention involves designing skills and interventions that facilitate generalization from the therapy to the family's daily life. Unless each family member becomes self-sufficient and all members are able to reinforce one another, the therapy is likely to fail once the therapist has left. As mentioned previously, researchers have established several steps to improve generalization from treatment to home: (1) maximizing the family's natural reinforcement potential; (2) assigning homework through therapy; (3) lengthening intervals between final sessions; and (4) predicting stressful life events (Truax & Jacobson, 1992).

RP Case History

The Shank family presented for treatment after a Thanksgiving celebration resulted in a family feud. Present at the initial session were the parents, Mary and Al, and children, Rich, 19, Bill, 17, Susan, 15, and Tammy, 11. Apparently the dinner was ruined for all family members by the constant bickering of the girls and boys. Their battles are described as "frequent" and "cruel."

Session 1

At the initial session, questions were asked to determine the family dynamics. It appears that the family is divided along gender lines with little overlap. This pattern appears long-standing, as both parents report similar dynamics within their families of origin. All family members stated that they wanted the fighting and bickering stopped, but they were not optimistic about whether this could actually occur, because each person believed the locus of the problem rested outside him or her and was therefore powerless to resolve this problem.

Most family members reported half-hearted attempts in the past to bring about change. The likelihood of effective change appeared low and the likelihood of relapse great. The therapist was careful not to own the problem and to make it clear that the family needed to discover their own resources to change the situation and to learn to help one another. Further questioning made it clear that effective communication, problem-solving, and encouragement skills were absent. The family seemed willing to change their responses and agreed to verbally congratulate each family member for a changed response at least one time before the next session. This activity was practiced within the session, and a simple encouragement strategy was taught (Dinkmeyer & Carlson, 1984).

Comment. This session began the relapse prevention process by empowering the family, tailoring the treatment, offering skill training and practice, and providing a homework assignment. The salient behavior identified to change was to increase the number of positive exchanges through encouragement. This seemed to be behavior that was reasonably changeable.

Session 2

The entire family returned for the second session. They reported no change in the family dynamics; however, the also reported not having done the homework assignment. The therapist asked the family members if they expected relationships to change while they themselves could remain the same. All laughed at this and recommitted to doing the homework in the upcoming week. The therapist asked each family member to encourage the others in the way they would have done during the previous week. This created a positive exchange, especially when done across the gender line. There was considerable joking and anxiety as this occurred. The family was asked what needed to occur to make sure the assignment was followed. A lively discussion took place; the family agreed to put up a chart for each family member to mark each time she or he encouraged another family member.

Comment. This session involved not overreacting to homework noncompliance and the development by the family of their own monitoring system. Further skill practice also occurred.

Session 3

Only the parents came to this session. A discussion occurred about the gender dichotomy within their families of origin. The couple indicated that this seemed familiar to them, although they did not like it. Each person agreed to write to each of their opposite gender siblings a brief "thinking of you" note. Additionally, they agreed to do one couple activity each week, and engage each opposite gender child in at least 30 minutes of conversation or shared activity during the next week.

Comment. This session strengthened the parent and child subsystem. The homework was geared to keeping them actively involved in treatment and to take charge of the family system. Increasing the number of out-of-session assignments keeps the therapeutic focus on between-session behavior. All assignments are "deceptively" simple and within the family members' existing behavioral repertoire.

Session 4

This session occurred 2 weeks after session 3. The session began by having each family member report what they had done differently during the previous 2 weeks. All seemed willing to share exactly what they had done. Comments were also made as to the decreasing feelings of hostility. The therapist indicated that the family needed to think about what could be done to insure that these changes were maintained and what should happen if they were not. The family wanted to continue the chart and agreed that any member could call for an unscheduled family therapy session if problems could not be resolved among themselves. The next session was set for 3 weeks.

Comment. The family is taking an increasing amount of responsibility for themselves. The therapist is gradually increasing the time between sessions and making the family more dependent on one another.

Session 5

The family reported a period of "uneventful" activity. All family members had 90% or greater compliance on the chart. There were no presenting problems, and all family members wished to stop treatment; however, they agreed to return at 2-month intervals for the next 6 months.

Comment. The family has taken responsibility for change. Each person is performing at a 90% compliance rate, and the family has agreed to stop treatment. Booster sessions have been scheduled.

Overall, This brief intervention was accomplished by creating a treatment alliance, tailoring treatment, managing stress, increasing the percent of positive and negative exchanges, and providing skill training.

Conclusion

Once skills are taught and learned, therapists can develop a follow-up program to monitor families in much the same fashion as automobile and other service contracts are prepared. Of course, we cannot be so bold to say that families need to come in every 10,000 miles, but it is not unreasonable to think that couples and families can benefit significantly from quarterly, semi-annual, or yearly checkups. At these sessions therapists can make sure that each family is (1) taking time for regular communication, (2) practicing encouragement, (3) setting aside regular time to resolve conflict, (4) having regularly planned leisure activities, and (5) developing clear plans and methods to insure implementation for future activities and time together. By monitoring these checkpoints it is possible for the family and therapist alike to be able to pinpoint areas that may need further work, just as a mechanic is able to spot carburation, acceleration, or wheel-alignment problems. Research on booster sessions (Whisman, 1991) seems to show a number of advantages to support conducting booster sessions, with a gradual decrease of treatment from regular weekly to less frequent visits. Although therapists are not trained to think in this fashion, it may prove to be the most effective solution to the high levels of relapse in marriage and family therapy (Sperry & Carlson, 1990; 1991).

Effective marriage and family life is not a privilege but a responsibility. Families and their therapists need to understand how to create and maintain effective relationships. Traditional methods of helping focus on the front end of change rather than on the maintenance of a successful intervention. We urge therapists who work with families to be aware of the important strategies to prevent relapse and increase treatment adherence. Again, as a recap:

1. Engage the family/couple and involve them in homework assignments throughout therapy

2. Match strategies to the family's unique needs

3. Use booster sessions and planned procedures to handle normal external stress

4. Train families in the essential skills

5. Gradually increase the time between visits allowing the family to be gradually less dependent on therapy

References

Bandura, A. (1977). *Social learning theory*. Englewood Cliffs, NJ: Prentice-Hall.

Baucom, D. H., & Hoffman, J. A. (1986). The effectiveness of marital therapy: Current status and application to the clinical setting. In N. S. Jacobson & A. S. Gurman (Eds.), *Clinical handbook of marital therapy* (pp. 597–620). New York: Guilford.

Bogner, I., & Zielenbach-Coenen, H. (1984). On maintaining change in behavioral marital therapy. In K. Hahlweg & N. S. Jacobson (Eds.), *Marital interaction: Analysis and modification* (pp. 27–35). New York: Guilford.

Carlson, J., & Dinkmeyer, D. (1991). *The basics of marriage*. Coral Springs, FL: CMTI Press.

Cummings, C., Gordon, J. R., & Marlatt, G. A. (1980). Relapse: Prevention and prediction. In W. R. Miller (Ed.), *The addictive behaviors: Treatment of alcoholism, drug abuse, smoking, and obesity* (pp. 291–321). New York: Pergamon Press.

Daley, D. C. (1989). *Relapse prevention: Treatment alternatives and counseling aids*. Blaze Ridge Summit, PA: TAB Books.

Dinkmeyer, D., & Carlson, J. (1984). *Training in marriage enrichment*. Circle Pines, MN: American Guidance Service.

Epstein, L. H., & Masek, B. J. (1978). Behavioral control of medicine compliance. *Journal of Applied Behavioral Analysis, 11*, 1–9.

Gottman, J. (1994a). *What predicts divorce: The relationship between marital processes and marital outcomes*. Hillside, NJ: Lawrence Erlbaum Associates.

Gottman, J. (1994b). *Why marriages succeed or fail.* New York: Simon & Schuster.

Holtzworth-Munroe, A., Jacobson, N. S., DeKlyen, M., & Whisman, M. A. (1989). Relationship between behavioral marital therapy outcome and process variables. *Journal of Consulting and Clinical Psychology, 57*(5), 658–662.

Jacobson, N. S. (1989). The maintenance of treatment gains following social learning based marital therapy. *Behavior Therapy, 20,* 325–336.

Jacobson, N. S., & Holtzworth-Munroe, A. (1986). Marital therapy: A social learning/cognitive perspective. In N. S. Jacobson & A. S. Gurman (Eds.), *Clinical handbook of marital therapy* (pp. 29–70). New York: Guilford.

Jacobson, N. S., Schmaling, K. B., & Holtzworth-Munroe, A. (1987). Component analysis of behavioral marital therapy: Two year follow-up and prediction of relapse. *Journal of Marital and Family Therapy, 13,* 187–195.

Lebow, J. (1995). Open-ended therapy: Termination in marital and family therapy. In R. H. Mikesell, D. Lusterman, & S. H. McDaniel (Eds.), *Integrating family therapy: Handbook of family psychology and systems theory* (pp. 73–86). Washington, DC: American Psychological Association.

Lewis, J. A., Sperry, L., & Carlson, J. (1993). *Health counseling.* Pacific Grove, CA: Brooks/Cole.

Ludgate, J. W. (1995). *Maximizing psychotherapeutic gains and preventing relapse in emotionally distressed clients.* Sarasota, FL: Professional Resource Press.

Marlatt, G. A., & Gordon, J. R. (1985). *Relapse prevention: Maintenance and strategies in the treatment of addictive behaviors.* New York: Guilford.

Meichenbaum, D., & Turk, D. C. (1987). *Facilitating treatment adherence: A practitioner's guide.* New York: Plenum Press.

Minuchin, S. (1974). *Families and family therapy.* Cambridge, MA: Harvard University Press.

O'Hanlon, B. (1994). The third wave. *The Family Therapy Networker, 18*(6), 19–29.

Skinner, B. F. (1974). *About behaviorism.* New York: Vintage Books.

Southan, M. A., & Dunbar, J. M. (1986). Facilitating patient compliance with medical interventions. In K. Holroyd & T. Creer (Eds.), *Self-management of chronic disease.* New York: Academic Press.

Sperry, L. (1986). Contemporary approaches to family therapy: A comparative and meta-analysis. *Individual Psychology, 42,* 591–601.

Sperry, L., & Carlson, J. (1990). Introducing relapse prevention into family psychology. *The Family Psychologist, 6*(4), 28–29.

Sperry, L., & Carlson, J. (1991). *Marital therapy: Integrating theory and practice.* Denver, CO: Love Publishing.

Sperry, L., & Carlson, J. (1993). *Psychopathology and psychotherapy: From diagnosis to treatment.* Muncie, IN: Accelerated Development.

Sperry, L., & Carlson, J. (1994). *The basics of stress management.* Coral Springs, FL: CMTI Press.

Truax, P., & Jacobson, N. S. (1992). Marital distress. In P. H. Wilson (Ed.), *Principles and practice of relapse prevention* (pp. 290–321). New York: Guilford Press.

Whisman, M. A. (1991). *The use of booster maintenance sessions in behavioral marital therapy.* Unpublished doctoral dissertation. University of Washington, Seattle.

White, M., & Epston, D. (1990). *Narrative means to therapeutic ends.* New York: W. W. Norton.

Wilson, P. H. (Ed.) (1992). *Principles and practice of relapse prevention.* New York: Guilford.

10

Epilogue

Ensuring effective treatment is the most important task of family therapy. Without enduring results, the profession will not continue in
these times of managed care. This book has presented the concept of
matched/tailored treatment as being the primary ingredient of effective
care. Tailored treatment yields consistently effective results.

To achieve effective tailored treatment, the therapist needs to be
aware of the widest variety of treatment possible. This knowledge needs
to be not just at the theoretical level but also at the practical level; the
therapist must be able to use each treatment modality. The theories
and techniques presented in Chapter 3 must be more than familiar
to the therapist; each approach and technique must be within the
therapist's repertoire.

The treatment issues of today are complex, dealing with the new
realities of family life. More and more families will need help dealing
with the multiple problems facing them. Without clear working knowledge of the multimodal therapy process, the therapist cannot succeed.
Therapists need to be able to accurately assess couples and families and
implement meaningful treatment within the first session. The broader
context of family life can no longer be ignored. The effect of work, gender, and culture present major challenges.

We remain hopeful that family therapists will learn to operate using
the principles of this book. We also hope that this book will serve as
a springboard for further development and refinement of the concepts
of matching and tailoring treatment. The goal of effective, enduring
treatment for families can become a reality

Index

TO THE OWNER OF THIS BOOK:

We hope that you have found *Family Therapy: Ensuring Treatment Efficacy* useful. So that this book can be improved in a future edition, would you take the time to complete this sheet and return it? Thank you.

School and address: ————————————————————

Department: ——————————————————————

Instructor's name: ——————————————————————

1. What I like most about this book is: ———————————————

————————————————————————————

————————————————————————————

2. What I like least about this book is: ———————————————

————————————————————————————

————————————————————————————

3. My general reaction to this book is: ———————————————

————————————————————————————

4. The name of the course in which I used this book is: ——————————

————————————————————————————

5. Were all of the chapters of the book assigned for you to read? ——————

   If not, which ones weren't? ——————————————————

6. In the space below, or on a separate sheet of paper, please write specific suggestions for improving this book and anything else you'd care to share about your experience in using the book.

————————————————————————————

————————————————————————————

————————————————————————————

————————————————————————————

————————————————————————————

Optional:

Your name: _____ Date: _____

May Brooks/Cole quote you, either in promotion for *Family Therapy: Ensuring Treatment Efficacy* or in future publishing ventures?

Yes: _____ No: _____

Sincerely,

Jon Carlson
Len Sperry
Judith A. Lewis

FOLD HERE

- -

FOLD HERE

Brooks/Cole is dedicated to publishing quality publications for education in the human services fields. If you are interested in learning more about our publications, please fill in your name and address and request our latest catalogue, using this prepaid mailer.

Name:_____

Street Address:_____

City, State, and Zip:_____

IN-BOOK SURVEY

At Brooks/Cole, we are excited about creating new types of learning materials that are interactive, three-dimensional, and fun to use. To guide us in our publishing/development process, we hope that you'll take just a few moments to fill out the survey below. Your answers can help us make decisions that will allow us to produce a wide variety of videos, CD-ROMs, and Internet-based learning systems to complement standard textbooks. If you're interested in working with us as a student Beta-tester, be sure to fill in your name, telephone number, and address. We look forward to hearing from you!

In addition to books, which of the following learning tools do you currently use in your counseling/human services/social work courses?

_____ **Video** _____ in class _____ school library _____ own VCR

_____ **CD-ROM** _____ in class _____ in lab _____ own computer

_____ **Macintosh disks** _____ in class _____ in lab _____ own computer

_____ **Windows disks** _____ in class _____ in lab _____ own computer

_____ **Internet** _____ in class _____ in lab _____ own computer

How often do you access the Internet? _____

My own home computer is:

_____ Macintosh _____ DOS _____ Windows _____ Windows 95

The computer I use in class for counseling/human services/social work courses is:

_____ Macintosh _____ DOS _____ Windows _____ Windows 95

If you are NOT currently using multimedia materials in your counseling/human services/social work courses, but can see ways that video, CD-ROM, Internet, or other technologies could enhance your learning, please comment below:

_____

_____

_____

Other comments (optional): _____

_____

Name _____

Address _____

Telephone number (optional): _____

You can fax this form to us at (408) 375-6414; e:mail to: info@brookscole.com; or detach, fold, secure, and mail.